D0897766

Grossman, Louis H
    Department store merchandising in changing environ-
ments, by Louis H. Grossman. East Lansing, Bureau of
Business and Economic Research, Michigan State University, 1970.

    xii, 229 p.   24 cm.   (MSU business studies)

    Bibliography : p. 223–229.

    1. Department stores—U. S.—Case studies.   I. Title.   (Series:
Michigan. State University, East Lansing. Bureau of Business and
Economic Research. Business studies)

HF5465.U4G7   658.87'1'0973   71–628430
                                              MARC

Library of Congress   70 [4]

Department Store Merchandising In Changing Environments

Department Store Merchandising In Changing Environments

by

LOUIS H. GROSSMAN
Associate Professor of Marketing
College of Business
Arizona State University

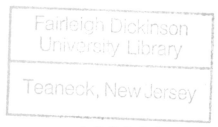

1970
MSU Business Studies

Bureau of Business and Economic Research
Division of Research
Graduate School of Business Administration
Michigan State University, East Lansing

Library of Congress Catalog Card Number: 71-628430
© 1970 by the Board of Trustees of Michigan State University
East Lansing, Michigan

Printed in the United States of America

Contents

Tables

ix

Acknowledgments

This book is based upon research originally conducted to ascertain how and why business firms alter strategies in response to external environmental change. More specifically, the book focuses upon a familiar trading institution, the department store, and reveals how and why four of these firms altered merchandising strategies in response to changes in competition and in demand.

I am unable to designate many who deserve acknowledgment because of an agreement to use only fictitious names and disguised sources of information. However, I trust that I have accurately reflected their thoughts and have properly used what they disclosed or transmitted to me. I thank all of them.

There are some individuals whose contributions I can publicly acknowledge. Mr. Clarence Judd, president, the George Nuestadt Research Organization, New York, and the late George Neustadt, generously provided valuable research data which enabled me to compare interview data with objective measurements of newspaper advertising. Mr. Samuel Feinberg, columnist of Fairchild Publications, New York, discussed at length some of his observations concerning the department store industry. Miss Ethel Langtry, executive director, the Retail Research Institute of the National Retail Merchants Association, New York, encouraged this research.

My experience in the merchandising and management of department stores and of specialty stores was invaluable in conducting research by personal interview. I wish to acknowledge the influence, insights, and inspiration I gained from the many years of association with my brother, Herman Grossman.

Several professors at the Graduate School of Business Administration, Michigan State University, provided personal guidance and aid, enabling me to build a bridge from the business realm to the academic world. They also supervised the research for this book. I wish to thank Dr. William J. E. Crissy and Dr. Paul E. Smith for their constructive and encouraging comments. Professor Stanley C. Hollander served as chairman of the faculty group supervising the research. I wish to acknowledge Dr. Hollander's high standards of scholarship and his ever-present willingness to assist me in my pursuit of knowledge. Further, I wish to acknowledge the assistance of Dr. Anne C. Garrison, also of the Michigan State University faculty. In preparing the manuscript for this book I received the meticulous and creative assistance of Mrs. Esther Waite, Division Editor, Bureau of Business and Economic Research. I thank all of these colleagues.

Personal acknowledgements are very much in order. My children— Jeff, Laurie, and Rachel—can all rightfully claim some credit for efforts in typing, clerical, and other services, including maintenance of quietude. While conducting the basic research for this book, writing the original manuscript, and then revising for this book, I received the unstinting, selfless, and constant aid of my wife. I dedicate this book to Gloria.

I

Introduction

For more than one hundred years the department store has been an institution fundamental to the American distribution system. The basic principle of the department store is the assembly of an enormous variety of consumer goods and services under one roof for the convenience of the one-stop shopper. Such traditional stores as Macy's, Bloomingdale's, Hudson's, Rich's, Dayton's, Lazarus', Marshall Field, and thousands of others flourished as they developed on this principle.[1]

Two environmental changes in the last twenty years have significantly influenced traditional department stores. In the first instance, increasing population, improvements in family income, and changes in income distribution have brought about an escalation in the quality of products demanded. The National Industrial Conference Board uses the term *demography of demand* to describe changes in population, family incomes, patterns of income distribution, and to reflect generally the effects of demographic differences and economic changes on consumer buying habits.[2]

The second change concerns competition. Population and income increases, as well as suburban growth, impelled traditional department stores to open branches in shopping centers and in outlying communities. As a result they competed more intensively with their own main stores as well as with traditional rivals, which also expanded. Simultaneously, the same underlying conditions of demography of demand provided the opportunity for many innovative retail firms, such as discount stores, to enter the market. In addition, several

1

different kinds of retailers offered commodities that traditionally had been sold only, or primarily, in department stores.

Marketing theory suggests that when two such significant external variables change, the firm must respond by adjusting some or all of the components of its marketing mix in order to survive and grow. In the marketing literature, both retail practitioners and authors deem merchandising a key management function. Presumably, then, if a firm were to adjust to these two changes it would alter its merchandising strategy decisions. The focal point of this book centers equally on how and why department stores adjusted certain merchandising strategies in response to particular changes in their external environment.

Consumers in America spend approximately 65.1 percent of their personal disposable income for retail purchases. Sales in 1963 amounted to $244.2 billion[3] and by 1966 were estimated to be $303.6 billion.[4] Department stores ranked third in sales (after food stores and automotive dealers) among retail institutions and accounted for approximately $20.5 billion in sales in 1963, or 8.4 percent of the total.[5]

Among the literature sources that provide guidance and enlightenment concerning retail institutions and their changing environments are two recently published bibliographies: *A Selected and Annotated Bibliography of Retailing,* by A. Hamilton Chute, and *A Bibliography for Students of Retailing.*[6] In addition to such standard references as the *Journal of Marketing* and the *Journal of Retailing,* the revised editions of well-known retail texts are valuable sources,[7] as are a group of articles originally published in the *Harvard Business Review,* entitled "The Retail Strategy Series."[8]

Many authors deal extensively with merchandising, with adjustment to new forms of retailing, and with other important functions and concepts related to strategy. More specifically, some authors point to the alternative courses of action open to the strategist whose objective may be to gain additional gross margin or to secure new customers or to change the store image.[9]

The literature suggests that the phenomenon of retail revolution is a recurring one that is not peculiar to the last two decades only.[10] Since the most probable event in the business realm is change, an account of how and why department stores have adjusted to change makes it possible to cope more successfully with this certainty.

In the remaining portions of this chapter, three critical subject areas are examined. First, strict definitions of generally used marketing terms are set forth. Second, certain environmental forces bearing upon traditional department stores are examined. In this connection, managerial forces that implement marketing strategy are detailed. Third, the way in which this strategy is brought to bear is shown.

Definition of Terms

Department store is defined in the *Standard Industrial Classification Manual* as "an establishment normally employing 25 or more people and engaged in selling some items in each of these three merchandise lines: furniture, home furnishings, appliances, radio and television sets; apparel for men, women, and children; and household linens and dry goods."[11]

The famous stores cited earlier are typical of this category. Some are independently owned and managed by the owners or owning families; others are publicly owned and managed as a part of a larger operating firm, such as Federated Department Stores, Inc., or Allied Stores Corporation. For the purpose of this book, the term excludes such firms as Sears, Roebuck and Company and the J. C. Penney Company. Operating results from such firms are not included in reports of the National Retail Merchants Association or in the aggregate reports of sixteen department store groups, which are used here for comparative purposes. During most of the 1945-1965 period the Penney Company did not carry furniture or major appliances. Further, these firms, as well as Montgomery Ward and Company, are regarded by trade associations as national department store chains rather than traditional department stores. The latter usually confine their retailing to a metropolitan or regional area.

The *SIC Manual* does not identify the discount department store as a separate type of retail store. One authority identifies a discount store "as a retail store that is called such because of the fact, belief, or claim that it sells at a discount off the list, 'usual,' or 'regular' price."[12] A trade publication defines a discount store as "a departmentalized retail establishment utilizing many self-service techniques to sell hard goods, apparel, soft goods, health and beauty aids, and other general merchandise. It operates at uniquely low margins. It has a minimum annual volume of $500,000 and is at least 10,000 square feet in size."[13]

Discount department store, as the term is used in this study, means a discount house that sells at least the three merchandise lines ascribed to a regular or traditional department store. By way of example, this definition includes such foremost retailers as E. J. Korvette, the Topps and White Front divisions of Interstate Department Stores, Woolco division of the F. W. Woolworth Company, Zayre's, and Arlan's among others.[14]

"**Merchandising** consists of those activities leading up to and including active selling. It includes determination of customer wants and desires and determination of the store's character as to merchandise and services offered to those customers. It also includes the promoting of merchandise and the conducting of selling and related services functions."[15] This definition is given by the NRMA and is used throughout the present study.

The American Management Association defines this activity as "the planning involved in marketing the right merchandise, at the right place, at the right time, in the right quantities, and at the right price."[16]

Edmund D. McGarry considers merchandising as the most comprehensive term to express the process of fitting merchandise to potential customers' desires.[17] Two textbook authors, Delbert J. Duncan and Charles F. Phillips, write that "the responsibilities of this division are centered in buying and selling activities, and these functions are considered the 'heart' of the retail business."[18]

Strategy is an overall plan or concept for carrying on the firm's business. More specifically, it is a plan to achieve certain objectives or goals, and includes a set of guidelines or decision rules to be employed to reach these goals. As used here, it is the plan that directs the merchandising activity. A merchandising strategy for a retail firm designates a specific market target, identifies the kinds of merchandise assortments and promotional appeal to be used for that target, formulates decision-making rules to govern executive action, and distinguishes between proximate and ultimate goals.

Price-lining for a merchandise classification "consists of selecting certain prices and carrying assortments only at these prices, except when mark-downs are taken."[19] This decision establishes the range of prices for that classification.

Several writers have pointed out that a soundly conceived price-lining decision is advantageous for both the customer and the retailer. William R. Davidson and Alton F. Doody claim that price-lining helps the customer "to identify significant differences in available prices with (her) concepts of desired quality and within the budgetary considerations that guide her merchandise selection."[20]

For the retailer, price-lining simplifies the buying function. Because of the predetermined range of retail prices, the retailer eliminates those suppliers whose merchandise does not fit the plan. Fred M. Jones has pointed out that there is "a tendency of customers of a given income group to pay about the same prices" for a merchandise classification.[21] If a merchant identifies his market target by income group, he can built assortments around a limited number of price-points and thereby improve his selection within the given price-range.

Trade up is closely allied to price-lining, and refers to a merchandising decision to emphasize upper price-points within a range or to extend the upper limits of the range. In addition, the retailer could decide to eliminate some lower price-points.

Advertising is "the preparation of visual and aural messages and their dissemination through paid media."[22] Department stores expend the largest percentage of advertising budgets in newspapers. Hence, this form of advertising is the continuing reflection of store character and often may be the first communication between store and customer.

Demand refers to people with needs and desires to satisfy, the financial capacity, including credit, to purchase, and the willingness to buy.

Demography of demand, as noted previously, describes conditions such as population, income, and social interaction, which influence consumer behavior.

Competition, as used in this volume, is the kind and degree of rivalry among retailers in a given market. The term also refers to the activities by which these rivals search for and attract customers and suppliers. It also refers to the rivalry in other merchandising decision areas such as pricing, advertising, or selecting assortments, for example.

Influential External Forces

Like all marketing institutions, the department store faces a set of external environmental factors usually regarded as uncontrollable.[23] Among these are demand, competition, law, and population. Marketing writers, notably Stanton, Duncan and Phillips, Alderson, Davidson and Doody, and Hollander, among others, have analyzed these forces to which the firm must adust.[24]

A legitimate business enterprise is sanctioned by law at birth and is partially constrained by law throughout its life. The state of technology often determines what the retail offering shall be. The structure of communication and distribution influences operational costs and may also determine retail location. While it does not minimize the influence of these other dimensions, this study is concerned only with conditions of demand and competition.

Demography of Demand

In its report on changes in the demography of demand for 1950-1960, the National Industrial Conference Board concluded:

All in all, the consumer market in the Fifties was marked by an enormous upward escalation in the quality of demand. . . . As the household's ability to buy expands and as cultural horizons are broadened, each additional dollar is spent differently than the last. In the lower and middle-income levels, where money often goes for improvements in the quality and quantity of necessities, this process is less pronounced. But in the middle and upper brackets, where everyday wants are already substantially satisfied, expanding buying power is likely to go for a wide range of luxury goods and services.[25]

Among other findings, the NICB particularly emphasized the rising entry into the work force by married women, the attainment of more education by a greater proportion of the population, and an extensive shift in the entire occupational mix from blue-collar to white-collar employment. With the greatly expanded middle-income class manifesting this change in income distribution, a significant number of families moved from the necessity to the discretionary income bracket.

The change in income distribution was accompanied by an increase in the average family's income. In 1961, two out of every five American family units belonged to the discretionary income group—those who earned more than $6,000 per year before taxes.[26] During the past thirty years, the national income in constant dollars increased at a greater rate than did the total population.[27] As income increases, the expectations of consumers also increase. Charles J. Collazzo reports: "Members of so-called upper income groups, in other words, put more emphasis upon being able to get what they want when they want it. They are also able to define their needs and to state their frustrations precisely."[28]

Competition

Competition for patronage of families with increasing amounts of discretionary income exists among all retailers. The management of a traditional department store thus is confronted with a paradox of consumer behavior. Malcolm P. McNair explains this phenomenon, one he calls the "crisis of expectation," as follows:

Many of our great middle class groups have suddenly experienced a widening horizon of the "economic good life" and these aspirations have grown more rapidly than has the disposable income of many of these same families. Too many dollars are tagged before they are received, and one of the consequences is a greatly increased receptivity to price bargains, especially in apparel, household furnishings, and food. Hence we find the seemingly incongruous situation of rising income and rising economic well-being accompanied by a substantially heightened interest in bargain merchandise.[29]

One of the leading forces in the retailing of bargain merchandise is the discount department store, which was born and has flourished during a period when all the aforementioned upward changes in the demography of demand also occurred. Shopping surveys indicate that all income classes patronize discount department stores. It is true that middle-to-higher income groups may patronize these retailers only for a limited number of department store kinds of merchandise. Just as they are challenged to design a strategy to compete for customers benefiting from positive trends in demography of demand, the traditional department stores have to adopt some strategy to compete most effectively with discounters.

In addition, the department store management has to compete with its own traditional rivals and with specialty and variety stores which have expanded their assortments both in price-range and kind. This phenomenon of "scrambled merchandising" has intensified competition in the entire industry. Scrambled merchandising is distinct from trading up within price-lines. The former term refers primarily to additional classifications of merchandise, which the merchant had not previously offered. For example, after 1945 several variety store chains added women's ready-to-wear and sportswear and children's outerwear classifications and thus began to compete with basement stores of traditional department stores. Or a more common instance is the addition by food stores of health and beauty aids classifications. Trading up, again, as used herein, describes a merchandising decision about the price-ranges. It should be noted, as well, that trade up can refer to such merchandise attributes as style and quality as well as to price.

Merchandising Strategy

Since this volume is primarily concerned with how and why stores have responded to the aforementioned external changes, it is appropriate to explain in greater detail what constitutes a merchandising strategy.

An increasing number of writers in marketing and retailing have emphasized strategy.[30] Perhaps this results from attention devoted to managerial rather than institutional aspects of the discipline. Most of these writers agree with one researcher of managerial philosophies who reports:

Effective application of management principles is largely dependent upon what is in the minds of those who apply them. While businessmen recognize that profit is essential to a healthy enterprise, they acknowledge that profit can be cut off at the source if all of management does not understand or is uninformed about the goals or objectives of the enterprise or has inconsistent attitudes about how the profit is to be made.[31]

The foregoing presupposes that a strategy, a plan, exists. Wroe Alderson asserts that "to adopt a marketing strategy is to take a stance or posture in the search for customers."[32] Wendell R. Smith describes a marketing strategy as

being primarily concerned with the creative elements of a goal-directed marketing plan . . . which includes the basic elements of the way in which the firm plans to get from where it is to where it wants to be . . . and it becomes the central theme that integrates and coordinates the many and diverse components of effort to be stipulated in the plan.[33]

Strategy formulation helps a retail firm to differentiate itself from competitors, since it forces the firm to a thorough analysis of itself, its competitors, and the marketplace. Finally, it requires a calculated forecast of the outcome.

By arbitrarily designating a strategy as offensive or defensive, the retailer can differentiate his own strengths and weaknesses from the complementary weaknesses and strengths of a rival. An offensive strategy leads to plans to capitalize fully on the relative strengths or advantages the firm enjoys, or conversely, upon the relative weaknesses or disadvantages the competitor has. A defensive strategy compensates for and corrects weaknesses in the firm's present operation or counteracts strengths or advantages the rival enjoys.[34]

It is axiomatic that a strategy should be formulated on the basis of the opportunity the retailer perceives in the marketplace. But successful execution of a strategy may depend on when as well as how the merchant interacts with his environment. A retail historian has observed:

> . . . [one] reason for believing in the importance of environment (upon the retailer) is the number of times the same innovation has been introduced simultaneously by a number of separate individuals. Closely allied to this are the number of unsuccessful similar ventures that have preceded many successful innovations. . . . Such experiences suggest that retailers are constantly probing the empty sectors of competitive strategy with many failures until someone uses exactly the right technique at the right time. In at least some cases, the merchant prince's skill may have been in judging opportunities rather than in originating techniques.[35]

An executive vice-president of Federated Department Stores commented on the significance of timing as it relates to changes within the market and the ability of the merchant to take action. He wrote:

> When you look back over the history of retailing, there have been quite a few major breakthroughs, and in every case they were made by the ability of a brilliant individual to look ahead of his immediate problems to foresee some great new trend in the future . . . there was one common denominator to all these innovations . . . first, they were introduced by a brilliant owner or manager who sensed more or less instinctively the need for change, and who had the power to take the necessary risk in making it. Second, they arose from existing or anticipated–but always real–customer needs. Third, all had profits as their objectives. . . .[36]

The statement was made earlier that in formulating a strategy the retailer must spell out his objectives. Only one objective, profit, can head the hierarchy of objectives. Others can only be the means to this one supreme end. Because these others are encountered in the literature and in research, they warrant explanation. In addition to profit, two objectives most often mentioned are market share and store image or store character.

Profit serves as a means as well as an end. The decision rule, for example, in selecting a classification or a price-range within it, or in determining when to place it in the store may simply be: can the firm generate a profit by merchandising this classification, per se? This must be contrasted with another decision rule which says, in effect, if it attracts customers and adds to the store's prestige, or if it differentiates the firm from others in the marketplace, it can be added to the assortment. When this objective also serves as a criterion, the strategist is constrained to measure every merchandising alternative solely by its impact upon the three primary components of profit: sales, gross margin, and expense.

A merchandising strategy may have as one of its objectives a certain share of the market. The term may apply to the total store volume compared with the total retail trading area, or to the store's sales volume compared with other department stores. For example, the J. L. Hudson Company's strategy stipulates that it must obtain a certain percentage of the total amount of retail sales in its trading area for every classification it merchandises. Bloomingdale's perceives itself as a merchant to a particular market segment whose incomes permit purchases on the basis of taste and quality and to whom price may be secondary.

The strategy must establish priorities so that the merchandise assortment, pricing, and services are provided in proportion to the demand characteristics of the selected market target. Some theorists in marketing have analyzed this dimension of target selection strategy as it applies to retailing. Alderson, for one, has contended that

the notion that any store could handle everything became a hollow illusion. . . . It is not clear that department stores as a group are in the extinction mode and some may have many profitable years ahead without demands for change which exceed the capacity of their executives to manage change. But those who survive will have to renounce the universal marketing task of matching all goods with all people.[37]

Many practitioners as well as researchers commented on the need by management to define "what kind of a store it is." Charles E. McCarthy, former Allied Stores president, now a St. John's University professor, remarked: "One requisite for survival and for success must be continuous striving for individuality and leadership in merchandising and services to the public. . . . Many department stores have failed because they did not achieve or maintain a distinctive personality in their particular community."[38]

Pierre Martineau's frequently quoted admonition concerning the customer's perception of the store is apropos. His research indicates that the force that draws a shopper to one store rather than another is the store's personality or image, "the way the store is defined in the shopper's mind, partly by its functional qualities and partly by an aura of psychological attributes."[39]

Significance of the Merchandising Function

In adjusting to the changing conditions of demography of demand and to competition, management considers alternatives pertaining to location and physical plant, merchandise assortment, promotion, price, and personal selling. In addition, management is also involved with functions such as finance, personnel, and store supervision. Management regards these factors of retailing as controllable when devising a total strategy. Hence, the merchandising function becomes especially significant for the following reasons:

Customer. Merchandising is responsible for matching the firm's offering to customer needs and wants. The merchant interacts between two markets, buying from suppliers or resources those goods he believes he can sell to customers. In this process he influences managerial definition of what kind of a store the firm aims to be.

Organization. Merchandising has been the organizational core of department stores. Whether seen in the 1927 Mazur plan or in the recent NRMA recommendations for multistore operations, the merchandising function is the one that has persisted as the central element in store organization.[40]

Gross margin. Merchandising is responsible for generation of gross margin, the excess of sales over the cost of sales. Since earnings result primarily from the interaction of gross margin and total expense, the relationship of merchandising to the objective of profits is obvious.

Inventory. Merchandising is directly related to the management of the inventory. This usually is the largest or the second largest investment of the firm's assets.

Expenses. Merchandising affects the majority of expenses in the department store. As defined, merchandising includes both the selling and sales promotion functions. Personal selling is the largest single, controllable expense, approximately 25 percent of the total expense structure. Effective personal selling can differentiate the department store from kindred or related forms of competition.[41] The cost of the management of the merchandising function itself usually exceeds 3 percent of sales. The second largest controllable expense, ranging from 4 percent to 6 percent of sales, is sales promotion.

Sales promotion. This function includes advertising, display, and publicity and bears significantly upon the firm's profitability. Within this function the largest budgetary share is expended for advertising, essentially for the newspaper medium. As "the outside face of the store," newspaper advertising can differentiate a store from its competition even when the merchandise is homogeneous.

Relationship of Merchandising Strategy to External Conditions

In devising a merchandising strategy to cope with changes in the external conditions of demography of demand and of competition, the traditional department store can consider several alternatives. It can imitate, ignore, or partially adopt the merchandising strategies of its rivals; it can manage change by catering to particular segments of its market. And, of course, it can design a merchandising strategy to encompass all of these.

To illustrate this range of possibilities, a department store, in response to either a positively changing demography of demand or increasing discount store competition, could trade up. Or the firm might alter its sales promotion function by adjusting the balance between various forms of advertising and display so as to reflect modified objectives. In the personal selling function, it might elect to increase the quantity and quality of salespeople, or it could substitute self-selection.

Both in the literature and among merchants there is frequent reference to "trading up" and to "increasing the fashion appeal" as desirable means for adjustment. These terms merit further discussion.

To exemplify the term *trade up* as previously defined, let us suppose that a knit dress department stocks garments ranging from $29.95 to $79.95 at retail prices. A change in policy could affect the emphasis within that range, say, from $39.95 to $49.95, or extend the range from $29.95 to $100.00, or extend upward to $100.00 and eliminate the $29.95 price. There are usually many reasons for the change in policy: change in resource market supply at various price-points; change in style or fabric, which affects resource market prices; change within the retail firm requiring higher gross margins, which may be obtained by shifting the range.

Another cause for trading up might be a change in demography of demand. That is to say, if consumer affluence and taste level are both increased, a department store could adjust its price-range emphasis to include those types of merchandise its new or changing customer groups would find satisfactory. A second external force, competition, particularly price competition at lower points within the range, could force the department store to trade up. In the former instance, the strategy would be offensive; in the latter, defensive.

A second merchandising strategy the traditional department store could consider is style emphasis. Should the buyer modify stocks to include style newness and style uniqueness at earlier rather than later stages in the cycles through which styles are prone to travel?[42] Should he assert leadership and thereby increase risk? As demography of demand moves in a positive direction, should the merchant await a shift, say, in style emphasis, or a change in taste level? Or should he attempt to stimulate or accelerate these changes by means of merchandise assortments, sales promotion, and fashion leadership? As low-margin retailers seek to widen their own assortments of fashion merchandise and trade up, can the traditional department store respond successfully by increasing style emphasis?

Competition for patronage of families with increasing amounts of discretionary income arises from new forms of retailing such as discount department stores. There may be alternative adjustments the traditional department store can make other than those already mentioned, such as trading up and catering to the escalated taste levels. The traditional department store could choose to compete more vigorously on price, discontinue services such as personal selling, and even trade down.

What strategy should a traditional department store adopt in order to compete most effectively with discounters? Stuart U. Rich and Bernard Portis propound a three-part set of alternatives: one, to convert to self-service, drop other services, and feature discount prices; second, to trade up, drop some of the more competitive hard-goods lines, emphasize fashion, and offer more services; and third, to upgrade merchandise lines and emphasize fashion, but at the same time add certain features of the discounters on a limited basis.[43]

The authors point out that the first alternative might mean leading from weakness rather than from strength, providing the store is already a strong or superior contender in the local retail competitive race. On the other hand, if a department store is second- or third-rate to start with (stressing price appeal and having no particular standing in the community, anyway), then to join the ranks of discounters will probably not harm its position and may boost its sales, at least temporarily.

Selection of the first alternative can result in the death of a business. "Temporarily" is rather tenuous. The danger in this alternative is that the retailer, while achieving temporary sales gains, may overlook or fail to look for the causes of his present marketplace position. In Philadelphia, for instance, F. E. Brown and George Fisk analyzed the reasons why certain stores failed. They report that both a traditional Philadelphia department store and a discount department store committed two errors. First, both stores underestimated the desire for quality among consumers in their market areas. Second, they gave too little weight to the importance of consumer desire for reliable information in retail advertising. The authors conclude that "both mistakes contributed substantially to the deaths of these stores."[44] The essential point here is that to formulate a strategy of trade up or trade down without careful judgment of the consumer's desires or without scrutinizing the assumptions the retailer makes about the consumer's desires can result in failure.

Some stores did choose to compete directly with discounters, indeed, to ape them. One notable example was the Famous-Barr Company in St. Louis, a division of May Company Stores. This store's volume about equalled the combined sales totals of its next two largest competitors. Although the Famous-Barr Basement Store had operated successfully for many years, the company, in responding to discount competition, "rushed to self-selection in basement operations in 1961. This turned out to be a bomb. The project was dropped several weeks later after massive customer complaints. The quality level of the merchandise was too high for self-service."[45]

The second alternative is to trade up, drop some of the more competitive hard-goods lines, emphasize fashion, and offer more services. This would capitalize on the distinctive attractions of the department store. The danger of the strategy lies in the possible loss of the middle-income customer who would then purchase hard-goods lines elsewhere. Further, self-service in these classifications of merchandise is accepted by a very large number of customers from all income groups.

The third strategy is the one Rich and Portis believe to be most promising in the light of their findings about shopping behavior. This recommendation is to upgrade merchandise lines, to emphasize fashion, and to adopt certain features of the discounters on a limited basis.

It points to the significant fact that the very nature of the merchandise itself may determine how it may be handled most profitably, congruent with the store's objectives and yet offered or sold or serviced in accordance with the customer's desires.

Fashion apparel exemplifies this last consideration about merchandise. Apparel lends itself to personal selling, and it frequently requires alterations. In addition, apparel satisfies psychological as well as physical needs. For these reasons it is the kind of merchandise for which women rely on the quality and reputation of the individual store. In contrast, such classifications as housewares, children's clothes, some lines of domestics, can be displayed and sold by means of self-selection and even self-service, even in department stores.

In a recent study of strategies used by major department stores that compete with low-margin retailers, Walter Gross notes that those who adopted a successful strategy did so early in the rivalry, anticipating the entry into their local markets of these innovators, and planning and effecting new marketing programs. This proved far less costly in the long run than if they had waited until the innovators were established.[46] He also observes that

the pathways for different departments within a store may vary. The proper direction for a particular department to follow should not be determined by wishful thinking about margin requirements but rather by trends which appear to be emerging in the nature of the major demand component for that particular merchandise line.

In his conclusions, Gross agrees with Rich and Portis that major department stores may choose to follow one of three fundamental strategies to meet the competition of low-margin retailers: one, to cater to groups primarily interested in low-price merchandise; two, to cater to groups primarily interested in high-price merchandise; or, three, to attract substantial numbers of customers from both of these groups.

A fourth alternative, which apparently these investigators did not consider, is the possibility that a firm could resolve this marketing problem by creating its own discount store subsidiary, and thus rival itself. The decision by the Dayton Company, Minneapolis, to open its Target Stores, a series of discount stores in the Minneapolis market, is consistent with its avowed objective of being all things to all people.[47]

Among the writers cited, Rich and Portis, and, again, Gross, concentrate on a single, external, force—discount competition. Other external forces cited in the literature and frequently mentioned by merchants are the changes in conditions underlying demography of demand. Therefore this investigation was expanded to include the responses of traditional department stores to both external forces: discount store competition and demography of demand.

Authors and merchants stress that all merchandising activities are interactive and interdependent. If a store decides to trade up, for example, it must also consider the effects of this decision upon such activities as personal selling, or display, or advertising. Of these latter-named activities, the role of advertising has often been associated with trading up in the development of a merchandising strategy.

Edward A. Filene, a merchant who expressed his views in *The Model Stock Plan*, advised the retailer to base his advertising upon his merchandising.[48] That is to say, the retailer should reflect in advertising those items the store stocks and sells most effectively. Since he advocates the Model Stock Plan as the foundation for merchandising, he logically claims that advertising should be based on that plan as well. Two writers in the area of retail advertising urge that effective advertising requires planning by price-lines. They suggest that "the (advertising) appropriation may be distributed to price-lines proportionate to the dollar values that each contributes in total department dollar sales."[49] From a study conducted in 1932 by the New York University School of Retailing, it was found that half of the stores surveyed concentrated their advertising appropriation on the three best-selling price lines.[50]

The foregoing suggests that, in responding to selected external forces, the retailer would alter his strategy with regard to trading up and advertising by adjusting both in the same direction. The retailer must consider price-lining in reaching a decision about these activities. Price-lining, by the nature of the function, is one of the more accessible merchandising elements for research purposes. Hence, these two interactive merchandising elements are the basis for this investigation of changes in merchandising strategies. Further, the following hypothesis was selected as a guideline for the investigation:

Traditional department stores facing an increasing demography of demand and increasing low-margin (discount) store competition alter their merchandising strategy as follows: they trade up within their price-ranges or increase their price-ranges upward; and they adjust their newspaper advertising to reflect these policies.

II

Methods
of
Investigation

The investigation on which this book is based consisted of case studies of how and why four department stores adjusted to external change during the 1945-1965 period. In undertaking the investigation, two alternative methods of inquiry were considered. One was to extensively study a large sample of stores by means of a questionnaire survey. Another was to conduct an intensive study of a small number of stores by personal interview. Some researchers believe the personal interview can be more revealing than a questionnaire when the purpose of the investigation is to determine *how as well as why* a firm selects a particular course of action. For example, the manager of research projects for the American Management Association comments:

We are using questionnaires less and less in our research. We lean a lot more heavily on the interview method now. There are simply too many nuances of any subject that a questionnaire does not bring forth, even an expertly designed one. Face to face conversation seems to be the only way that we can find out things in depth.[1]

There are no patents in the retail industry. However, there are individual leaders whose superior judgment of situation and opportunity, when combined with personality or conviction or entrepreneurship, enables them to lead their companies through adjustment to survival and growth. It appeared that more revealing data could be obtained by interviewing executives responsible for formulating and executing merchandising strategy.

In an impersonal survey some of these executives might have been unwilling or unable to disclose judgmental factors pertinent to particular decisions. A personal interview provides a better opportunity to detect the subtle reasons for change. The interactive process of interviewing can encourage recollection of conditions and decisions that significantly affected the courses of events.

Another reason for selecting this method was to secure in greater detail a review of events by more than one executive in each firm. This provided a check for consistency and continuity. In addition, I believed my own experience in the department store industry might also encourage respondents' cooperation and disclosure. I had participated in the management of a retail enterprise for a number of years, serving as a buyer, then as director of the merchandising, sales promotion, and personnel functions and had acquired an intimate knowledge of the industry.

The 1945-1965 period was selected for study for several reasons. First, many profound changes in marketing, retailing, and department store institutions occurred subsequent to World War II.[2] Second, as previously noted, external environmental changes accelerated rapidly at the same time. Third, one objective of the study was to interview executives directly involved in management during these adjustments. Selection of a previous period might preclude such a possibility either because current top management members might not have been in decision-making levels prior to World War II, or because many executives who were in those positions at that time had retired or left their companies by 1966.

The firms studied were selected on a three-criteria basis. First, the department stores had to have been in business for at least fifty years. This meant that the firm had operated during turbulent economic conditions, had competed with various kinds of retailers, and undoubtedly had been managed by different men or groups.

Second, firms were selected whose managements possessed considerable discretion and autonomy in resource allocation and in merchandising judgment. If a national headquarters or an absentee ownership imposed bureaucratic requirements upon management, it would become even more difficult to ascertain both how and why the particular firm responded.

The third criterion was that the firms investigated be located in large, urbanized centers on the presumption that the impact of both external environmental factors to be studied would be more pronounced in these areas.

Each of the enterprises selected met the minimum test of successful adjustment—survival. In 1965, the youngest was sixty-six years old; the oldest, ninety-three. During at least six decades each has been exposed to economic turbulence, sociological and political changes, and changes in population. Each exceeds $12,000,000 in annual volume (1965) and operates at least one branch store; and each is located in a Standard Metropolitan Statistical Area comprising a trading area of at least 250,000 population. All of the executives interviewed were active in their respective companies. Fictitious names are used throughout this report.

Procedure

All communities and all trading areas in the United States did not change in the same direction or to the same degree during the 1945-1965 period. An attempt was made to ascertain what had been the major changes, if any, in demography of demand and in competition in each community represented in this study.

The following demographic and economic criteria were used to trace trends within each subject store's trading area: population, net effective buying income, total retail sales, general merchandise sales, and income distribution. Although individual newspaper research departments and public agencies have published numerous analyses of their respective areas, it was decided to use standard references for all areas. Accordingly, data were obtained from the *U.S. Census Reports* and *Sales Management Buying Power Guide*.

Due to company prohibitions, it was not possible to secure the same kinds or amounts of financial information from all firms. However, a thorough search of a retail trade publication file for all of the firms and of the newspaper files in each local community was conducted. These sources afforded an opportunity to augment both financial and historical accounts given by company executives. The sources also revealed changes in local competition, including the opening of shopping centers and of discount stores.

These investigations provided objective reports on changes that occurred in each market during the 1945-1965 period, and a basis for evaluation of managerial perception of its external environment.

Thirty executives in the four firms were interviewed. Their responsibilities ranged from chairman of the board to buyer, and included staff executives. In some instances these officials were interviewed a second time. Each was asked the same set of questions germane to merchandising strategy.

"To have the right goods at the right time at the right place at the right price," a merchant must read his market accurately and with some foresight. Interviewing several executives within one firm provided a check for consistency among those responsible for merchandising strategy. Further, by comparing the interviewee's version of the external market with objective demographic, economic, and competitive data, the executive's knowledge of his market could be appraised, and his opinion obtained on which tactics were most significant in the merchandising strategy.

Direct interview questions sought information about the history of the firm; the merchandising strategies currently formulated and implemented; and changes for which the individual executive had been responsible in conception, formulation, or execution. While the questions were intended to elicit information pertinent to the hypothesis, additional inquiries were made when it appeared that causes other than those hypothesized might underlie apparent changes in merchandising strategy.

Corroboration of Interview Data

Subsequent to personal interviews questionnaires were sent to those executives interviewed and to additional respondents in each store. There were several objectives: The first was to corroborate interview data by comparing what executives said the firm did with the way in which the firm in fact behaved, as revealed by actual records. The second was to compare the relationship of changes, if any, between merchandise and advertising price-lining, two elements of a merchandising strategy. Toward that end, the respondents were asked to provide information about merchandise and advertising price-lining in their respective areas of responsibility. The third was to secure the retailer's own records or his estimates of changes in price-lining, which, in turn, would indicate a trend in trade up. Fourth was to provide the opportunity for the respondents to state whether they attributed merchandising events to the external environmental events. Appendix B is a copy of the questionnaire.

Four methodological problems were forestalled. The first pertained to the question of which merchandise classifications the questionnaire should include. Although the National Retail Merchants Association divided the total merchandise offering of a department store into seventy-three major departments, it was deemed unnecessary for the objectives at hand to inquire about all of these.

The second problem emanated from the first. Price-lining, of course, is a decision about items or classifications of merchandise, not about departments. Which classifications should be included?

The third problem was how to evaluate price-lining changes due to general price-level changes. Unless this was resolved there could be no answer to the question: did the store trade up or did it simply move with the general trend of the market prices as reflected in the price index?

The fourth problem was to locate some independent source whose data could corroborate store records of the price-lining of merchandise advertised. Since newspaper advertising is a public record, the measurement of advertising price-lining would provide both a check of store records supplied and also some indication of the merchandising strategy.

To solve the first and second problems, merchandise departments were selected on the basis of the following criteria: they should represent major kinds of goods included in accepted definitions of a department store, including those which emphasize fashion; they should represent major sales volume contributions to total store volume.

The departments selected for study are listed in Appendix A. Nationally, they account for 22.8 percent of the total "Main Store" volume. Of the total newspaper expenditures, 27.2 percent is allocated to these departments. In turn, the respective classifications within each department are listed in Appendix A.[3]

To solve the third and fourth problems, it was necessary to find indexes applicable to price-lining of merchandise advertised, and that also took into account changes in the price level. The discussion now turns to these.

In his study of the American department store from 1920-1960, McNair concluded that "the so-called Lifo index, the Department Store Inventory Price Index (hereafter referred to as DSIPI), is the best current department store price index."[4] The DSIPI reflects both the methodology of the regular Consumer Price Index and the particular array of commodities a department store normally carries.

Therefore this index serves as a basis of comparison for merchandise price-lining throughout the study.

The Neustadt Price Studies

There was need also to find or devise an index applicable to price-lining of merchandise advertised as well as merchandise stocked and sold. Since 1932, department stores and newspapers have used the Neustadt Price Studies of Retail Advertising.[5] These studies measure all newspaper advertising published over a signature of a retail store for a selected list of seventy-six items of various classifications of merchandise, including those previously designated for this investigation.

Advertising of each selected commodity is grouped into six price zones, which are considered natural zones for the commodity. The price zones are flexible and are subject to change annually, dependent upon current patterns of retail prices. For example, a current range of women's and misses' silk or wool dresses is zoned as follows: zone 1, under $10.00; zone 2, $10.01-$18.00; zone 3, $18.01-$28.00; zone 4, $28.01-$38.00; zone 5, $38.01-$50.00; and zone 6, over $50.00.

Although the Neustadt research is sponsored by retail and newspaper clients the documents are now available publicly. A preliminary investigation revealed that while some department stores may have been advised of the results of these surveys, they did not possess nor could they currently obtain data from 1945-1965. In a few localities where newspapers could locate data covering the time period of 1945-1965, the stores had not collected nor had they retained merchandise price-lining data.

Store executives advised that while they had traditionally related advertising expenditures to sales by departments, they infrequently maintained a record of these expenditures by classification or by price-line of goods advertised. In addition, there was frequent executive turnover among those operating officials who normally would supply and interpret department or classification data.

Although the concept of classification thinking had been discussed for several decades prior to 1960, it did not make a real impact until after that date. This is borne out by trade press statements that in 1963 the National Retail Merchants Association initiated a program to formalize classifications of merchandise. Since classification merchandising and advertising data were to provide corroborative evidence of interview data, it appeared that meaningful data for this study could only be generated for a period after 1960.

From 1960 to 1965 the BLS DSIPI remained steady.[6] Whereas the total increase amounted to 4.5 percent, the index did not rise by more than 1.5 percent in any one-year period. During this period the Neustadt price zone ranges generally remained unchanged.[7] The five-year span, 1960-1965, is a period in which the criterion of price-level stability of both merchandising and advertising was met while the external environment changed.

Given the paucity of price-lining information prior to 1960 and the price stability of the 1960-1965 period, it appeared obvious that more meaningful information could be secured for this limited span. Therefore, corroborative evidence was sought by analyzing Neustadt data for this time period and by means of a questionnaire. In order to facilitate understanding, the chart (Table II-1) is given at this point rather than later.

Complete Neustadt measurements of advertising price-lining for the subject stores and respective cities were obtained in two of the four cases; in the other two cases, only a limited amount of data could be obtained from either Neustadt or from respondents.

In Table II-1, three designations and descriptions are stated for each commodity measured. The broadest is that used in the Bureau of Labor Statistics, DSIPI. The next most inclusive is the National Retail Merchants Association's department number. The most specific is the Neustadt code number, which pertains to a classification of merchandise.

The DSIPI divides all department store merchandise into twenty-one groups. Illustrative of these is Group IX, Women's Outerwear and Girls' Wear. This group includes the following subgroups used in this study: coats and suits, dresses, and blouses and sportswear. In addition, the following DSIPI groups were included in the advertising price-lining measurements: Group II—Domestics and Draperies, Group X—Men's Clothing, Group XI—Men's Furnishings, and Group XVI—Furniture and Bedding.

For each of the commodities measured, the data include changes in the DSIPI, which uses 1941 = 100 as the base year. More specifically, as seen in Table II-1, the DSIPI index in 1960 was 185.9, and in 1965, 192.5. The relative change was 2.8 percent.

Although the NRMA department numbers represent subgroups within the DSIPI descriptions, they are not used in the analysis. The

TABLE II-1

Analysis of Advertising Price-lining in 1960 and 1965

Name of Mdse. Class. Women's and Misses' Dresses
Neustadt Code No. 10. *Neustadt Description: Silk Dresses, Rayon and other Synthetics, Woolens in Women's and Misses' Sizes, Dresses for street wear, afternoon, and evening wear included. Junior Sizes excluded.*
DSIPI Description: *Women's Wear–Dresses.*

NRMA Dept. No. 42-11
DSIPI Group: IX
DSIPI Index, *1960:* 185.9 (1941 = 100)
DSIPI Index, *1965:* 192.5 (1941 = 100)
Relative Change in Index, 1965/1960: 102.8

Price Zone No.	Price Range	Analysis: 9-Cities				Analysis: Monroeville				Analysis: Staplinger's			
		1960		1965		1960		1965		1960		1965	
		Percent of Adv./Zone	Index of Adv.	Percent of Adv./Zone	Index of Adv.	Percent of Adv./Zone	Index of Adv.	Percent of Adv./Zone	Index of Adv.	Percent of Adv./Zone	Index of Adv.	Percent of Adv./Zone	Index of Adv.
(1)	Under $10.00	13	13	14	14	11	11	12	12	13	13	12	12
(2)	$10.01 to $18.00	28	56	22	44	29	58	26	52	31	62	33	66
(3)	$18.01 to $28.00	15	45	14	42	21	63	16	48	21	63	10	30
(4)	$28.01 to $38.00	12	48	12	48	12	48	12	48	12	48	6	24
(5)	$38.01 to $50.00	12	60	14	70	10	50	12	60	8	40	18	90
(6)	Over $50.00	20	120	24	144	17	102	22	132	15	90	21	126
	TOTALS	100	342	100	362	100	332	100	352	100	316	100	348
	1965/1960 Index:		105.8				106.0				110.1		
	Price Center:	$ 24.00		$ 28.00		*Below*		*Below*		*Below*		*Below*	

Monroeville less than 9-Cities both years but proportionately higher in 1965 than in 1960. Staplinger's less than Monroeville and less than 9-Cities both years even though its price center was proportionately higher in 1965.

1. Comp. their own adv. indexes, did 9-City group trade up?   x Yes;   No.
2. Comp. its own adv. indexes, did Monroeville trade up?   x Yes;   No.
3. Comp. its own adv. indexes, did Staplinger's trade up?   x Yes;   No.
4. Comp. with Monroeville did Staplinger's trade up, relatively?   x Yes;   No.
5. Comp. with 9-Cities, did Staplinger's trade up, relatively?   x Yes;   No.
6. Comp. relative changes in DSIPI and its own adv. indexes, did Staplinger's trade up?   x Yes;   No.
   Its change was (greater) than DSIPI change by 7.3 percent.
7. Other comments: Store traded up relative to itself but it traded in lower zones than either the city or 9-City aggregate. It shifted to higher-priced merchandise within upper three ranges. In 9-Cities this classification uses more lineage than any other. Based on interview data one would expect higher index and price center by store. See Chapter II, pp. 23-26, for an explanation of the terms "Above" and "Below" as used in this and all similar tables.

24

relevant department numbers are shown on the charts for the sake of convenience. For example, the DSIPI Group IX includes NRMA department number 42-00, described by the NRMA Controllers' Congress as Dresses. More specifically, Table II-1 concerns NRMA department number 42-11, Women's and Misses' Dresses. Table II-1 also illustrates the use of price zones and price zone ranges, terms discussed earlier.

Four additional measurements and comparisons are shown in this table.

The first is the "Percent of Advertising Per Zone," which shows how the total linage that was devoted to a given commodity classified was distributed among each of six price zones.

The second is the "Index of Advertising." This is the product of the first column multiplied by the price zone number. If a firm expended all of its linage (or dollars) in price zone 6, the index would read "600." These indexes have been successfully used for many years by Neustadt and newspaper clients and some retailers to analyze advertising strategies and campaigns. Some firms claim they can trace merchandising strategies from extensive series of these indexes on the assumption that the advertising strategy reflects the merchandising strategy.

The third is the "1965/1960 Index," obtained by dividing the 1965 Index of Advertising total by the 1960 total. This became the significant measurement of advertising price-lining trade up. An absolute change was deemed less significant than a relative change because an upward (or downward) change in the index of, say, twenty, was significant only in relation to the magnitude of the initial or ending index figure. Further, the relative measure permits a comparison with the DSIPI. Again referring to Table II-1 for illustration, the absolute change in advertising indexes for the 9-city group was 20, from 342 to 362. However, the more significant measurement was that the 1965 index was 5.8 percent greater than the 1960 index.

The fourth measurement is the "Price Center." This represents the mid-point price, the price with 50 percent of the linage expended above it, and 50 percent of the linage expended below it.

Neustadt measurements of this median figure could be obtained only for the 9-city group and these are stated precisely. The 9-city group includes New York, Brooklyn, Philadelphia, Washington, Pittsburgh, Cleveland, Detroit, Chicago, and St. Louis. Coincidentally, six of these nine cities are also among the eleven cities used by the Bureau of

Labor Statistics for construction of the DSIPI. In these cities, Neustadt measures linage for ninety commodities, all traditionally found in department stores.

Price-center measurements for individual cities and stores are stated as either above or below this 9-city standard. Such judgment is based on inspection of advertising linage expended for each zone in each instance.

The inquiry was: in what price zone does the 50 percent of the linage expenditure fall? Referring again to Table II-1, the price center for the 9-city group in 1960 was $24.00. In 1960, retailers in Monroeville, one of the cities studied, expended 40 percent of their linage in zones 1 and 2, and 61 percent through zone 3. Again, the median must be in zone 3. Since the Monroeville total through zone 3 was greater than the 9-city total, it was assumed that the Monroeville price center fell at some point below $24.00.

It should be pointed out that an assumption could also be made about the importance of the first two zones. In the example cited, the Monroeville retailers in 1960 devoted 41 percent of their linage in zones 1 and 2 as compared with the 9-city expenditure of 40 percent in these zones. One could argue that the median or price center might have been below rather than above the 9-city figure. For some of the comparisons, this possibility may obtain. For others, the judgment will seem more obvious. For instance, consider the same comparison for 1965. The 9-city price center falls at $28.00. In this instance the 50 percent expenditure is at the high end of price zone 3 so that the judgment by inspection coincides with the Neustadt measurement. The Monroeville price center is less than $28.00 because retailers in that city expended 54 percent of their linage in zones 1-3.

Accordingly, it seems valid to assume that price centers for cities as well as for individual stores were above or below the 9-city price center. In the respective tables these terms will be found beneath the tabular forms of "Percent of Adv./Zone" and "Index of Adv.," as seen in Table II-1.

By the same process, comparisons were also made between the 9-city group, individual cities, and specific stores studied. However, these less precise comparisons of price centers reinforced the decision to use the Index of Advertising as the essential criterion for evaluating advertising trade up.

Using the Index of Advertising as a basis, six comparisons for each classification were drawn in order to focus on the trade-up trends.

The reader should be aware of one additional condition underlying this analysis. The advertising price-lining data are for the July-December period for the respective years. Detailed investigation disclosed that this is not as serious as first supposed because more than 50 percent of the annual linage is expended during this period.

In ten of the seventeen commodities studied, more than 50 percent of the linage was expended in the July-December period over a period of years which included both 1960 and 1965. Of the seven below 50 percent, the lowest was the Men's Sports Coats classification, expending 45.5 percent of its annual linage in the last six months. Of the ten which were above 50 percent, the highest was the Women's and Misses' Sweater classification, expending 72.3 percent in the July-December period.

Results of Efforts to Obtain Corroborative Evidence

A considerable amount of data was secured concerning price-lining as revealed by the Neustadt measurements. It was anticipated that respondents at the stores would be able to provide data from store records. This, however, was not the case.

There were several reasons to believe the information regarding price-lining would be at hand. The questionnaire had been pretested at Eppley's (fictitious), a well-established department store which, while managed by the original founders, is now owned by a national department store chain. Merchandisers at Eppley's understood the questionnaire and were able to ferret out a great amount of information for 1964 and 1965.

In addition, the information sought by the questionnaire should have been available because for many years the department store industry, in general, and certain individual stores had been claiming that an information revolution was about to take place. By employing electronic data processing, it was said, stores would collect and retain details about their merchandising as well as about their environments. A third reason for believing the information could be obtained was that the executives had granted ample time and had generously answered questions during personal interviews.

Despite general assent to a request for cooperation prior to the dispatch of the questionnaires, the executives were unable to provide the information requested. The small response can be attributed, perhaps, to several conditions.

There is the possibility, of course, that the questionnaire was inadequately designed. Another explanation is that the questionnaire required too much time in addition to that which these executives had already given. The questionnaire required that specific data be obtained from store records or estimated by the respondent, but it also requested the executive to detail whether events represented by such data influenced his decision making.

The information was solicited as corroborative evidence and not as the primary substance for study. However, the lack of this information, in view of the proclaimed industry-wide efforts to generate more complete information, deserves additional comments, which will be made later in the book.

Basic Limitations

There are three basic limitations in this study. The first inheres in the subject. A basic assumption of the marketing concept is that external events, the environment outside the firm, act as the triggering agent, the cause, the reason for the action to be taken. This assumption is the limitation. However, the firm could adjust, could change its merchandising strategy for other reasons. One reason might be, as previously stated, not because a force impinges upon the firm but because the firm sees opportunity. Another reason might be that to continue the present strategy would not generate sufficient profit. That is to say, change could emanate from an internal as well as from an external cause.

A second limitation pertains to the methodology of investigations. The researcher must reckon with what one philosopher called the "egocentric predicament," the inability of a person to get outside or beyond his own experience. When asking an official to recall the business situation before, during, and after change, the following risks exist: the error or distortion of memory; the self-judgment, which the incumbent or the successor renders; and the subjective process of retrospective selection of facts and relating these to strategies that existed or were created ten or twenty years previously. And, of course, the investigator is also subject to the same circumscriptions during interviews and, again, later when selecting those data deemed most relevant.

The third limitation is the very small number of firms included in the research. The question arises whether these are special cases or whether they are representative of the industry. The answer will determine if any generalizations can be drawn. Again, the limitation is an assumption that more knowledge could be secured by means of a smaller number of intensive case studies.

The degree of the first and third limitations could be ascertained only after conducting the research. To diminish the effect of the second limitation, a second investigation was conducted to seek corroborative evidence. The limitations, however, did not appear to be so severe as to preclude the proposed research method.

In each case report, a four-part sequence is followed:

1) **History of the firm to 1945.** This includes data about the founding and the founders, demographic and economic characteristics of the market until 1945, and changes in merchandising strategies from founding until 1945.

2) **The 1945-1965 period.** This includes statements of demographic and economic characteristics of the market from 1945 to 1965, and managerial evaluation of those characteristics for that period based upon interview data and as reported in questionnaire responses.

3) **Managerial decisions regarding merchandising strategies for the 1945-1965 period.** Again, this is based upon interview and questionnaire data. In addition, sources outside the firm were used in this section, including the Neustadt data and the trade press and other publications.

4) **Comparisons between hypothesis and findings.** This includes an explanation of the congruence or variance between the hypothesis and findings.

Each case is examined in a separate chapter: Chapters III through VI. Chapter VII consists of a comparison of the four cases, and follows the same pattern as indicated for the individual cases. This chapter also sets forth conclusions of the investigation and proposes areas for additional research.

A great deal of interview information was secured on the basis of a pledge that names of individual stores and cities would be concealed. It has been necessary, therefore, to disguise all names of individuals interviewed as well as names of pertinent publications. Other literature sources, however, are cited as published.

III

Staplinger's

History of the Firm to 1945

Throughout its ninety-year history the retail firm of Staplinger and Rausch (hereafter referred to as Staplinger's) has earned several distinctions in the distribution trades. Its long business life is to be noted, of course. At times, Staplinger's led both the retail and wholesale industries with merchandising innovations, and currently it operates in these and other segments of the marketplace. Thus diversification has characterized its business life. The firm is also distinct by virtue of the continuity of family management and ownership. The current board chairman, Amos P. Rausch, represents the third generation engaged in active management. Families of the founders retain a controlling financial interest in the firm whose stock is traded publicly.

In 1873, two immigrants, Harry Staplinger and Robert Rausch, after serving an apprenticeship in a New York dry goods store, traveled westward and secured employment in a small Midstate community. Within two years they accumulated sufficient capital and credit to purchase a dry goods store in Beardon, Midstate. During the next four years they opened three additional stores located in comparably small Midstate communities, thereby creating one of the earliest chain store operations. Another dry goods merchant, Alexander Belmont, sought their counsel on whether or not he should open a store of his own in Monroeville, a leading city in Midstate. Staplinger and Rausch persuaded Belmont to join them as a partner instead. The triumvirate agreed that Belmont would open the fourth and largest store in Monroeville and also would organize a wholesale dry goods firm to supply themselves and other merchants in the state.

As the retail division grew in the flourishing Monroeville community, the wholesale division was expanded by opening branch offices in other states. The new business combination engrossed the partners' attention so extensively that they liquidated the smaller stores and moved to the larger city. Subsequently, they physically separated the two businesses. On land adjacent to the downtown section, Staplinger's erected a warehouse for the wholesale business. Simultaneously, it secured a leasehold on one of the city's choicest corners for the enlarged retail store.

A better understanding of the events after 1945 can be gained by noting some of the problems which Staplinger's faced, and some of the decisions reached, prior to 1945.

Managerial Decisions Prior to 1945

One decision pertained to the development of branch stores. As early as the 1920s several rival department stores opened branches in central business districts of Monroeville's booming suburbs. Staplinger's did not participate in such expansion. Many years later, in 1954, the president of the company said:

I agree that the management in the 1920s apparently erred on the conservative side. Staplinger's did not move, as did a number of others, to open branches in the heart of the big suburbs. The only compensation now is that we don't have the headache of operating branches in the center of suburban cities where parking is almost as much a problem as it is in downtown Monroeville. Our expansion now, and in the future, will be in shopping centers.[1]

A second problem which affected merchandising strategy prior to 1945 can be traced to the firm's dual role in distribution as a wholesaler and as a retailer. For many years Staplinger's was a retailer whose main interest was wholesaling. In retrospect it becomes apparent that one of America's oldest, best-known department stores has, almost since its founding, never devoted itself solely to the retail business.[2] One executive who started his career in the firm's wholesale division but who is now a corporate vice-president in the retail division said:

Prior to World War I we expanded the wholesale business by opening offices and branch warehouses in major cities throughout America. After the World War I boom, however, the wholesale segment of our business declined. Successive presidents of the firm continued to headquarter at the wholesale distribution center. The wholesale division did less business and generated less profit than the retail, but, nonetheless, the tail wagged the dog.[3]

Investigation confirmed this executive's appraisal. During the last seventeen years of its existence as a full-line wholesale business, from approximately 1925 to 1942, this division lost money in all years except two.[4]

A third major problem arose from the real estate lease governing the main downtown location. Harry Parrish, the general merchandise manager, pointed out that the high occupancy cost handicapped the firm both before and after 1945. A news report on the company's 80th Anniversary in 1955 elaborated: "There were times when the store earned a profit equal to 3 percent of sales. It appears the firm is definitely headed in that direction again. Until 1960, however, it will be hobbled by total occupancy costs of perhaps 4.5 percent of sales whereas the average is about half that figure."[5]

These conditions—failure to develop branch stores, the burdens of the wholesale division, and the real estate lease—influenced merchandising strategy before 1945 and again after 1945.

Merchandising Prior to 1945

Asked to describe Staplinger's merchandising prior to 1945, one executive responded:

We tried to be, and we were, a carriage-trade store, catering to upper-income groups. Quality-wise, I think we had a higher trade than we have today. We stayed in downtown Monroeville even as some of our customers moved to the suburbs. And we didn't make the kinds of profits needed to refixture and adequately maintain our plant.[6]

While reviewing the store's history, several executives (but not all) emphasized that Staplinger's pioneered in a number of personalized services, which enhanced the store's image and also rang the cash register profitably. One of these was a bridal service. Brides were invited to register their gift desires and pattern preferences in china and silver. Staplinger's also conceived the idea of hiring and training professional bridal attendants to go to weddings. By 1960, the store was reputed to cater to 5,000 weddings a year.[7]

Staplinger's also claimed a first in personalized service when it organized a shop for men only during the Christmas shopping season. In 1936, it reputedly transacted $250,000 in sales, an impressive sum in that year.

The store was one of the first in the 1930s to transform a portion of its ready-to-wear division into a College Shop. Supplementing this organization of merchandise classification in terms of customer needs and desires, the store selected a college board from among students.

Prior to 1927, home furnishings were limited in storage and display space. Confined chiefly to linens and domestics, draperies, and a few furniture items, categories which were carried in the wholesale business, the home furnishings division nonetheless managed to garner large-size contracts for convention halls, hotels, and other enterprises requiring complete interior decoration services. Impressed by this performance, the management constructed an addition to the retail store to house home furnishings departments. The depression thwarted major inventory expansion, however.

Staplinger's was one of the first to recognize possibilities of modern furniture after several merchandisers visited Sweden in 1935. Soon thereafter the buyers discovered that the California market could supply "simplicity of line and design," which epitomized what the division meant by modern design.

The Monroeville store earned the national attention of the decorative home goods trade in 1938 when it launched an ensemble called the Wishmaker House, a coordination of color and design in the home furnishings field. A trade journal reported:

The decorative home goods trade is impressed with this new coordinated idea Staplinger's has brought together. Many other stores signified their interest when a total of 20 other department stores asked to be franchised in their own cities to sell the ensembles made up by various producers according to Staplinger's specifications as to design and color.[8]

Subsequently, seventy-five department stores were licensed, and the participating manufacturers developed a home furnishings volume of several million dollars. The program continued until halted by the war in 1942.[9]

These ideas are commonplace today. However, the innovative quality at the particular time of introduction tends to belie some disparaging estimates, including those by its own executives, of the firm's force as an independent department store. An explanation for the less-than-favorable appraisal may lie in a general attitude concerning the store's management, which can best be summarized by the following:

Prior to 1945 we didn't integrate plans. We drifted through the 30's and even partially through the 40's. It was a family-owned, family-managed business, insulated and isolated, not quite alert to the need to develop a distinctive personality. Rather we tended to be a pale shadow of Smith's, who did a better job of getting trade from higher income groups.[10]

Changes in Monroeville Environment:
1945-1965

Some of the oldest and most famous traditional department stores are located in Monroeville. In this same market, several local and regional discount department store chains opened their original stores. In the period before 1945, the department stores of this city were among the first in the nation to establish branches in central business districts of suburban communities. Yet these same stores hesitated to participate in the shopping center movement after 1945. As income distribution widened considerably and residential relocation proceeded rapidly among both white and nonwhite groups after 1945, many traditional department stores in Monroeville couldn't make up their minds what to do about it. A description follows of some of the important changes in Monroeville from 1945 to 1965.

Changes in Demography of Demand

Monroeville population, total net effective income, and total retail sales increased during each five-year period measured, as seen in Appendix Tables A-1 through A-3. General merchandise sales declined by 1950 but increased thereafter, as Appendix Table A-4 shows.

More specifically, population did not increase proportionately as much as in the nation. The Monroeville index (1946 = 100) rose to 127.5 in 1965, while the U.S. index reached 137.0 in that year. Among the cities compared in this study, Monroeville's total net effective income ranked second, but the magnitude of change was less than in the nation. As expected, the change in total retail sales and in general merchandise sales (except for 1950 for the latter) followed income patterns, and the rankings were the same as for net effective income.

Appendix Table A-5 shows the changes in income distribution among families as measured by changes in percentage of households in each income group. The data reflect trends. They do not necessarily indicate that the percentage of households in each income bracket is actually more or less than in another city. The purpose of the data, in the case of Monroeville, is to indicate that the percentage of households at each end of the income scale increased. Despite the rise of the median family income in the nation from 1955 to 1965, the percentage of households in Monroeville with incomes of $0,000 to $2,499 rose from 1960 to 1965, but the percentage remained less than in 1955. The change in the income group of $7,000 and over in Monroeville was, of course, more favorable for retailers.

Changes in Competition

In Chapter I the discount department store was examined as a focal point for analyzing changes in merchandising strategy. It is also necessary, particularly in the Staplinger case, to account for two other changes. The first is the competition of three department store rivals. The second is the advent and growth of shopping centers.

Traditional department stores. During discussions concerning competitors, the Staplinger interviewees frequently referred to their neighbor, Smith and Company, the oldest retail establishment in Monroeville. One executive remarked:

A preponderance of our customers were older than the average shopper. They were in the top income brackets, engaged in white-collar occupations. But we had tolerated ourselves as a second-best competitor to Smith's for this so-called better business. In retrospect I am sure this influenced our decision of where we should go in our merchandising.[11]

Historically, Smith and Company balanced its appeal by offering in one portion of its store elegance, high fashion, quality, and the best of service. By merchandising its Basement Store as a store within a store, it also appealed to value-seeking customers. During both depression and prosperity the company pursued this policy.

Smith and Company had established branch stores in the 1920s and thus was one of the first department store retailers to recognize the opportunities outside of its own central business district. Fortunately for Staplinger's, the rival management did not resume this practice until 1950, when Smith opened its first branch store in a plaza shopping center. Aggregating 500,000 square feet of retail selling area, this giant shopping center was the largest constructed in Midstate to that date. During the next fifteen years, Smith and Company opened as the dominant store in three additional Monroeville shopping centers.

A second traditional department store rival, Werner's, had, until 1945, emphasized its convenient neighborhood locations and moderate-priced assortments of branded merchandise. The firm featured home furnishings as its merchandising forte and in its newspaper advertising placed considerable emphasis on sales events. From 1945 to 1960 the firm followed, first, a trading-down policy and then turned toward a trading-up policy. One handicap was that in its older locations Werner's could not provide adequate parking.

From 1950 to 1962 Werner's vacillated between a direct confrontation with discounters and an attempt to become a fashion store. Its erratic sales performance can be seen in Table III-1. After 1962, the firm expanded into shopping centers and became, as a Staplinger executive remarked, "a very formidable competitor who now knows where it belongs and what it is doing."[12]

A third department store rival, Coulder Brothers, adjusted to a similar set of problems. For thirty years before World War II, it had grown spectacularly as a price-cutting, unbranded merchandise firm located in neighborhood shopping districts, in central business districts of suburban and neighboring communities, and in Monroeville's central business district.

As in the Werner instance, the neighborhoods had changed. Price-cutting brought neither sales nor profit gains. From 1950 to 1960, Coulder Brothers altered its merchandising strategy. It traded up and emphasized branded merchandise in all classifications. However, before sufficient investment in time and inventory could bring about the desired impact, a declining sales and profit performance precipitated a change in merchandising policy. The firm reverted to a price-emphasis appeal in both merchandise assortment and sales promotion. One competitor observed: "Coulder Brothers did not know itself. One day it was trading up; the next, down. It is very difficult to overcome a specific reputation or image you have established so positively with the public."[13]

After suffering a loss in 1963, the board of directors changed the management. Pursuing a policy of "appealing to those whose desire for value is limited by a budget," the management located new branch stores in shopping centers and balanced its price appeal with merchandise lines, including national brands, which offered a higher gross margin. Banner sales and profit results were reported for 1964 and 1965. Relative sales for these three firms, and for Staplinger's, are shown in Table III-1.

The shopping center. Development of the plaza type shopping center also intensified competition. The first of these opened in 1950, as noted, and then the number and size of centers and the variety of tenants increased until, by 1963, over fifty-eight such shopping opportunities were located throughout Monroeville. Each of the three largest contained over 1,000,000 square feet of retail selling space. In aggregate, these fifty-eight comprised well over 12,000,000 feet of retail selling space.[14]

Discount stores. In addition to adjusting to the aforementioned changes by traditional department store rivals, the Staplinger management also faced the competitive thrust of discounters. Definitional problems and lack of authoritative data preclude precise measurement of discount department store growth in Monroeville from 1945 to 1965. Indeed, by 1961, one noted writer in retailing claimed that the discount house had already lost its identity as a distinctive type of retailing.[15] While no precise figures for discount stores in Monroeville could be obtained, one source estimated that 132 stores operating there at the end of 1964 accounted for 3.07 percent of total retail sales.[16]

It should be made clear that discounting as a merchandise strategy did not suddenly develop after 1945.[17] Monroeville illustrated this contention. Indeed, the executive vice-president of Coulder Brothers was one of the first after 1945 to decry "discounting," even though his firm had invaded and successfully built a profitable regional chain of department stores during the 1920-1940 period on precisely this pricing strategy.[18] In this same market, one of the most successful trading area chains of home furnishing specialty stores flourished on discounting strategy.[19]

To what extent did these discount stores draw customers from traditional department stores? Many studies show that customers today patronize both kinds of retailers. One survey conducted in Monroeville revealed evidence that at least 75 percent of those customers who patronized Staplinger's also visted some discount stores.

TABLE III-1

Comparison of Staplinger's Sales and Profit Performance with Other Department Store Firms, 1946-1965

Year Ending 1/31	Staplinger Company Sales Index: 1946=100	Werner's Sales Index: 1946=100 (1)	Coulder Bros. Sales Index: 1946=100 (2)	Smith's Sales Index: 1946=100 (3)	16-Store Aggregate Sales Index: 1946=100 (4)	Federated Department Stores Sales Index: 1946=100	Staplinger Net Profit Percent to Sales Index: 1946=100 (5)	16-Store Aggregate Net Profit Percent to Sales Index: 1946=100
1947	100.0	100.0	100.0	100.0	100.0	100.0	100.0	100.0
1948	107.4	107.6	107.3	107.3	100.7	130.0	59.5	101.1
1949	112.8	119.8	110.0	113.9	N.A.	148.0	46.1	69.2*
1950	103.9	114.2	105.1	105.0	N.A.	153.0	11.2	84.6
1951	118.2	119.0	109.7	113.1	N.A.	162.2	43.9	50.5*
1952	117.4	126.2	114.8	114.6	125.5	174.6	37.6	46.7
1953	118.4	127.2	116.1	114.6	130.0	191.3	20.2	51.1
1954	126.1	120.7	115.9	110.7	131.7	204.5	25.4	58.2*
1955	136.3	117.9	120.0	104.7	136.3	213.9	28.5	58.9
1956	143.4	120.1	123.7	102.2	144.4	229.7	30.7	62.7
1957	159.3	112.7	128.1	107.2	159.9	256.9	35.1	60.7
1958	159.7	122.5	132.9	111.2	165.4	271.5	30.0	57.8
1959	162.8	132.4	133.1	110.7	169.3	279.0	34.4	56.4
1960	229.8	135.4	125.2	119.0	183.9	324.6	40.0	62.4
1961	232.8	153.1	125.8	118.9	185.9	335.5	29.3	57.6

TABLE III-1 (Continued)

Comparison of Staplinger's Sales and Profit Performance with Other Department Store Firms, 1946-1965

Year Ending 1/31	Staplinger Company Sales Index: 1946=100	Werner's Sales Index: 1946=100 (1)	Coulder Bros. Sales Index: 1946=100 (2)	Smith's Sales Index: 1946=100 (3)	16-Store Aggregate Sales Index: 1946=100 (4)	Federated Department Stores Sales Index: 1946=100	Staplinger Net Profit Percent to Sales Index: 1946=100 (5)	16-Store Aggregate Net Profit Percent to Sales Index: 1946=100
1962	245.7	167.0	135.0	119.7	198.7	365.8	27.6	59.1
1963	253.3	181.1	147.1	123.1	208.9	383.0	20.5	54.9
1964	270.2	185.6	156.8	130.3	238.5	398.5	28.0	60.7
1965	289.0	196.4	177.5	142.2	248.7	519.1	44.4	76.9
1966	306.2	206.6	188.1	155.4	266.7	568.5	53.6	84.0

*Harvard Business School figures were used because 16-store aggregate data were not available for those years. The Harvard figures are extracted from McNair and May, *The American Department Store, 1920-1960*, Bureau of Business Research Bulletin No. 166 (Boston: Harvard Graduate School of Business Research, 1968), pp. 24-25. A comparison between these two sets of operating statistics shows that when an index of the fiscal year 1946 (ending January 31, 1947) is used, the indexes for the 20-year period under study usually vary between 5-8%. Federated Stores was chosen as a standard because it is the department store sales and profit leader.

SOURCES: Published financial statements of individual firms, public records such as *Moody's Industrials, Fairchild Financial Manual*, for respective years. The 16-store summary source is the Harris Trust and Savings Bank, Chicago. The roster of 16 stores, or more accurately, firms, includes: Allied Stores Corp., Associated Dry Goods, Broadway-Hale Stores, Carson Pirie Scott and Co., City Stores, Emporium Capwell Co., Federated Dept. Stores, Gimbel Bros., R. H. Macy & Co., Marshall Field, May Department Stores, Mercantile Stores, Rich's Inc., and Wieboldt Stores. In aggregate these firms sold $6,770,700,000 in goods and services during the fiscal year ending January 31, 1966. This is 27% of the approximate $25 billion in department store sales during 1965.

TABLE III-2

Discount Department Store Shopping in Monroeville in 1963 by Traditional Department Store Customers

Firm	Percent of Each Department Store's Customers Who Shopped at Discount Stores	Median Number of Visits to Discount Department Stores by Shoppers of Each Department Store During Preceding Year	Total Family Income Reported by Shoppers of Listed Department Stores
Coulder Bros.	81	7.9	$6,524
Sears, Roebuck & Company	80	7.5	6,780
Montgomery Ward	79	7.5	7,082
Werner's	78	7.1	6,779
Staplinger's	*75*	*5.9*	*7,277*
Smith & Co.	74	5.6	7,399

SOURCE: *Monroeville Gazette*, "How Monroeville Shops," IV (February 1963). Based on a total of 2,000 weighted interviews in Monroeville. Interviewees drawn from systematic probability sample in Monroeville by an independent research organization. Two national discount department store chains had announced intentions to open stores in Monroeville but were not included in this survey.

Based upon the median number of visits to discount department stores by shoppers of department stores, as seen in Table III-2, one can assume these customers also patronized discount stores.

The survey revealed two other significant facts. First, Staplinger's customers, who had heard of the listed discount stores, mentioned most frequently two local discount chains that opened for business after 1950. Staplinger's customers also stated that, among all discount stores, these two were the easiest to reach. Second, the list of discount department stores shown to Staplinger's customers did not include specialty discount store organizations, thus excluding from the survey discount stores specializing in such classifications as home furnishings, appliances, toys, housewares, drugs, and health and beauty aids. Further, two nationally-famous discount department store chains had not yet opened in Monroeville. Presumably, if the survey had been repeated in 1965, the percentage of those who visited discount stores would have been higher.

Changes in Merchandising Strategies:
1945-1955

In addition to the foregoing external changes, the Staplinger management had to consider internal factors. Interview responses suggested that these internal pressures were as compelling as the external forces. Three of the internal factors deserve brief mention.

One factor, the inhibiting real estate contract, was cited previously. Another was family management—its capacity to manage, its appraisal and response to external change, and its succession. A third concerned the total interests of the firm: whether it should concentrate solely on retailing.

Alternatives

Within constraints imposed by both external and internal conditions the management chose from among the following alternatives:

1) It could continue its high-fashion, specialty-shop appeal to a limited market segment.

2) It could broaden its appeal to an increasingly affluent segment who were seeking moderate- to better-priced merchandise.

3) It could continue to compete with Smith and Company on terms that would be determined more by Smith than by itself.

4) It could seek its own niche in the marketplace.

5) It could continue to concentrate its operation at the central business district location and plan for branch stores eventually.

6) It could diminish downtown operations, continue to pay the high rent, and immediately invade suburban or neighborhood shopping districts or suburban central business districts.

The firm also needed to consider these additional internal alternatives: Should it continue management succession within the family, or should it groom others for these responsibilities? Should it remain completely independent regarding its resource and buying office affiliations, or should it seek the advantages of some form of confederation? Should it continue to be a corporation of many businesses, or should it allocate its resources solely for retailing?

From interview data and from evidence garnered from external sources, the decisions, and reasons for those decisions, appear to be as follows:

First, the management abandoned its dependence upon family for succession. It sought, found, and developed outside talent. Together with some of the older management, these newer executives formulated different merchandising policies.

Second, Staplinger's decided to devote considerable effort to its merchandising activities within the Monroeville central business district while simultaneously planning for future suburban shopping center expansion. Four additional retail outlets were opened between 1950 and 1955.

Third, Staplinger's decided to appeal to an increasingly affluent middle-class group. This appeared to be the most feasible basis by which the firm could build a sufficient sales volume per square foot in its only store and thereby overcome the leasehold handicap. By directing the merchandising toward Monroeville's broadest concentration of buying power, the management foresaw an opportunity to build a more lasting profit structure.

Fourth, it decided to continue as a corporation with many interests. For example, it became a real estate firm in order to relieve the pressure of an onerous lease and to hedge against an obdurate landlord, a step that was necessary if it was to execute its basic merchandising strategies.

These four major decisions established the guidelines for the next twenty years. They were not reached simultaneously nor were they necessarily implemented in that order. The order is used here for convenience of reporting and analysis. The pattern of change during each decade from 1945 to 1965 will be discussed in terms of these decisions.

Management Succession

Two financial developments undoubtedly caused Staplinger's to resolve the management question as it did.

In 1946, several directors, who also constituted the management and who were descendants of the founders, registered with the SEC and sold to the public 100,000 shares of cumulative preferred stock. This marked the first time families of the original founders had disclosed actual ownership. In this instance, it also indicated that the company required additional capital for eventual expansion.[20] More than ever before management became aware of the need to generate sales.

The second development, as reported by an executive, was the postwar performance, which was not reassuring to either new participants in ownership or to the financial community. Commenting on the 1945 to 1950 period, Ed Strong, the vice-president and sales promotion director, said: "Though we increased our volume the first few years after the war we did not increase our profits. In fact, for fiscal 1949, our profits measured as a percent of sales declined 89 percent from our first postwar (1946) performance. We still had only one store."[21]

The entire department store industry profit-to-sales ratios declined after 1945. As shown in Table III-1, Staplinger's performance was considerably poorer than average. By 1950, the firm declined dangerously close to its 1946 fiscal sales volume and perilously close to a loss. On a sales volume in excess of $50,000,000, it earned less than $50,000.00 after taxes. In later years the president of the firm (then its general manager) referred to this "as an occasion when we nearly went broke."[22]

One of the corporate officers described the decision about management succession:

In 1947, the real change occurred. We went from family to professional management. Amos P. Rausch, then president, went outside and hired as general manager Austin Worth with the intention of grooming him to become the chief executive officer. (Worth is now president of Staplinger's.) Rausch realized we didn't have the management team nor manpower reserve necessary to grow. I think, too, he realized there was room for new leadership needed for a changing market. Mr. Worth's background consisted of considerable experience in personnel both in and outside of the retail industry. Also, because of previous experience, he had a propensity to emphasize the financial perspective in all of his thinking. Further, he seemed willing to delegate to others what we normally considered merchandising; that is, the essentials and techniques of buying and selling. The result was that we broadened merchandising to include men and money as well as merchandise itself.[23]

This concept of merchandising as the management of "the three M's—men, money, merchandise"—became the central technique of merchandising and has continued to the present time. This technique was employed to reach one objective, profit. Austin Worth has repeatedly referred to this strategy. In 1957, for example, he remarked at a professional meeting:

Many retailers are unaware that they did not improve their services or their facilities because they did not pay attention to their cash flow . . . but this is only one phase of operations which heads up to a fundamental belief . . .

verything we do goes back to a very simple "How can I use my money
?" . . . that is why you will see a much greater emphasis in total merchandising on the use of space, the amount of dollars you have invested in
space . . . after all, the cost of real estate in retailing is basic . . . if the real
estate cost goes up to $2 a square foot annually, we have to decide how we
are going to merchandise so that we get the same rate of return on the $2
cost space that we get on a lesser cost, say, $1.20. And this cannot be done
overnight.[24]

Definition of Market

The "sleeping giant of Monroeville,"[25] as the trade press tagged the
store, attempted during the 1945-1950 period to redefine its market
and the store's future.

A merchandising vice-president who participated in management
throughout this adjustment period described both the needs of the
store and the alternatives available:

We were not obtaining business from a sufficiently broad income segment by
which we could increase both volume and profit. The economic and social
forces had already changed both our traditional customers and those who
might become ours. A newspaper survey showed that customers under 30
years of age comprised only 19 percent of our total sales, less than Smith's or
some of our other competitors.[26]

Guided by a strategy requiring increased sales volume per square
foot, aiming at a middle rather than an upper-class segment, demanding profit as well as volume, Staplinger's strove to attract customers to
its sale location. To do this, it increased emphasis on lower price-lines
both in goods stocked and in the advertising. Ten years later, Austin
Worth commented on these attempts to discover just where the merchandising effort had to be placed in order to establish a new identity:
"We had to find out where the price-line was for the customer, where
the customer stops being appealed to by a good, friendly, aggressive,
middle-class store, and that is what we are if we really want to be
honest about it."[27]

Seeking a new market segment and implementing a new strategy
apparently faced internal opposition as well as the usual external
competition. Although president Rausch had brought Austin Worth
and others into the company, some stockholder-management members
in the first postwar recession year, 1949, favored a return to past events
as a guide. The board chairman, for example, regarded 1949-1950 as a

period in which consumer buying would return to "normalcy," that is, the prewar pattern. He predicted: "Customers are now buying when they want merchandise and not because they fear scarcities. Our store is taking its cue from our 1939 pace, a typically normal year. This trend will affect our own buying pattern, too. We will buy closer to our needs."[28]

However, both the board chairman and the president approved, and one year later lauded a major change to implement the new strategy. This change concerned resources.

Change in resources. To execute this major change in its merchandising strategy, Staplinger's decided to change its residential buying organization. If it was to appeal to middle-class segments as well as retain the upper-class trade it had cultivated throughout its history, the management needed to reassess and alter its resource relationships. A merchandising executive explained:

It is paradoxical that with all of the corporate experience as a wholesale resource and our partial involvement in manufacturing we didn't do a more effective job in our relationship between the retail division and market resources. We also knew that we could only be as strong as our resources. But how could we know what was best in the market? How could we learn how successful retail firms merchandised what they found or developed in the markets? Should we continue to operate our own separate buying office in New York, abroad, and on the West Coast? These were questions we had to answer as we went about the task of changing our offering.[29]

Staplinger's decided to discontinue its own resident buying organization and to affiliate with Consolidated Retailers, a confederation of large department stores which had formed their own buying syndicate. This also provided a communication link for ideas and standards. One merchandising executive who was a buyer at the time of change explained the impact:

I was buying ladies' shoes in our Basement Store at the time. We were operating only one store. Somehow the store had permitted the Basement to become a dumping ground for all the mistakes upstairs. Our gross margin was low, of course. We were behind the season because of a poor showing. We had actually reached the point where we were ready to eliminate the department. Our displays resembled a discount house. Our stocks looked more like distressed goods. And, of course, some of them were. After we changed our buying organization and joined a merchants' confederation, we discovered some merchandising facts of life which altered our planning. First, we learned that other stores in our volume class ran very successful, profitable basement shoe departments. But they were on their own. Each department or classification was accountable for its own profitability. We had found a standard, a basis for comparison, a pattern for emulation. It provided me with a basis for planned merchandising, gave me access to other stores, and of course gave me entree into market resources I might not have used otherwise. Personally, I regard this as one of the most significant moves during the twenty years I have associated with the store.[30]

This basic decision enhanced Staplinger's position among market resources for several reasons. It became a member of a combine with enormous total buying power, providing more adequate access to moderate-to-medium priced markets. And very importantly, as several executives stressed, it exposed Staplinger executives to the operations and operating figures of several successful American department stores. It also, of course, revealed Staplinger's performance to the remaining affiliates. One interviewee remarked: "For some time it was a joke around the New York office. Whenever another firm's performance slipped the buyer or merchandiser was told he would be sent to Staplinger's. This indicated our standing at that time."[31]

This decision proved providential for additional reasons. For many years Consolidated Retailers had represented Smith and Company in foreign markets, but the latter refused to join the association on a full membership basis. Hence, Staplinger's actually supplanted Smith and Company.[32]

During the next fifteen years many department stores differentiated their offering from competition and increased their profits by staging coordinated promotions of imported merchandise. The reference here is not to low-priced, mass-produced merchandise in such classifications as sportswear for women, girls, men, and boys, or to electronic or photogenic goods. Rather, the reference is to better quality, often custom-made, merchandise featuring excellent design and the finest materials. These coordinated promotions tended to concentrate in the home furnishings classifications and in some women's apparel and accessories classifications.

As will be evident by review of Staplinger's merchandising program, especially after 1955, these foreign import promotions and the inclusion in the inventory of these kinds of goods, proved to be significant contributions to the strategy changes. There is no evidence that either Smith and Company or Staplinger's foresaw this upsurge in merchandising of imports. Suffice it to say that Staplinger's did not seek the affiliation primarily for that reason. Rather, the objective seemed to be, as stated, to aid management in establishing internal controls as well as to broaden its domestic resource base. For example, five months after affiliation, the firm's board chairman was quoted in the trade press: "I feel this move was one of the most important in our long history. This association with other large stores, particularly with the retail research division, will be very helpful."[33]

The 1949 fiscal report reflected this search for standards and guidance. The chairman pointed out advantages the firm had already obtained by its new residential buying office affiliation; with help from the association, Staplinger's installed a new system of work center expense accounting about which the chairman said ". . . it gave us by far the most effective means of expense control we have ever had. This has helped us to locate and identify where the responsibilities for profit are. We are beginning to delegate that responsibility downward."[34]

Apparently these guideposts provided a basis for optimism, even though the chairman reported a decline in such measurements of activity as sales per square foot and the amount of the average sales check. On the other hand, he stated that the number of transactions during the year had increased. While this may indicate that the company had already traded down somewhat, the most meaningful fact is that the chairman and the management dwelt on those merchandising activities which bear on profitability.[35]

By replacing Smith and Company, the Staplinger management served notice it intended to compete vigorously to become a distinctive retail enterprise, and as one official expressed it, "to anticipate rather than wait for change." In the 1951 fiscal statement, company officials again acknowledged the merits of this decision: "This has helped in the exchange of figures and in obtaining merchandise. We initiated several research projects of our own and modified our cost accounting system as a result of this."[36]

Sales Promotion Changes

The drive for sales volume and the need to procure results immediately caused the firm to modify its sales promotion strategy, particularly its newspaper advertising. Two buyers expressed their recollections of this change:

In the late 1940s we took double shots of adrenalin. We went very promotional. Some people thought we damaged our image. We extended Anniversary Sales from a week to ten days to three weeks. As a result, we were competing with Smith's Basement Store and Werner's and Coulder's. At a later date when we attempted to reestablish our image as a fashion leader it became very costly in terms of extra effort in personal selling, in advertising expenditures, and in extra mark-downs we had to take.[37]

Store records to relate advertising price-lining to merchandise price-lining for this period (1945-1955) are not available. The consensus of those interviewed was that the store had advertised below its volume selling price in a given range. This represented a departure from prewar and wartime policies of advertising at or above the volume selling point in a given price range.

Emphasis on credit selling represents another change in the strategy, a logical extension of the merchandising concept. The company campaigned to sell credit as a means of purchasing at Staplinger's. It encouraged people to use this service and promoted the new liberal program at Staplinger's. By 1950, credit volume reached 48 percent of total transactions compared with an average industry performance of 45 percent.

Handicapped in securing suburban business because of its lack of branch locations, the store encouraged customers to use their credit by more frequent telephone purchase. By inaugurating an "Enterprise" telephone service to some sixty suburban communities considered a part of the Monroeville trading area, the store invited the suburban customer to call the store without incurring a toll charge to herself.[38]

The store also established a mail-order campaign to its credit customers. It dispatched card inserts and mailers different from monthly charge enclosures. The messages included announcements about physical improvements, special events, and specific merchandise offerings.[39]

Location Decisions

Real estate decisions significantly affected and reflected merchandising decisions during 1946-1955. They can be summed up as branch store and main store decisions and will be discussed in that order.

Branch stores. It was surprising to learn of the initial expansion program. While constructing a new warehouse in the far north side of Monroeville, the management decided to utilize a portion of the 350,000 square foot building for a branch store. Staplinger's opened this branch in 1950 as a 75,000 square foot Warehouse Store. It featured "low prices, self-selection, evening and Sunday shopping, ample space for free parking."

That same year the firm opened a specialty appliance and hard home goods (excluding furniture) store in a suburban Monroeville community. A trade press reported this event: "Subsequent to its affiliation with Consolidated Retailers in 1949, Staplinger's developed a tidy volume in such fields as major appliances, and housewares, where previously an appreciably smaller effort was made. This has given the store a complete personality in home goods retailing."[40]

However, these classifications were among the most competitively priced in Monroeville. Despite the optimistic report cited, the venture was not successful and closed within the year. One explanation may be that the temporary advantage in procurement Staplinger's gained by its new buying office affiliation was quickly offset by an increase in total supply of consumers' durables.

Staplinger's did not succeed in either venture in which it aped discount retailing. Inventory investment in both instances was in lower zones of the normal price-range the store stocked. It is not clear whether the store actually extended the normal range downward, but by emphasizing lower price-points within its normal range, it can be said the store traded down in these classifications. According to interviewees, the store supported both efforts with newspaper advertising. It is reasonable to expect that the advertising price-lining also emphasized these lower price-points.

In explaining why merchandising was so important a function, the statement was made that the inventory represented the largest or second largest investment for the department store. Since 1945, the administration and promotion of credit as a means of obtaining patronage has become of extreme importance to retailers. For some department stores, the investment in accounts receivable has become the largest asset in the business. By 1950, many large and small retailers learned they were, indeed, merchants of money as well as of goods, and that they could profit from their accounts receivable as much as they could from inventory turnover.

In view of the foregoing, it was surprising to learn from an examination of the records that Staplinger's in 1950 sold to the Monroeville Bank its conditional sales contracts for an amount in excess of $1,500,000. One explanation may be that Staplinger's chose liquidity in preference to the interest income from sales contracts. The action to hasten liquidity under such circumstances can be a sign of stringent financial constraints and tends to confirm interview data concerning the firm's financial capacity as it affected merchandising strategy. More specifically, as will be related shortly, a tight financial condition may cause loss of discounts, delay the taking of markdowns when needed, and may cause the store to forgo opportune purchases.

During the following year the company announced it would open its first branch store in a shopping center. This 50,000 square foot unit opened on schedule in 1952 and occupied 10 percent of the shopping center's total selling area. The store stocked merchandise primarily in the apparel and textile classifications. Simultaneously, the firm announced plans to open a second branch in Northside Shopping Center within a year.

Before this materialized, Staplinger's reversed its field. It opened, instead, another warehouse store, a 33,000 square foot unit selling primarily home goods, which would help Staplinger's put up a stronger fight against discount house competition. Located five miles from its first shopping center branch, the unit was designed as "strictly warehouse."

Eight months later, Staplinger's introduced its second shopping center branch store. This center included twenty-eight stores in 220,000 square feet of retail selling space. The Staplinger store occupied 64,000 square feet.

Main store. In 1948, to hedge against a possible loss of lease on its main downtown location (the leasehold was to be renewed or renegotiated by 1955), Staplinger's purchased the real estate adjacent to the main store, which housed a portion of its downtown retail business. This property did not front on the main street, however. Because it did not require additional retail space at that time, the company leased all but the ground and first three floors as prime downtown office space. This obligation, as well as the uncertainty about the main store, may have delayed company branch expansion.

The capital to open the first shopping center branch was obtained from the sale in 1951 of its share in a downtown delivery garage. When the firm started leasehold negotiations in 1952 on the downtown location building, it believed itself better fortified than ever before to deal with the onerous real estate situation. Even by 1954 the downtown store accounted for 85 percent of the firm's retail sales. But to renew the lease on the old terms was untenable. A merchandising vice-president commented: "Simply put, we weren't doing enough business for the size of tent we had leased. We had to merchandise the space either by increasing the dollar volume per square foot or reduce the space used for selling goods and services."[41]

Local newspapers and the trade press reported in 1955 that Staplinger's had been unable to renegotiate its lease satisfactorily under the terms of the trust agreement controlling the rental of its site. Consequently, it planned to vacate the premises it had occupied for fifty years. Rather than leave downtown Monroeville, the firm decided to build a new store on the site acquired in 1948. However, the Probate Judge of Monroeville finally consented to the trustees' request to sell the original land and building to Staplinger's. In late 1955 the store concluded this multi-million dollar purchase.

To finance this acquisition, the company issued promissory notes due within the next fourteen years, bearing $3\frac{3}{4}$ to 4 percent interest. Staplinger's used part of the proceeds to remodel a portion of the Main Street building. Subsequently, it leased a portion of this space, with openings into the Staplinger street floor, to two specialty stores, which, despite the fact that they were competitive, brought additional traffic. The company also used a part of monies received from the notes to help finance the construction of a shopping center in which it opened its third and largest branch store in 1956.

Becoming a landlord to other retailers seems consonant with the company's historic pattern of diversification and was repeated in the following decade. Also, the steps outlined may underscore the management contention that the retailer must be a merchant of money as well as of goods.

Summary: 1945-1955

In response to external change, the Staplinger firm was guided, if not constrained, by internal factors. The most notable of these was change of management, which brought about a different concept of merchandising strategy. In one of its first major decisions, management identified a new market segment. The strategy required additional sales volume in broader price-line ranges and more aggressive sales promotion in order to reach the designated market segment. Management sanctioned competition with discounters and permitted both sales promotion and location decisions which either encouraged or required trading down to accomplish the mission. Resource changes were made which would help management become internally profit-minded and enable it to secure merchandise consonant with its new strategy. The logic of merchandising, the interview data, and literature sources all tend to support the proposition that Staplinger's traded down during this period.

Changes in Merchandising Strategy:
1955-1965

Recapitulating previous observations concerning internal factors which might affect merchandising strategy, the data in Appendix Tables A, 1-5, show that general trends in population, income, and retail sales continued to increase in Monroeville from 1956 to 1966. One demographic change which proved advantageous to Staplinger's was the resurgence of residential construction for middle-to-better income groups in locations very near the central business district. Another development during this decade was the increasing intensity of Negro and nonwhite population growth within Monroeville, which partially accounts for the variance of income distribution, as seen in Appendix Table A-5.

Severity of competition also increased. Approximately 20,000,000 square feet of retail area were added. Three-fourths, it is estimated, were constructed in plaza-type shopping centers in which such traditional competitors as Werner's and Coulder Brothers occupied sites. Smith and Company became the largest tenant in Midstate's largest shopping center.

Discount stores occupied approximately 5,000,000 square feet of retail area in Monroeville by 1965. Two local discount department store chains, which started in business after 1950, reached a collective sales volume of $63,000,000 by 1965. In addition, such national chains as Korvette, Interstate, Zayre, and others, deemed the giants of the discount store industry, established branches in Monroeville.

Internally, the management did not reduce its emphasis on merchandising strategy. The experiences of the previous decade intensified its desire to develop appropriate merchandising tactics. For example, regarding discount stores, Ed Strong remarked:

As discounting increased, we recognized that our quest for volume brought our merchandise and advertising price-lining closer to this kind of competition than we should have been. We were trading down too far. Besides, this program was not providing the profit and return on investment we had to secure. So we attempted to change.[42]

Certain internal constraints continued to inhibit merchandising, however. Failure to generate sufficient profit and constant pursuit of sales volume affected liquidity. One buyer succinctly expressed the effects: "We wanted sales volume. We were always short of working capital. We weren't taking our discounts. We held back on markdowns. Under these conditions you always have a tendency to trade down in quality and pricing."[43]

Ten years later, Austin Worth, in speaking about the need for long-range planning, reminded his audience of Staplinger's experiences: "We started our long-range planning 10 years ago because we were a deficit corporation and had to be able to offer some hope to our stockholders and directors. We built carefully over the years—our sales by classifications, our cash flow program, our profit projections."[44]

Management Succession

Both Rausch and Worth continued as the chief architects and executives of the merchandising strategy, and currently serve as board chairman, and president, respectively. They claimed they had succeeded in developing a reservoir of management talent. In 1966, before a professional association, Austin Worth declared:

We have a group of 25 younger executives who can and will manage this corporation in 1980. They currently serve as store managers and merchandise and administrative managers. Each has been transferred from one middle management line promotion to another at almost regular three-year periods. The younger members run in age from twenty-six to thirty-five. Some merchandise managers are in their forties and have been with us now for fifteen to twenty years.[45]

These executives are encouraged to attend business administration courses at nearby universities. The company brings academic experts to the main store headquarters for executive seminars.

For its employees, the management demonstrated and conducted schools and training sessions on the need to exploit its long-established reputation as a friendly store. The general training program did not appear to be different from that encountered throughout the industry or in other stores studied. Staplinger's instituted a profit-sharing plan in 1954 to reward its veteran employees. As a result of the relatively poor profit performance, as can be inferred from the data in Table III-1, the contributions to the pension fund were not as large as anticipated. Nonetheless, throughout this period, the management regularly attempted to communicate to its employees, particularly sales personnel, the need and desire to draw patronage from a wider segment of the public.

Definition of Market

During the 1956-1960 period, Staplinger's attempted to reverse its trading-down strategy but did not succeed. Interviewees stated that the company recognized it had traded down too far but that the turnabout did not occur until 1959, when the company expanded beyond Monroeville. Strategies of sales promotion and resource development appear to conflict rather than complement each other during this period.

Sales Promotion: 1955-1960

Despite its desire to trade up in the advertising price-lining as well as in its merchandise price-lining, Staplinger's found it necessary to prime the pump for sales volume. During 1957, for example, it staged a gigantic extra-hours, one-day, store-wide sales promotion event in its central business district location. For this event, Staplinger's purchased the largest amount of retail newspaper advertising space ever used by a single Monroeville store in a single day. The store succeeded in "setting a peak in sales for any day in its history, surpassing even the Christmas season."[46] Staplinger's one-day sale was repeated later in the year, but the firm barely managed to equal the previous years' sales and declined in profits, as Table III-1 indicates.

This conflict between sales volume and gross margin continued for the next two years. The one-day sale increased in frequency to five such events in a given year. The company had already expanded its Anniversary Sale to three weeks. By apportioning this much advertising expenditure to price promotion events, and by diverting inventory investments to support them, the company was impeded in its effort to trade up.

Yet, especially in its downtown location, Staplinger's accompanied these thrusts for volume with a number of merchandising and sales promotion events designed to secure day-in, day-out business and to establish itself once again as a fashion leader. For example, in one of the first attempts by a retail store in Midstate to sell art, the main store, in 1957, staged a double-feature art show. It included a one-man exhibition by a contemporary French artist. In addition, the store sold fifty original paintings by great masters.

Imported merchandise, as noted, had become an important part of Staplinger's assortment. For the first time in Midstate, a department store coordinated and assembled in one specific location items from all countries and all classifications for a two-week event. Sufficient interest and patronage justified extension into a third week.

Some large department store affiliates of Consolidated Retailers devised a merchandising technique called "Customer Preference." This analytic technique helped a retailer to concentrate on characteristics of the item rather than on the item itself in order to detect what the customer preferred. The primary analytic effort was to identify the attributes of an item—with respect to material, color, design, and price, for example—which the consumer preferred as evidenced by her purchasing behavior.

Stores that used the techniques claimed they could gauge demand more accurately and, therefore, could respond more profitably. However, both store timing and customer demand could, and did in some cases, wreak havoc among departments within stores. Interviewees reported that buyers, in their zeal to capitalize on a trend, overstocked on certain features which customers decided they no longer desired. Or, in other instances, buyers neglected basic stock assortments in order to exploit a momentary upsurge in demand for a particular item or idea.

Customer preference also required an orientation based upon consumer habits and desires rather than store buyer habit and preference. For example, in 1958, Staplinger's reorganized the dress departments to provide increased shopping ease and customer convenience. The president reported:

We found out that the average customer buys dresses more on impulse than by careful calculation. Now she can find anything in dresses she wants on our Third Floor of Fashion. More significantly from her viewpoint and ours, too, the same salesperson can wait on a customer shopping for an entire wardrobe of dresses from better priced casuals, town types, afternoon frocks, and she can select and try on in the same fitting room.[47]

Resource Changes

While Staplinger's attempted to secure volume and yet attract customers interested in fashion and quality it also strove to increase its merchandise gross margin. A buyer summarized the situation:

After we achieved volume, and after we began to build branch stores resembling our main store and not discount houses, we started a drive for increased gross margin. We had to get that in order to increase our profits so that we could continue our expansion program. Our instructions were to make money on goods, including sale merchandise.[48]

The press for additional gross margin affected merchandising of home furnishings and housewares during this period. The previously cited attempts to secure profitable volume and to simultaneously compete with discount stores had not improved the company's performance.

One major effort was to reduce the total number of resources supplying the company. It reduced the number of television and electronic equipment lines from seven to three, the number of houseware resources by 30 percent, and, in furniture, the number of upholstered resources from fifteen to five, case goods from fifteen to five, and occasional tables from twenty to five.

During this 1955-1959 period, Staplinger's again seemed to be ahead or behind the times. In several of the merchandising techniques cited, such as customer orientation, coordinated stocking and shopping, it presaged the current emphasis on classification merchandising, boutiques, and the shop concept. It expanded its appeal to one segment by means of individualized, personalized, specialty-store type of merchandise assortments and presentation. In other techniques, however, Staplinger's more closely resembled the discounters as it supported homogenized, massive, store-wide price promotions aimed to "buy volume the next day."

This last phrase signifies changes in emphasis. First, it means that the store seeks only a proximate goal of achieving a given sales volume for the next immediate period, usually a day or a week, or even a month. It subordinates long-range goals, which may be more difficult to define and may require a different allocation of resources. Second, it usually implies a willingness to expend funds on a short-range basis in order to achieve these results. Thus a store may reduce expenses for maintenance and shift the difference to advertising, expending a disproportionate share for that activity, in the expectation that this will stimulate immediate consumer response. Every merchant must constantly allocate resources on a basis of priorities, which includes a time consideration. The significance of this decision will become more apparent in this as well as in the other case reports.

Location and Expansion Decisions

Staplinger's continued its branch expansion program, opening three additional shopping center stores by the end of 1958. However, none of these were as large as the branches opened by Smith and Company or those by Sears, for example. By the end of fiscal 1958, the firm obtained 31 percent of its retail sales volume from branch stores and reported that for the first time in five years the main store gained in sales. Table III-1 shows that profit did not increase proportionately, however.

When Staplinger's opened its third branch store, the management announced that it planned to eventually encircle Monroeville with two rings of branches. The closer one would be the group of regular branch department stores in shopping centers. The more distant one would consist of department stores to be opened in shopping centers in other population centers that surrounded Midstate.

However, the first acquisition in the outer circle was a traditional department store located in the central business district of a neighboring community. Originally a branch of Smith and Company, this store was sold to an independent merchant whose family in turn sold to Staplinger's. This presented an opportunity to acquire immediate sales volume in a medium-to-better price store. While this acquisition did not fit the proposed pattern, it was in line with the long-range strategy of the firm.

Midstate Department Stores Merger

The largest single expansion of the twenty-year period occurred in 1959, when Staplinger's acquired Midstate Department Stores, a regional chain. These retail firms were either first or second in sales in their respective communities. Executives offered several explanations for this unusual amalgamation. They can be summarized as follows:

These were reliable, quality stores which would add immediately to our volume. This acquisition really made a mature corporation out of us. It increased our assets. Because we paid for this principally with convertible debentures we did not have to deplete our cash or liquidate other assets. We gained considerable leverage which enabled us to borrow more readily. This really financed our expansion.[49]

Inspection of data in Table III-1 confirms these estimates. The substantial increase in sales in fiscal 1959 (year ending January 31,

1960), indicated by a rise in the index from 162.8 to 229.8, can be attributed only to this acquisition. The increased net profit index figure (from 34.4 to 40.0) applied, of course, to a substantially higher sales volume which soared above $100,000,000, again resulting primarily from the acquisition. Further, the 1959 profit-to-sale ratio was the highest since fiscal 1950.

Financial circles expected that this acquisition would lay the foundation for appreciable expansion. Net worth increased 43 percent; working capital, 53 percent. Trade spokesmen estimated "it would have taken Staplinger's ten to fifteen years to build up the volume in the respective areas where these stores are located."[50]

The acquired company bore some blemishes, however. Its management had failed to develop new leadership from within or to bring in new vigorous aspirants from other retail firms. Also, it had failed to modernize its physical plant and merchandising equipment and methods. Hence the Staplinger management inherited those kinds of problems with which it was familiar—family management, aging inventory, real estate deterioration, and personality difficulties. But, for the acquired company, the opportunity to sell out the entire property at one time to one buyer was unusual and served well its desire to liquidate. And for Staplinger's, the opportunity was at hand to expand outstate, immediately boost its corporate sales volume, and carry out modernization plans as well as those plans relating to shopping center expansion.

This acquisition proved to be an engrossing test of what merchandising meant at Staplinger's. Questions about merchandise, money, and men abounded both before and after the transaction. Five years later, after shakedown experiences with the acquired stores and with other acquisitions, the company's president remarked:

Our 1964 results highlight the culmination of a five-year expansion program which placed severe pressure on both working capital and management. This is the first year in which our operation reflected the full effect of this program, of increased and modernized store facilities, of our management objectives, of aggressive merchandising and promotional activities, and a constantly improving expense control.[51]

Expansion during 1961-1966 period. After acquisition of Midstate Department Stores in 1959, Staplinger's announced it would construct a new ten-story addition to its Main Store. In this structure it leased out the main floor, mezzanine, and basement floors and used the upper eight stories for its own merchandising. A company official explained that the cash flow from depreciation and income would enable the company to expand even faster in the future.

Several demographic changes in the early 1960s bolstered Staplinger's confidence in the Monroeville central business district. An 896-unit, upper-middle-class apartment house project was constructed near the downtown shopping district. The University of Midstate relocated its campus and facilities, including faculty and student housing, at the other end of the downtown district. Three new superhighways from different suburbs and construction of two additional 600-unit apartment houses nearby encouraged and justified the management investment in downtown real estate.

Two developments in 1962 absorbed both Staplinger's capital and its attention. The first was a Staplinger-financed construction of a 200,000 square foot shopping center in Monroeville. This included a restaurant and the first basement store to be operated in a store branch. A second development, also financed by Staplinger's, consisted of a 100,000 square-foot department store and an 85-home subdivision in the $15,000-$22,000 price-range. These were located in a community that included one of the Midstate Department Store's units.[52]

Although it had not engaged in the food service business prior to 1960, the company apparently believed its merchandising strategy could include this segment of the retail industry. Therefore, it bid for, and won, the contract to provide food and beverage service at the Monroeville Transportation Center.

Commercial and residential activity in the vicinity of its second branch, built nine years earlier, had increased substantially by 1965. Staplinger's decided to double the size of its store there and to construct a 105,000 square-foot office building. The president explained that this would "localize commercial activity in the Center and increase the attraction of the shopping project."[53]

The physical expansion and the management of capital affected other elements of the merchandising strategy, particularly sales promotion and resource development. Referring to the 1961-1966 period, the sales promotion director defined the objectives:

We tried to emphasize the difference between discounters and our kind of retailing. We planned and staged more special events, more intensive fashion promotion, traded up in our advertising. We used our downtown store to project an image of a friendly institution and a demonstration of the quality and assortment of goods. The branches were to imitate this.[54]

Despite these statements, Staplinger's continued to promote sales volume events. It was not until 1965, after returning to its promised profit performance, that the company diminished the one-day sale events from five per year to two per year. The Anniversary Sale was also reduced from three weeks to one week that year.[55]

The program of resource selection and partnership continued during the various expansion and volume drives. Parrish, the general merchandise manager, cited an example:

In our affluent economy, what is important is the idea, not the price, not even the item. When bonded jersey dresses came on the market it was the idea which was important. Ten years ago each dress department in our firm would have tried individually to promote the item. Today, we coordinate everyone's efforts to promote the idea for all size and price-ranges. You can only do this, however, when you work with a limited number of resources to whom you are important and who have a stake in your success.[56]

Another Staplinger merchant, Carl Trine, associate merchandise manager of home furnishings, illustrated the importance of resources by referring to the electric household knife.

I think ten years ago we would have handled it differently in two respects. First, we probably would have attempted to compete with everyone, discounters included. We would have advertised that we have the lowest price on all makes. Second, we would have bought from every and all resources so we could represent every line. In short, we aimed at volume. Today, in fact, right now, we are merchandising this differently. We aim to handle in depth those kinds of goods and those price-lines where we can make some gross margin. To do this, we cut down the number of lines handled and became important to fewer resources.[57]

Diversification

By 1965, Staplinger's merchandising operation included six divisions. Trade sources estimated that two retail divisions, Monroeville, and Midstate Department Stores, accounted for 80 percent of corporate sales. The main downtown store contributed 50 percent of total retail volume or about 40 percent of corporate sales.

The specialty wholesale division generated approximately 12 percent of corporate sales. Remaining divisions—food service, contract sales, and real estate—contributed the balance. In 1965, the food service was growing faster than the others.[58]

By 1945, the first year of the period studied, Staplinger's had divested itself of all nonretail businesses except for a specialized portion of its wholesale division. Twenty years later, the company had expanded and included a chain of retail stores, a flourishing specialized wholesale business, a food business, a contract decorator and furnishings business, and a substantial portion of an insurance company as a result of its successful pioneering in the distribution of insurance to its credit customers.

There are additional measurements of the strategy. Financially, Staplinger's resurgence in fiscal 1959 was followed by sales volume gains at a declining rate and proportionately poor profit performances. Indeed, by the end of fiscal 1962, the profit-to-sales ratio had dropped to the second lowest point in the twenty-year period and the actual dollar profit was less than that of fiscal 1958.

A vice-president claimed that earnings between 1960 and 1962 were adversely affected by a number of largely nonrecurring factors. "We bought some markdowns, in stores and goods, when we acquired Midstate Department Stores. We had some start-up expenses for two major suburban units, we modernized our downtown store; we were delayed in our construction at the city transportation terminal. We expect earnings to rebound in fiscal 1963."[59]

The prediction proved correct. As he reported on the company performance for fiscal 1964, Amos Worth, the company president, referred to the effects of some of these previous years on the immediate past:

We will report substantially better profits after the lean year of 1962 and after the 1960 growing pains. Our institutional banking friends tell us that 1962 to 1964 was the hump–and that we're over that hump. We think this trend will continue. We are on the threshold of a radical change in retailing, the shift in emphasis in assets from inventories to receivables. We're in the banking business. The single greatest asset is not inventory; it is accounts receivable. Our accounts receivable are currently 130 percent of our inventories.[60]

In terms of its market targets, two attempts can be gauged. One attempt was to attract younger customers. The trade press reported:

Customers under 30 years of age now comprise about 30 percent of Staplinger's total sales. Just 15 years ago this group accounted for 19 percent of the store's business. In the home furnishings division, for example, the company accented its home planning center called "Interiors for You." It also hired more young decorators who "talk the language of the under-20 customer." The firm also made this service available in all of the Monroeville branch stores.[61]

One of the significant demographic changes throughout these twenty years was the rapid increase of the Negro population in Monroeville. Staplinger's was one of the foremost among retailers to open its sales and supervisory employee ranks to this minority group. As a pioneer in public as well as personnel relations, it sent executives to various Negro neighborhoods to communicate the firm's desire to hire members as well as seek their patronage.

Did these efforts help Staplinger's to secure patronage from this segment of the market? There is some evidence which suggests that despite its obvious appeal, in terms of personnel policies and practices, merchandise allegedly stocked, sales promotion and public relations programs, the total effort as measured by Negro patronage has not been especially successful. During this period both the nonwhite proportion of the total population and the income level of that segment increased. The results of an intensive personal survey conducted among Monroeville shoppers indicate that Staplinger's has not fared any better than has its traditional rival, Smith and Company, which purportedly had not expended similar efforts to influence buying behavior within the nonwhite community. As shown in Table III-3, of 2,000 interviewees, 1,208 said they were customers of Staplinger's, while 1,171 claimed to be customers of Smith and Company. Of these latter two groups of customers, 8 percent and 7 percent, respectively, were nonwhite. And of the nonwhite patrons who traded at Staplinger's, the majority shopped only at the main store in the central business district. The nonwhite patronage of Sears, Werner's, and Coulder Brothers is also shown.

During this second decade, Staplinger's reached a new sales volume peak and achieved the best profit-to-sales performance since fiscal 1947. The company believed it had the best-prepared management personnel reserves in its history. It was contributing the largest sums ever to the profit-sharing fund. It had reached the trading level sought for twenty years, having traded up in merchandise and advertising price-lining to the tastes and capacities of a broad middle-income group. Executives interviewed believe the company had succeeded in changing its merchandising strategy.

Price-Lining Investigation
and Results

As detailed in Chapter II, an attempt was made to verify interview data by two different methods. The first consisted of sending a ques-

TABLE III-3
Nonwhite Shoppers in Central Business District Units and Branch Store Units of Major Department Stores in Monroeville

Shoppers	Sears	Coulder Bros.	Werner's	Smith & Co.	Staplinger's
Total shoppers	1,465	1,270	1,153	1,171	1,208
Nonwhite shoppers	203	182	136	78	102
Percent nonwhite shoppers to total	13.8	14.3	11.8	6.6	8.4
Nonwhite who shop central business district only	48	60	49	79	78
Percent of total nonwhite	23.6	32.9	36.0	89.7	76.4
Nonwhite who shop branch stores only	82	48	36	2	6
Percent of total nonwhite	40.5	26.4	26.4	2.6	5.9
Nonwhite who shop central business district and branch stores	73	74	51	6	18
Percent of total nonwhite	35.9	40.7	37.6	7.7	17.6

SOURCE: *Monroeville Gazette Research*, 1964. Based on 2,000 weighted personal interviews in Monroeville.

tionnaire to interviewees and other executives at Staplinger's. The objective was to obtain numerical data pertinent to merchandise and advertising price-lining for two years, 1960 and 1965, for the eighteen classifications listed in Appendix A.

Several executives stated orally and by written communication that they did not have the records to answer the questions. That is to say, they could convey neither merchandise nor advertising price-lining information. They reiterated their general claims that Staplinger's had traded up during the 1960 to 1965 period. Further, they emphasized

TABLE III-4
Analysis of Advertising Price-lining in 1960 and 1965
Women's and Misses' Dresses, 9-Cities, Monroeville, and Staplinger's

Name of Mdse. Class. Women's and Misses' Dresses
Neustadt Code No. 10. Neustadt Description: Silk Dresses, Rayon and other Synthetics, Woolens in Women's and Misses' Sizes, Dresses for street wear, afternoon, and evening wear included. Junior Sizes excluded.
DSIPI Description: Women's Wear–Dresses.

NRMA Dept. No. 42-11
DSIPI Group: IX
DSIPI Index, 1960: 185.9 (1941 = 100)
DSIPI Index, 1965: 192.5 (1941 = 100)
Relative Change in Index, 1965/1960: 102.8

Price Zone No.	Price Zone Range	Analysis: 9-Cities 1960 Percent of Adv./Zone	1960 Index of Adv.	1965 Percent of Adv./Zone	1965 Index of Adv.	Analysis: Monroeville 1960 Percent of Adv./Zone	1960 Index of Adv.	1965 Percent of Adv./Zone	1965 Index of Adv.	Analysis: Staplinger's 1960 Percent of Adv./Zone	1960 Index of Adv.	1965 Percent of Adv./Zone	1965 Index of Adv.
(1)	Under $10.00	13	13	14	14	11	11	12	12	13	13	12	12
(2)	$10.01 to $18.00	28	56	22	44	29	58	26	52	31	62	33	66
(3)	$18.01 to $28.00	15	45	14	42	21	63	16	48	21	63	10	30
(4)	$28.01 to $38.00	12	48	12	48	12	48	12	48	12	48	6	24
(5)	$38.01 to $50.00	12	60	14	70	10	50	12	60	8	40	18	90
(6)	Over $50.00	20	120	24	144	17	102	22	132	15	90	21	126
	TOTALS	100	342	100	362	100	332	100	352	100	316	100	348
	1965/1960 Index:		105.8				106.0				110.1		
	Price Center:	$24.00		$28.00		Below		Below		Below		Below	

Monroeville less than 9-Cities both years but proportionately higher in 1965 than in 1960. Staplinger's less than Monroeville and less than 9-Cities both years even though its price center was proportionately higher in 1965.

1. Comp. their own adv. indexes, did 9-City group trade up? x Yes; _____ No.
2. Comp. its own adv. indexes, did Monroeville trade up? x Yes; _____ No.
3. Comp. its own adv. indexes, did Staplinger's trade up? x Yes; _____ No.
4. Comp. with Monroeville did Staplinger's trade up, relatively? x Yes; _____ No.
5. Comp. with 9-Cities, did Staplinger's trade up, relatively? x Yes; _____ No.
6. Comp. relative changes in DSIPI and its own adv. indexes, did Staplinger's trade up? x Yes; _____ No.
   Its change was (greater) than DSIPI change by 7.3 percent.
7. Other comments: Store traded up relative to itself but it traded in lower zones than either the city or 9-City aggregate. It shifted to higher-priced merchandise within upper three ranges. In 9-Cities this classification uses more lineage than any other. Based on interview data one would expect higher index and price center by store.

64

TABLE III-5

Summary of Responses to Questions Concerning Seventeen Selected Merchandise Classifications

Commodity	Question 1 Yes	Question 1 No	Question 2 Yes	Question 2 No	Question 3 Yes	Question 3 No	Question 4 Yes	Question 4 No	Question 5 Yes	Question 5 No	Question 6 Yes	Question 6 No	Totals Yes	Totals No
Women's & misses' dresses	x		x		x		x		x		x		6	0
Junior dresses	x			x	x		x		x		x		5	1
Women's & misses' untrimmed cloth coats	x		x		x		x		x		x		6	0
Women's & misses' sweaters	x		x		x		x		x		x		6	0
Skirts	x		x		x			x		x		x	3	3
Blouses		x	x		x			x	x		x		4	2
Men's dress shirts	x			x	x		x		x		x		5	1
Men's suits	x		x		x		x		x		x		6	0
Men's slacks		x		x		x		x		x		x	0	6
Men's sportcoats	x		x		x		x		x		x		6	0
Mattresses	x		x		x			x		x	x		4	2
Sofas	x			x	x		x		x			x	4	2
Bedroom suites	x		x		x		x		x		x		6	0
Drapes	x			x		x		x –		x		x	1	5
Towels		x		x		x	x		x			x	2	4
Blankets	x		x		x			x		x	x		4	2
Bedspreads	x		x			x		x		x		x	2	4
Totals	14	3	11	6	13	4	10	7	11	6	11	6	70	32

NOTE: The six questions at the bottom of Table III-4 were also asked about sixteen additional commodities.

that during 1960 and even more in 1965, they allocated advertising at or above their volume selling price points. Consequently, the questionnaire technique could not be used in this case.

A second method of corroboration was to obtain measurements of Staplinger's newspaper advertising by price-line and to compare the actual allocations for two years. It proved possible to obtain such data for Staplinger's for 1960 and 1965, and to ascertain how other retailers in Monroeville allocated their newspaper linage by price-lines. Finally, similar data for nine major cities was obtained.

In Chapter II, a table of data concerning Women's and Misses' Dresses illustrated the Neustadt advertising price-lining analysis. As such, it was labeled Table II-1. The reader will recognize this in the present chapter as Table III-4. As noted in the illustration, the questions at the bottom of the table provide a basis for comparing data for individual classifications in the 9-city group and in the subject city and store. A summary of the answers to these questions is contained in Table III-5.

The conclusions of advertising price-lining analysis are threefold. First, Staplinger's started at a substantially higher price-lining level than the other two groups measured. Second, despite the sales promotion events revealed in the interview data, and despite the drive for sales volume, Staplinger's not only started at a higher price level but it succeeded in reaching an even higher one, both relatively and absolutely. Third, this case illustrates that trading up and trading down are relative. The attempt of a store with higher-priced assortments to reach a newly affluent group at a lower level of the income distribution scale is somewhat different from a general trading down by all stores.

Summary

Staplinger's has always fulfilled the mission of a traditional department store—to assemble an enormous variety of consumer goods and services under one roof. During the last twenty years it has extended this offering through many branch stores in Monroeville and to many Midstate communities. In addition to providing the basic merchandise lines expected in a department store, this venerable firm has expanded its merchandising to include other kinds of goods and services. Further, it entered many activities related to retailing, in some instances to achieve retailing objectives and in other instances to earn a profit, by applying merchandising principles to that particular enterprise. Indeed, even in its concept and function of merchandising, Staplinger's has, from its inception, differed from both text descriptions and classic definitions of this industry.

During the period studied, the external environment changed. Trends in demographic conditions and in economic factors favored retailing in Monroeville. The city enjoyed population and income increases and responded by demanding both better-quality and lower-priced merchandise. There were changes in competition as traditional department store rivals, especially after 1950, expanded into suburban and shopping center locations. Amidst these changes the discount department stores flourished as well.

In response to these changes, the Staplinger Company attempted to redefine its marketplace position. Essentially, it decided to increase its share of the growing middle-income demand for department store types of merchandise. Initially, the store traded down. Later, in order to more adequately meet demand and also to differentiate itself from discount, low-margin, and promotional price stores, it attempted to trade up. During the last ten years, as the firm expanded by opening new stores and by acquisitions, as it became more financially stable, it tended to trade up toward the price-lining level it had established prior to 1945.

These responses, different from those hypothesized, can be traced as well to internal influences. Management succession and development, financial requirements, leasehold contracts, among others, were major limitations and constraints which determined the course of action.

Evaluation of Staplinger's strategy requires acknowledgement of where it stood at the beginning of the period as well as at the end. For all the reasons cited, the management perceived a different opportunity in a different market than ever before in its long history. The means of seizing the opportunity were remarkably similar to the Staplinger historical pattern.

The following conclusion is based upon data derived from interviews, publications, research agencies, and Neustadt analysis.

In response to an upward shift in demography of demand and increasing low-margin (discount) store competition, Staplinger's, during the first decade of the period studied, initially traded down from its former level. It attempted to secure a marketplace gap it perceived to exist among traditional department stores. During the second decade, it faltered during the 1955 to 1960 period as it attempted to trade up to a level below its traditional pattern. The impact of discount department stores caused it to reevaluate and redefine its market target. Thereafter, from 1960 to 1965, Staplinger's succeeded in trading up to a level it intended to reach when it redefined its merchandising strategy after 1945. In both decades the newspaper advertising reflected these policies.

IV

The Fair

History of the Firm to 1945

A recent account of the history and development of department
stores points out: "single-unit department stores generally originated
from two sources: specialty stores which expanded the breadth of
types of merchandise and variety of lines carried; or a joining
together of formerly independent merchants."[1] Often the latter group
consisted of lessees who operated under the sponsorship or management of an outside party or under the sponsorship of a fellow lessee.
The Fair, subject of this chapter, originated in this classic pattern.

The Fair was organized as a department store in 1900 in Keelim,
Northstate. It began as a confederation of leased departments, most
of which traded in low-quality merchandise. Managers or individual
owners operated their businesses as if they were sole proprietors who
had rented single store spaces. A merchant acquainted with The Fair
said: "The result was a hodge-podge. Some departments carried low-
grade merchandise; some, high grade. There was no definite policy;
hence, there was really no basis by which customers could establish
an opinion of the store."[2]

Three lessees were more successful than others. William Delzer,
Sanford Lipson, and Stanley Tanner leased and operated the notions,
hosiery, and underwear departments respectively, and managed them
profitably. These three men were road salesmen for wholesalers and

manufacturers, and had invested in these departments to assure themselves of retail outlets in the booming Keelim market.

As the business and profits increased, the three salesmen-retailers formed a partnership headed by Delzer. All three moved to Keelim and gradually purchased the assets of less successful lessees. By 1906, the partnership controlled the entire store and its real estate.

The merchandising policy that evolved was undoubtedly influenced by the salesmanship-resource experiences of the three partners. Management insisted that buyers seek strong resources, especially national-brand manufacturers if possible. A bulletin issued in 1925 by The Fair on the subject of image is as current today as it apparently was then. Marketing and retailing literature today includes many articles concerned with image and with the need to cultivate consumer belief in a firm, a label, or a particular product. In 1925, The Fair admonished its buyers:

> The image of a store is the total impression it makes on the community. Given a favorable image of our store, the franchise you have to do business in your department is a very valuable thing. Given a less favorable image, your franchise would be much less valuable. One department isolated from the rest of the store is not likely to get the customers in the door. Just remember that the only thing you offer that is unique is the store's image or reputation. The merchandise you carry, the credit you provide are all available in other places in town. They should be important when *you* offer them.[3]

Neither the trade press nor any of the interviewees could provide information about the company's progress during its first twenty years. During the third and fourth decades of its history, The Fair, as portrayed by interviewees, was a medium-to-better price store. While always competitive in its pricing, it was not necessarily a price leader. Rather than seeking volume leadership, The Fair stressed profitable volume by means of excellent customer service and quality merchandise procured from strong resources.

To achieve that end, The Fair in 1934 applied for membership in and was accepted by the Department Store Buying Syndicate, a group of independent department stores organized for wholesale resident buying, and research functions. A store secures several advantages by such affiliation as was exemplified by the Staplinger case. For The Fair, this new association brought the management into contact with executives from many of America's best known and most successful department stores, most of which were larger than the Keelim store. The Fair benefited by the greater amount of information and buying assistance it could command. Also, this association became the contact through which the store was sold in 1949.

Only one of the executives interviewed had been associated with The Fair prior to 1945. Gilbert Moran, personnel director, reiterated the claim that the store had always inclined toward customer service and community participation and attempted to stress quality and fashion.

A review of trade press and local news files tends to confirm these generalizations. For example, as early as 1933, The Fair purchased property behind the store to use for customer parking.[4] In 1936, it sponsored a special science exhibition, displaying two sets of television-telephones. Again, it won the bid to furnish a home constructed and sponsored by *Life* magazine to serve as a model for Keelim.[5] However, inspection of the files disclosed that The Fair was perhaps more price competitive than interviewees indicated. For example, in December, 1936, a local liquor distributor filed suit in Circuit Court to restrain The Fair from selling Schenley liquor products at less than the minimum prices set by Schenley.[6]

A brief review of the Keelim demographic and economic development can help explain the retail market structure prior to and after 1945. Until 1930, Northstate's economy had been predominantly agricultural. As industrialization increased, the city of Keelim became the manufacturing and distribution trade center. Heavy industry in Keelim attracted and then employed large numbers of immigrants from 1875 to 1925. The community could never boast of the business-government-education combination that will be noted in the L. H. Kane Company case, for example, or of spectacular growth prior to 1945, as in Monroeville. Hence, Keelim tended to be a "feast or famine" town, one in which merchants, according to one interviewee, developed a strategy of price appeal. He added:

Schmidt's and Samuelson's (the two other traditional department stores in Keelim) and The Fair, too, taught the people to wait for sales and to judge by price. These "Big Three of Keelim" fought for years for volume supremacy and they all acted as if a middle class didn't exist in Keelim. Every time The Fair started to merchandise the better price-lines it would run into an economic reversal in the town, and, boom, the store would run a sale.[7]

Apparently no one of the three major department stores had established a clear position as a fashion and quality leader. Indeed, no one of the three achieved a dominant volume position. Most interviewees credited The Fair, however, with being the quality and brand-name resource store in Keelim.

Changes in Keelim Environment: 1945-1965

It was stated earlier that strategy formulation requires thorough analysis by management of the marketplace, of its competitors, and of itself. For example, the merchant must select that part of the income spectrum toward which he will direct his efforts. Strategy formulation will also depend upon a retailer's perception of his competition. A third factor in this decision concerns self-knowledge: an appreciation of the kind of merchant a man is or wants to be. The Fair's merchandising strategy reflects this triple analysis. In this section, the discussion centers on the second factor, the changes in demographic and economic conditions in Keelim and among competitors. It then relates how executives at The Fair perceived these factors during the period from 1945 to 1965.

Merchandising strategy changes among all retailers in Keelim, including those who entered this market after 1945, seemed to depend on who interpreted what demographic and economic developments. For example, it is ironic that while local retailers, including The Fair, remained undecided about their plans for expansion, two nationally famous retail firms entered the Keelim market and by diverse strategies exploited opportunities the hometown stores overlooked.

Changes in Demography of Demand

Tables A, 1-5, Appendix, show that the overall changes in demographic and economic conditions in Keelim from 1945 to 1965 were positive. Its population increase was gradual, second to Haverford's (another city in this study), and almost at the same pace as recorded for the nation. Appendix Table A-2 shows that the relative changes in Keelim's total net effective buying income were greater than in Freeport. But they were less than those experienced in Monroeville, Haverford, or in the nation as a whole.

Based on an index of 1946=100, Tables IV-1 and Appendix Table

TABLE IV-1
Selected Operating Data of The Fair and Keelim

Item	1945	1946	1947	1948	1963
The Fair, total sales, fiscal year end, 1/31 of year following. (Index: 1946 = 100)	73.8	100.0	102.3	114.6	121.9
The Fair, net profit percent of sales, fiscal year end, 1/31 of year following.	2.27	5.60	3.97	2.63	N.A.
Expressed on index: 1946 = 100	40.6	100.0	70.9	54.2	47.3
Keelim, total retail sales, calendar year (1946 = 100)	64.9	100.0	128.1	140.1	201.5
Keelim, general merchandise, sales, calendar year (1946 = 100)	83.6	100.0	124.5	144.3	225.3

SOURCES: *Sales Management Buying Power Guide; Keelim News;* Federal Trade Commission; and *Market Publication No. 1,* August 28, 1963, and August 29, 1963.

A-3 show the uneven growth in Keelim retail sales. Although the total retail sales and the general merchandise sales increased from 1945 to 1948, at which time the index figures reached 140.1 and 144.3, respectively (as seen in Table IV-1), the two figures declined by 1950 to 121.4 and 128.6, respectively. Nonetheless, the interview data suggested that the initial increases helped to attract the interest of the company that purchased The Fair in 1949.

Income distribution changes also explain why various retailers invested in Keelim. As seen in Appendix Table A-5, not only did the "$7,000 and over" income group increase substantially from 1950 to 1965, but the "$10,000 and over" group increased proportionately even more. In the first category, the Keelim index in 1965 equalled the U.S. index. In the second category the Keelim index in 1965 reached 175.9, exceeding the national index of 148.3. Also, the Keelim index ranked second among the four cities compared. The percentage of families with incomes of less than $7,000 annually was not substantially different from the national figure. In 1955, more than three-quarters of Keelim households had incomes of less than $7,000, while the national figure for the same year was 80.9 percent.

Executives at The Fair in the 1950s continued to view Keelim as a factory town, a beans and beer, a meat and potatoes town, according to statements made by interviewees. Reading the economic data

furnished by the *Keelim News*, and recalling the city's periodic unemployment in the past, The Fair's management concluded it should
merchandise to factory workers whose wages were approximately
$66.00 per week in 1950, $77.00 in 1952, and $82.00 in 1954.[8] Or,
again, in 1955 these executives focused on data showing that more
than one-third of the Keelim households had disposable incomes of
$3,999.00 or less.[9]

The reader should bear in mind that Keelim, like other heavy-
industry towns, had known many periods of feast and famine. As
could be expected, these conditions influenced retailers as they assayed their market. One official at The Fair summarized the perspective that prevailed until the 1960s:

I think a depression psychology typified Keelim. Historically, the people
had always been a penurious group and thrift was a way of life. People
always lived in the shadow of unemployment. Strong ethnic and religious
mores governed the style of life here. Retailers were always scrambling to
stay alive.[10]

Other executives, but not all, reiterated a similar theme—that
business conditions in Keelim were either depressed or suffered by
comparison with other metropolitan areas in the middle United
States. They attributed many merchandising strategy decisions on
assortments, pricing, promotions, or expenses to these external conditions.

Since the data in Tables A, 1-5, Appendix, do not suggest such
unfavorable conditions for retailing, these same variables were analyzed in greater detail. The *Keelim News* has records relevant to
employment, factory earnings, gross personal income, and retail, general merchandise, and department store sales from 1950 to 1965. Data
sources include the Federal Reserve Bank, the U.S. Department of
Commerce, the *Keelim News* Research Department, and the *Sales
Management Survey of Buying Power*. Table IV-2 summarizes those
findings.

Generally, the data do not support the aforementioned claims.
Except for the 1956-58 period, the total employment increased steadily. While the number of factory production workers fluctuated, the
decline was never more than 9 percent of the numbers employed in
1950. Indeed, from 1950 to 1965, the number of factory workers employed had increased proportionately more than the total employment. Retail, general merchandise, and department store sales in-

TABLE IV-2

Summary of Selected Economic Measurements for Keelim, Northstate, 1950-1965

(1950 = 100)

Item	1950	1952	1954	1956	1958	1960	1962	1963	1965
Total employment (annual average)	100.0	112.2	113.3	120.0	118.9	122.8	129.6	130.6	140.0
Factory production workers	100.0	107.9	94.2	106.2	91.0	98.1	134.9	134.5	144.3
Percent of factory production workers to total employed	35.8	34.4	29.7	31.8	27.5	28.7	37.2	36.9	37.0
Gross personal income	100.0	118.0	122.9	139.6	145.5	157.9	169.2	173.5	182.5
Retail sales*	100.0	111.5	112.9	123.7	127.3	141.2	151.4	158.1	170.7
General merchandise sales**	100.0	N.A.	106.9	118.8	121.3	153.4	173.5	175.1	247.5
Department store sales***	100.0	N.A.	98.6	110.4	109.0	123.7	123.7	N.A.	N.A.
Department store sales percent to general merchandise	89.6	...	83.3	83.2	80.7	72.5	64.3	N.A.	N.A.
Department store sales percent to retail sales	14.0	...	12.3	12.5	12.1	12.3	11.5	N.A.	N.A.

*In 1948, retail sales were 91.2 percent of 1950; **gen. mdse. sales, 96.3 percent; and ***dept. store sales, 100 percent of 1950.

SOURCES: *Keelim News*, Market Research Department, for respective dates.

creased, as might be expected in light of the 82.5 percent increase in gross personal income from 1950 to 1965. General merchandise sales increased proportionately more than total retail sales. Despite this favorable factor, however, Keelim department stores failed to increase their portion. That is to say, using 1950 as an index of 100, retail sales increased 51.4 percent by 1962; general merchandise sales by 73.5 percent; and department stores by only 23.7 percent.

During the 1945-1965 period, management executives at The Fair did not agree on what this market was or on what it should mean to the company. However, other retailers, representing different kinds of retail institutions, foresaw potential in Keelim's various market segments.

Changes in Traditional Department Stores

In 1955, executives at Dean and Company, a nationally famous quality department store, began to investigate Keelim. They had discovered that, although their store was located at some distance from Keelim, they drew both personal shopping and mail patronage from that city. Further, they too read the data relevant to demography of demand. What they noticed was that an increasing percentage of Keelim households were becoming more prosperous, that Keelim was steadily growing, and that diversified industries had located there. They hypothesized that if more than 25 percent of the households reached an annual income level of "$7,000 and over," there would be sufficient buying power to support a quality department store offering wide assortments at moderate prices. Subsequently, they decided these conditions would develop, and committed themselves to build a 293,000 square foot department store in a 1,000,000 square foot shopping center called Keelim Park, eight miles from the Keelim central business district. This store has been successful ever since it opened in 1958.

The Dean Company's success can be attributed to several positive factors. The store was located in an area where 50 percent of the households had annual incomes exceeding $8,000. The company offered, in Keelim's largest retail structure, very broad assortments of merchandise in all traditional department store classifications. Its prestige also proved to be a valuable asset.

The Fair's two traditional rivals—Samuelson's and Schmidt's—continued to emphasize price and also to expand into shopping centers. Each exploited its respective strengths. Samuelson's business in hard goods—appliance, furniture, and hard home furnishings—was especially large and well established among three generations of Keelim families. It did not operate a downtown location, having established a reputation with its four neighborhood stores.

Schmidt's built a business on "value" (which in this instance meant "low price"), wide assortments in lower price-ranges, heavy sales promotion efforts, and a very successful Bargain Basement in the downtown store. It opened two branch stores after 1945 but had not earned more than an average reputation for its fashion appeal.

Both Samuelson's and Schmidt's expanded into shopping centers, although neither altered their basic merchandising strategy. Each operated two stores in separate shopping centers. Rather than continue the rivalry, the two managements decided, in 1962, to merge into Samuelson's-Schmidt's, thus enabling a single firm to clearly claim and hold sales volume dominance in the Keelim market for the first time. Also, the merger enabled one firm to offer its merchandise in the three most patronized shopping locations—downtown, established neighborhood shopping districts, and newly constructed shopping centers.

Samuelson's-Schmidt's sales volume as a merged enterprise was now twice as much as that of its nearest rival, The Fair. Despite some legal difficulties, including Federal Trade Commission and National Labor Relations Board charges and suits, the new retail giant managed to accelerate its sales volume faster than other stores, as revealed by Federal Reserve figures for the area.[11] The combined management faced some sales volume losses in two declining neighborhood areas. As in the Staplinger case, the management converted the upper three floors of a neighborhood store to its own real estate purposes, using them for bookkeeping and other operations, gaining space it would otherwise have had to lease from outside sources.

Some trade observers claimed that the combination of a department store eminently successful in hard-goods classifications with one whose success lay in lower-priced promotional merchandise would make it difficult to emphasize the fashion elements of merchandising. For instance, the Samuelson-Schmidt combination ranks among the top ten retail advertisers in the country (excluding Sears, Ward's, and Penney's). Observers pointed out that the firm's giant size became both its strength and its weakness. For instance:

A consumer here finds it not unusual to pick up an issue of the *Keelim News* and see a sequence of Samuelson-Schmidt ads something like this: One or two fashion pages, a couple of pages of housewares, furniture, white goods, a page or two of clearance or Special Sale, followed by a couple of pages of "economy basement" offerings.[12]

Despite these criticisms, the firm increased fashion emphasis in three steps. First, it added to the assortments of fashion merchandise. Second, it constructed boutiques and shops within the stores to provide an atmosphere conducive to fashion selling. This program did not apply to apparel alone but included the home furnishings divisions as well. Third, the firm sponsored a consumers' panel composed of leading women in the Keelim area. The activities of the panel received wide and effective publicity.

Shopping Centers

Shopping center construction and occupancy also constituted a major external change in the Keelim environment. Six major shopping centers were opened between 1945 and 1965, as shown in Table IV-3.

Obviously The Fair did not spearhead these expansions and when it became a tenant the firm did not lease spaces as large as its rivals did. The largest single occupancy was by Dean and Company, an "outside" traditional department store. One advantage Samuelson-Schmidt enjoyed is apparent in this summary; the combined firm was the dominant store in four of the six centers.

Sears and Penney's did not participate in shopping center development during the period studied. However, both announced they would occupy major spaces in Keelim's largest shopping center, to be opened in 1967. This 1,250,000 square foot air conditioned shopping mall includes four department stores: Sears, 225,000 square feet; Penney, 225,000 square feet; Wier Co. (a specialty store in Keelim), 50,000 square feet; and The Fair, 175,000 square feet.[13]

Discount Department Stores

As noted at the beginning of this section, two outside firms eyed Keelim as a potential market. The first was Dean and Company. The second was a national mercantile company which decided to organize a chain of low-margin, partial self-service department stores. In these

TABLE IV-3

Statistical Summary of Six Major Shopping Centers in Keelim, 1945-1965*

Year Opened	Name of Shopping Center	Approximate Size (sq. ft.)	Number of Tenants	Approximate $ Sales Total Center (000)	Major Department Store	
					Tenants	Size (sq. ft.)
1951	West Gate	600,000	37	$ 27,200	Samuelson's	190,000
1954	North Gate	390,000	45	22,100	Sears Roebuck & Co.	85,000
					Wier Company	30,000
					The Fair	102,000
1956	Center Court	1,026,000	85	57,700	Wier Company	80,000
					Schmidt's	237,000
					J. C. Penney	93,000
1956	Murray Plaza	150,000	24	8,200	Samuelson's	30,000
					W. T. Grant	15,200
					Sears Roebuck & Co.	19,200
1958	Keelim Park	1,000,000	63	37,500	Schmidt's	207,000
					Dean & Company	293,000
1959	Beacon Point	287,000	29	12,750	The Fair	69,600
					J. C. Penney	58,100
Totals	6	3,453,000	283	$165,450	Samuelson's & Schmidt's	664,000
					The Fair	171,600
					J. C. Penney	151,100
					Wier Company	111,000
					Sears Roebuck & Co.	94,200
					W. T. Grant	15,200
					Dean & Company	293,000
						1,500,000

*Based on 1963 Census.
SOURCE: "The Keelim Market," *The Keelim Journal*, 1967.

new stores it planned to include a complete assortment of traditional department store classifications. The basic strategy was to design a "promotional, low-margin store" that would provide pleasant, comfortable, accessible shopping at prices below the level the chain charged in its other stores but slightly above the prevailing discount store level. In 1960, it opened Consumers World, a pilot store of 125,000 square feet.

Why had this eminently successful firm selected Keelim? Some observers pointed out that the firm had always operated successfully in Northstate, including Keelim, where it knew the market. This would seem to substantiate interview data that "Keelim is a bargain town, responds to price, and you have to promote sales and prices if you want to go ahead." The judgment proved correct. Within four years, by 1964, the firm constructed two additional Consumers World stores, thereby merchandising 375,000 square feet of selling area in Keelim.

While traditional department store firms added 1,500,000 square feet as tenants in shopping centers (Table IV-3), their new rivals, the discount department stores, added 1,160,000 square feet to Keelim retailing in the same period. Table IV-4 shows that these enterprises found Keelim a worthwhile market. Both the Consumers World firm, as noted, and Lander's, the two largest discount firms, are divisions of national mercantile chains. None of the discount stores located in the six major shopping centers. A census report of the discount market stated that in 1964 there were fourteen discount stores in Keelim, occupying 1,100,000 square feet of retail space.[14]

The discount department stores, in toto, supplied a wide range of prices and assortments to Keelim. Two of these firms, Lander's and Allison Brothers, had established national reputations primarily as distributors of low-end apparel and soft home furnishings, but they expanded their operations in Keelim and elsewhere to include hard goods. True-Value Stores was a local firm which included hard and soft goods from its beginning and also emphasized lower-priced merchandise. Consumers World, as stated, was a pilot operation by a national retailing firm to see if it could successfully offer medium-to-low-priced goods on a self-service basis. The background of the merchants placed in charge of Consumers World indicated that they would pay close attention to such fundamentals as basic stock maintenance, excellent housekeeping, signing, and display.

TABLE IV-4

Self-Service Department Stores in Keelim, Northstate, 1966*

Firm	Number of Stores	Number of Square Feet
Lander's	4	365,000
A.B.C.	1	110,000
Jack's	3	120,000
Roadway Stores (non-food stores)	4	20,000
Tru-Value Stores	2	220,000
Allison Brothers	3	280,000
Savemore Stores	2	200,000
Consumers World	3	375,000
		1,160,000
	Estimated sales volume	$$90,750,000**

*As defined by the *Keelim Journal*. Fictitious names, however, represent several nationwide discount department store firms.

**Based on industry-wide average of $55 sales per gross square foot occupied, *The Discount Merchandiser,* New York, 1966, p. 13. Data collected by University of Massachusetts, Bureau of Business Research.

Interim Summary

Both population and income changes in Keelim from 1945 to 1965 were favorable to the retailing industry. Traditional and discount department store firms expanded. One national firm launched a pilot chain of discount stores in this market. A traditional department store from another area invaded Keelim with the largest single store in the area. Management's "reading of the market map," or inter- pretation of these external changes, partially accounts for changes in merchandising strategy.

Ownership Change at The Fair: 1949

As World War II closed, The Fair expanded by acquiring two department stores in smaller Northstate communities. One year later, it opened a new electrical appliance and housewares specialty store in West Keelim. Aided by long-established resource relationships and the strong market positions of the Department Store Buying Syndicate, The Fair generated one of the largest sales volume increases in its history, to which the three additional stores contributed substantially.

The Fair, during the 1945-1948 period, solidified resource relationships and enlarged the stock assortments of higher price-lines. Neither the sales nor the profit performance, as shown in Table IV-1, were favorable when compared with the Keelim market, as noted earlier in this chapter, or with industry performance, as seen in Table III-1. However, two factors warranted the increasing attention manufacturers and retailers paid to this store. It appeared that The Fair would emerge as the quality and fashion store in the growing city of Keelim. In addition, the net profit on a large sales volume became attractive when measured as a return on investment rather than as a percentage of sales only. For both of these reasons, the United States Department Stores, Inc., a nationwide retail firm and also an affiliate in the Department Store Buying Syndicate, began an investigation that led to its purchase of The Fair in 1949.

What kind of a store was The Fair prior to its sale? What was its merchandising strategy then? Interviewees offered varying opinions. The executive with the longest tenure stated: "The image before the United acquisition was good. The Fair was well accepted, strong in home furnishings, perhaps weaker in ready-to-wear and accessories. But it was a quality store and since 1936 had recaptured leadership in department store merchandising."[15]

A buyer who started with the store's training squad after college graduation explained that "The Fair was really 'two stores.'" He elaborated:

When United purchased the store it had the best lines of merchandise. People in the upper 10 percent of the income range definitely considered The Fair as *the* department store of Keelim. But the store also appealed to those whose incomes were in the lower 50 percent of the range. Perhaps it was the Basement operation. I would say the weakness lay in failing to offer assortments to the middle-income groups. Yet, the store apparently repeated the same mistake just six years ago. In the home furnishings division, for example, we had $1.00 towels in great strength. Then we had a gap. And then we offered the city's largest assortment of $5.00 towels. But we were weak in between.[16]

The present president retrospectively appraised the store more favorably:

At one time The Fair must have had the fine reputation in town for good-to-better goods. Otherwise, why have people accepted what we have tried to do and tried to offer? No, I think United bought the store because it was that kind of fashion store which it could help to grow. Or, at least, it thought it was that kind of store.[17]

Merchandising Strategy Changes: 1949-1963

Interviewees and other sources indicated that from 1949 to 1963 The Fair management pursued a seemingly contradictory, two directional, merchandising strategy requiring antithetical tactics. One executive succinctly summarized these:

It is difficult to precisely evaluate what occurred after the United purchase. I think we were the leading fashion outlet among department stores in Keelim. But we were probably trying to combine a genuine concern about a long-run fashion business and an immediate scramble to stay alive. In pursuing that objective we did not hesitate to use any expedient.[18]

A buyer expressed the reaction of those executives responsible for implementing these two-directional objectives:

It was helter-skelter; one day we aimed in a fashion direction; the next, toward value, which meant price. Sale time was excitement time. Then everyone, from the top down, became excited. That was the big emphasis. Run a successful sale and you were a hero! The result was that at the buyer level you didn't really know what the store wanted.[19]

Executives at The Fair often used prosaic trade terms to describe the two-directional strategy. One of these words is *cargo*. It means that the merchant strives for sales-volume-at-any-price. More explicitly, the term implies the merchant will sacrifice quality of merchandise and gross margin and will tend to trade at lower price levels in order to sell ever increasing amounts of goods. The standard becomes sales volume rather than a quality level.

The second term used, *fashion*, meant, in this instance, discrimination in selection of merchandise so that the quality level becomes the standard and the decision-rule for assortments, even in determining the composition of a basic stock. Interviewees referred to a retailer as a cargo operator or as a fashion merchant.

The two-directional strategy manifested itself, according to executives interviewed, in four activities. They were identified as: planning, expansion, classification merchandising, and resource relationships.

Merchandise Planning: Cargo

Interpretation by The Fair of United States Department Store policies influenced merchandise planning. One United policy was to encourage each store to achieve dominance in its respective community by supporting all efforts to sustain and enlarge the anchor store located downtown. A management could expect to be judged in terms of the success of the downtown operation. Another way to gain dominance was to feature both lower-priced and middle-bracket merchandise, and to make sure that the store was not undersold. Perhaps more basic than all of these was a conviction by United that the key to long-range success was to stress return on investment to the management in each store. By insisting that every dollar produce a profit, the United headquarters encouraged a store management to find merchandise that would meet demand and sell quickly. Conceivably, these policies could be interpreted to discourage establishment of large, complete branch stores that might reduce downtown volume. This may account for the strategy of branch store operations at The Fair.

But at The Fair this admonition to dominate was also taken to mean "dominate at any cost, get volume at any cost." One merchandiser remarked:

We dynamited for business, adding almost $2 million volume in one year. We still had a reputation, at least the best of three bad ones in town. We started to sell toys at 40-50 percent off regular retail even before the discounters came. We forgot assortments, prestige, resources. If the public wants button-down oxford shirts, then be sure you have the largest selection of button-down oxford shirts in Keelim. Better still, try to find a resource, any resource, who can give you a $5.00 shirt for $3.50. But it should not have meant that the rest of the stocks were to suffer. And all this worked, for a couple of years. The volume and profits increased. Expenses lagged behind these volume spurts. But then they caught up. Soon you required assistant department managers and more help. And other expenses, such as advertising and merchandise handling, increased. The result was that profits hit the skids.[20]

Several merchants at The Fair reiterated the view that the local consumer market had changed. Granted that perhaps at one time this had been a factory town, the emerging demand was different, they claimed. One buyer stated that "the emerging market arose from the Taste Revolution." Asked to elaborate, he added:

There is a new middle market, one which demands or at least desires self-expression. These customers are tired of old kinds of goods and since neither we nor our competitors provided this individuality, our customers progressed beyond us. When we finally changed after 1964, consumer response indicated this demand already existed. So far as our industry is concerned I think this was the major shift in retailing during the 1940s and 1950s.[21]

But cargo merchandising prevailed. In stocking of the last branch opened in 1962, The Fair Village Store, the management inclined toward budget merchandise. A dress buyer commented:

They just didn't believe in this kind of merchandising, whether downtown or in the branches. It was difficult to launch and sustain volume in better dresses. And when it didn't take off they felt justified in adding more budget ready-to-wear. Of course, as you diminished stocks of better goods, the volume in those ranges declined even more.[22]

Dominance also required that The Fair never be undersold. To emphasize its pricing policy, the store expended considerable advertising for a tactic called "an island of loss in a sea of profit" merchandising. For example, the General Electric Company sued The Fair in 1955 for illegal price-cutting. The counsel for General Electric showed that during the first five months of 1955 The Fair promoted its own private brand of steam iron at a price varying from $9.99 to $12.99, claiming a $17.95 valuation. The counsel declared that the $17.95 comparison was fictitious and that this quality had never sold for more than $12.99 anywhere in the country. He forced The Fair's vice-president to admit that the store had sold only 297 steam irons during the period and had advertised it at least six times. He also produced records to show that a General Electric steam iron price-maintained at $17.95 had not been advertised by The Fair but had still accounted for 22 percent of the sales in that classification. During the sixth month, The Fair cut the General Electric steam iron to $13.99 and sold 333 irons on the basis of two ads.[23] Cargo merchandising did not produce profitable volume or effective resource relationships or customer belief in merchandise or promotion.

In their discussions of merchandising planning, interviewees frequently referred again to recession periods, depression psychology,
and the nature of demand in Keelim. However, one executive partially blamed the department stores themselves for their plight.

All three of the major stores were strong in home furnishings. But they
were always underfinanced, always looking for cash. You could always tell
when the 10th of the month was by the size of the sale each store staged.
They taught the people of Keelim to shop by comparative price, to ask
themselves how much they saved before they bought. Yes, there were some
fine specialty shops here but the general taste level was low because the
stores never sought to tell or sell or lead in quality or fashion or new goods.
The attitude seemed to be that we shouldn't tell the customer what they
might want; rather, we should find a common or average and try to dominate the market for that demand.[24]

Another buyer suggested that cargo merchandising was not the role
of the department store. "People don't need us for meat and potatoes.
When they want taste, fashion, the better goods, we should be able
to supply such goods because that is the mission of the department
store."[25]

This merchandising strategy resulted in a roller-coaster sales curve
and required recurring drives to beat last year's figures. Any prolonged failure triggered a batch of new sales promotion plans. The
failure, as one executive said, "was that we couldn't secure a day-in,
day-out business. The fear was always present that you might be
called on the carpet to explain why you didn't beat yesterday."[26]

Cargo merchandising, according to interviewees, was based on the
hope that sales volume increases would outdistance expense increases. In an environment where volume is king, there is a tendency
to favor those expenditures likely to bring immediate results. By the
same token there is also a tendency to postpone those expenditures
which are essentially an investment. Under such conditions the firm
might willingly increase its newspaper advertising for a limited
period, say, for a store-wide sales event. Again, however, that same
store might delay the expenditure, even of a like amount, to repaint
a floor or department.

Interviewees contrasted the different approaches utilized by the
new managements before and after 1963. Before 1963, in order to
gain additional volume, The Fair had opened only the Basement
floor of the downtown store for shopping six evenings a week and

opened the remainder of the store for business only two evenings a week. When the new president assumed his office in 1964, one of the first acts was to eliminate the six night openings. "This was a smirch on the entire Main Store as well as a very costly search for sales volume."[27]

A veteran executive explained that the massive refurbishing in the 1955-1958 period, to be noted shortly, was necessitated by a penny-wise, pound-foolish expense control program in the late 1940s and early 1950s:

We didn't take care of all the problems and let the physical plant run down. We cut back every time there was a sign of volume decline. . . . The environment in which the employee works affects how she handles the customer as well as the goods. Also, the wrong physical layout not only causes deficient customer service but it also increases expenses by the same token. Therefore, you can reduce expenses by constantly studying and modifying the environment in which you bring the customer, the clerk, and the goods together.[28]

Some executives advocated what might be termed "a creative approach to merchandising expense control." One proposal was

[to] do what's hard for our competition to do—to increase our costs by wider assortments for discriminating customers; to increase display costs to show off more effectively our best goods; to increase payroll costs in order to obtain the employment of quality salespeople who can be trained to sell $150.00 worth of coordinated home furnishings instead of seconds in towels by the pound; increase advertising expenses by not demanding an immediate turnover of goods; by increasing our markdowns so we won't be afraid to offer a selection of several colors and not just the one that happens to be "hot" at the moment.[29]

The management did not accept these kinds of proposals; management was unwilling to invest in this kind of a strategy over time, for at least a period of one or two years. Also, the management was unwilling to invest the resources required to effectively penetrate the proposed market segment.

Merchandise Planning: Fashion

A veteran ready-to-wear merchandiser who received his training in the East at one of America's most renowned specialty stores pointed out that the strategy prevailing in a store affected a buyer's behavior:

When price, sales, pushing for volume dominates, an attitude permeates
throughout the store. You begin to look at goods differently than when you
push for style. In the latter case, you look at goods more carefully. When
you continually buy off-price you look at goods as units or dollars rather
than as some kind of intrinsic value. It takes inventory in either case. But
when the pressure is to get volume you don't look for that extra markup,
that extra amount of gross margin dollars; you just buy for volume. And it
becomes a never-ending treadmill. You begin to bring in lower-priced
resources and you actually begin to change stock composition and quality
as this process continues.[30]

Despite the foregoing internal environmental conditions, some merchants at The Fair guided themselves by fashion merchandising objectives. The executive most sympathetic to the deposed administration acknowledged that "whenever we had a strong individual divisional merchant with firm convictions, we found ourselves apace with
the consumer. For example, we were ahead or abreast of the consumer
in decorative home furnishings and in furniture."[31]

Generally, the advertised price-lines in this division were at or
above the 9-city averages. These data will be analyzed in greater detail in the section "Questionnaire and Price-Lining Analysis" of this
chapter.

An executive in another division also claimed that a strong individual could countervail with fashion merchandising. The merchant
in the women's and misses' budget coat department demonstrated that
upgrading in both quality and price could be successful. Starting in
1961, he gradually increased the gross margin from 37 percent of sales
to a high of 42 percent by 1965, simultaneously increasing the sales
volume in successive years. He explained:

At the beginning they said—"don't change this department. It is too
good." They were satisfied with the volume at 37 percent markup. I wasn't.
I knew that more could be done, that customers would respond favorably to
better goods. I started to use branded resources and changed the mix of
goods. We cut down the number of sales. Sure, we missed the day but we
seldom missed the week.[32]

Again, the evidence derived from analysis of advertising suggests
that The Fair, at least in this ready-to-wear classification, expended
its advertising at higher price levels than the average store in the
9-city group.

Expansion

The second activity in which the two-directional strategy became apparent was in the program of expansion pursued by The Fair. Again, both cargo and fashion are appropriate terms by which these actions from 1949 to 1963 can be analyzed.

Expansion: cargo. The Fair appeared to follow two guidelines regarding branch stores. The first, which can be traced to the parent company, was that subsidiaries such as The Fair should concentrate on continued development and refurbishing of the "mother" store downtown. The second was a conviction that branch stores should not mirror the main store. However, this can only be attributed to The Fair management itself, since there is no basis for ascribing such a policy to the United corporation.

In 1949, The Fair converted the West Keelim branch, opened in 1946 as an electrical appliance, radio, and housewares store, to a Youth and Fashion Center. The immediate postwar demand for consumer hard goods had partially subsided and increasing competition had reduced gross margins. Retailers were allocating additional space and investments to the world of youth classifications.

The significant decision was not the reallocation of inventory or choice of classifications. Rather, it was the decision to carry children's wear in basement price-ranges in this branch store, although the income and demographic data of that area supported a proposal to include, if not feature, merchandise from the upstairs' departments.[33]

Northgate shopping center opened in 1954 with Sears and Wier and Company as major tenants. But The Fair did not open its branch there until 1958. The center was located in one of the three highest-income residential areas of Keelim. Yet one observer noted the store did not have all downtown departments or all classifications within each department represented. "Some fringe items such as handkerchiefs were missing in the men's section."[34]

The reader will recall that Dean and Company opened its huge store in 1958 with complete assortments. At a later date, The Fair did change its merchandising at this location. In 1965, the new management persuaded the Northgate owners to "take steps to get the price tenants out and get quality tenants in stores that will appeal to the wealthy suburbs.[35]

Soon after opening the branch at Northgate, The Fair management confirmed plans to open a "twig" unit in the Beacon Point shopping

center. This would open as a basement branch store. The president at
that time was quoted as saying: "The reasons for constructing a basement store are that experience has shown that the best-selling merchandise in outlying branches is popular-priced convenience goods,
exactly the sort of a thing a basement store carries. Also, this proposed branch exactly matches the space used by our basement store
downtown."[36]

For unexplained reasons, the store opening was delayed until 1959.
It finally opened as a department store supermarket, using checkout
counters and shopping carts. With the exception of shoes, hosiery,
jewelry, and cosmetics, it was essentially a self-service store. The store
highlighted basement and budget price lines. An observer noted that
"it featured dresses, for example, going as high as $14.95."[37] The
reader can note from the Neustadt tables that this would place the
highest price dress in price zone 2, even though incomes in this residential area were higher than the city average. (The Neustadt price
zone range in 1959 was the same as for 1960.)

These techniques were successful in attracting customers to this
branch store. Sales volume increased and, in 1961, The Fair announced plans to double the space and expand lines offered. Self-
service and check-out systems would continue. At that time the trade
press noted that store "representatives from all over the nation came
to see this new phenomenon in retailing. Store officials are highly
enthusiastic about the success of the self-service operation."[38]

Retrospectively, one executive, who manifested a sympathetic understanding of the previous management of which he had been a part,
evaluated the results: "There were unfortunate effects. We disap-
pointed and angered many customers. For years, The Fair had been
a quality store. Customers anticipated branches, wanted them, but
ours shocked them. And these branches confused our own organization."[39]

The Fair opened its third branch in 1962 at a site it called The
Fair Village store. Containing as much selling space as the Northgate
store, it opened largely as a self-service store with sales help in some
departments such as men's clothing. The Fair Village store shared its
building and common entrances with a national grocery supermarket
unit.

Over a longer period, however, this attempt to cargo merchandise
did not succeed, as will be explained. Those who innovate may be
hailed as heroic one day and ignored or even severely criticized shortly

thereafter. Called great innovators by industry observers, praised for daring, applauded for "correctly reading its market" at the time, the management at a later date could also read:

The Fair had to fight the discount image. In the early 1960s, the height of the discount mania, the management in power took the discount bait hook, line, and sinker. The branches were hailed as the first self-service branches by a traditional department store. The whole organization went "modern" in this way. Competition claims the stores were doing a lot of business. Unfortunately, they weren't making any money.[40]

The Fair was not alone. Several soundly managed department store firms experimented with discount merchandising. Famous-Barr tried the discount, self-service concept in 1961 and failed. L. S. Ayres, a traditional prestige department store in Indianapolis, acknowledged to its customers that it initiated, owned and managed Ayr-Way, a successful, self-service discount store in Indianapolis. Both the parent company and the offspring thrived not only in that city but in other Indiana communities as well. Others, such as J. L. Hudson, experimented with basement branches, succeeded in some, miscalculated the market in others. Dayton's of Minneapolis succeeded in launching a discount chain to its own market under the name of Target Stores. The point here is that The Fair's merchandising strategy in branches apparently ran counter to the total expectations of customers and was misaligned with the market opportunity. However, not all of The Fair's expansion was in this direction.

Expansion: fashion. In the downtown store, The Fair attempted to sustain its position as a quality firm. It transformed its Basement Store merchandising in 1955 from a promotional and price leadership basis to one emphasizing competitively priced basic stock assortments. Later, after the supermarket technique and cargo merchandising appeared to be successful, The Fair transformed the Basement Store into a branch operation. In that same year (1955) it started a $2 million refurbishing and remodeling investment in the downtown store. The objectives were to provide a more suitable environment for better merchandise, to emphasize the fashion elements, and to gain additional selling space. Included was a complete remodeling of the main floor, especially in the fashion accessories, shoes, and menswear divisions. The second floor was redesigned to include individual shops for separate customer groups and merchandise classifications. Rearranged traffic aisles and regrouped departments encouraged coordinated selling. There is reason to believe that both The Fair and its customers were satisfied. The store continued this kind of investment in its physical plant until the middle of 1960.

In 1959, The Fair sold the two branch stores it had acquired in 1945 in two communities outside the immediate Keelim trading area. Apparently the management believed it had developed a potentially more profitable strategy for branches within the immediate Keelim trading area.

Classification Merchandising

Amidst the contradictory merchandising policies already described, The Fair had a fundamental idea struggling for expression. Executives called it "Classification of Goods by Customer Preference." The concept is essentially one that is consumer-oriented.

Records and correspondence disclose that two merchandisers at The Fair prepared detailed expositions on this process in 1953. They presented their papers and demonstrations to store principals at national conferences of the United States Department Stores. Many of these ideas are similar to those promulgated by the National Retail Merchants Association at conventions during the past two years.[41] Classification merchandising is a dissection process within merchandising whereby a store can more profitably match its offering to consumer demand. In the Staplinger case, interviewees referred to this process as "Customer Preference." In the Mayfield case (Chapter V), the reader will note that management also required dissection of departments into classifications and subclassifications. The reader will learn that one of the purposes there was to ascertain both gross margin contributions and expenses attributable to every class of commodity.

The president exhorted every merchant at The Fair to study and develop practices in accordance with the concepts expressed in the classification and customer preference program. The following extracts from intra-store communication and interview data indicate the importance of this subject.

The important elements of the program are, first, the customer viewpoint as a simplifier of the complex retail business. Customer desire for merchandise is stimulated by the physical characteristics of the merchandise, by such features as style, color, material, pattern, and use benefits. Customer preferences in these features change, and it is therefore practical to analyze the degree of change so that stocks can be corrected, realistically, for the selling period ahead.

The second important principle involves the classifying technique. Classifying a business divides it into the customer demand areas. As the separate little businesses in a category of merchandise can be isolated, and separately analyzed and planned for, these separate little businesses can be maximized. Then, after segregating customer demand areas into classifications and sub-classifications, the task is to determine for each segment of the area which customer features need continuing analysis. These features become the basis of the record-keeping procedures and there should be just enough formal record-keeping to provide the degree of customer feature analysis that supervision agrees will be productive.

The third step is to conduct a semiannual review in order to isolate strengths and weaknesses. Such identification should become the basis for long-range planning.

The fourth step is to place in writing every bit of timing information that can be developed. One of the major objectives of this program is the proper flow of goods, because we believe that buying, or liquidation action, at the right times can be scheduled.

The fifth step is to aggregate all the information. If a business is as intensely classified as is recommended, it is possible to miss the forest through detailed study of the trees. Therefore, it is essential that the regularly scheduled *total look* of a classification of goods becomes a part of the decision-making procedures. The result should be the identification of duplicating assortments and of customer demand areas, or features that need accelerated or diminished support, in the selling period for which buying and liquidating decisions are being made.[42]

In a bulletin to the buyers, the merchandise manager cited an example of Classification by Customer Preference merchandising:

What we want to do is to identify the features that attract customers to certain items and represent these same features widely in the stock, at different quality levels and at different price-lines. For instance, if a polka dot cotton voile dress at $10.99 sold out quickly on the first shipment, should we represent polka dot cotton voiles in several price-lines in several styles? And what other features about that cotton voile dress, attracted customers? —was it the mandarin collar, the full skirt, the rhinestone buttons, or what?[43]

Perhaps Classification by Customer Preference was ahead of its time at The Fair. Intra-store communications dated in the 1950s certainly evidenced interest and enthusiasm and direction. According to interviewees, it did not succeed.

Some claimed that management employed the technique to the extreme. One executive commented:

There was no fluidity. If C. P. showed that black and white would be the number one preference at the peak of demand, we were supposed to stock 300 pieces, have it in depth, ready to power the item. But you can't always buy major resources that way; and you can't produce a stock which the market itself doesn't have. And the president was absolutely sure he was right and the reason the idea didn't work was that his subordinates were wrong or didn't know how to work the system.[44]

But perhaps a more searching appraisal is that offered by a merchandiser, no longer associated with The Fair, who was an executive there during the 1950s:

I think they were tops in merchandising but they forgot to be merchants. They fought branches until they couldn't continue without them. Then they selected secondary locations and ultimately imitated discounters. The technique and system kick showed up in the Classification by Customer Preference program. Everything was run by the book. The way they administered it was more like the Big Item, the runner item technique of the 1930s. But the Big Item didn't solve the problem of how to provide broad and right assortments for customers who wanted something a bit better or a little different. The C. P. Program really was aimed, presumably, at assuring the customer of this style-right assortment.[45]

Resources

The two-directional strategy also manifested itself in the selection and cultivation of, and in the continuity with, resources. Conflicts concerning resources arose, first, because each divisional merchandise manager interpreted differently, as already noted, what the strategy was; and second, because in the selection of resources the buyers often competed among themselves as a result of these individual interpretations. That is to say, buyers within the same division might seek merchandise from the same resource because, despite their nominal assignment, they pursued the same mission.

The retailer-resource relationship can be viewed as existing between two choices. On one hand, the retailer selects resources in accordance with what he believes his store should represent and in accordance with the retail market segment from which he seeks patronage. On the other hand, because he is a reseller, he is usually constrained to choose from what the resource market offers. Conflicts about resources within a store organization will intensify if the merchandising strategy is not distinctly expressed.

Executives pointed out that when an organization permits every merchandise manager to be a king unto himself, a conflict about resources is likely to ensue. These disagreements resulted in loosely defined price-lines, and such mixed merchandise presentations that a sixteen-year-old girl might be encouraged or required to shop in the same department as a fifty-five-year-old woman. Obviously, they added, they could not plan to maximize department store attributes of fashion, service, and individuality under such circumstances. A buyer at The Fair contrasted the merchandising of a specific dress department before and after 1964:

Resource selection affects presentation of the store itself to the public because, hopefully, what the customer sees is the merchandise itself. Consider our Avenue Dress Shop. It is defined now as a place in the store which caters to the career girl. We range in price from $12.00 to $25.00 with our strength at $15.00 to $18.00. We evaluate every resource in terms of its capacity to provide strength to the merchandising idea, to the market segment, we have selected for this department. We now use fewer resources. We have favorable positions with them. No other department uses these same resources. There is consistency in the assortment and in the presentation. Before this, however, I might have found that some other dress department used or was using the same resource and may have worked with it differently.[46]

Resource policy and related merchandising conflicts denied The Fair profit opportunities. Department and specialty stores in 1960 were already taking notice of the Villager, a relatively new resource in ladies' sportswear. Concentrating on classic styling and design of silhouette, on fabric selection, and on the use of conservative color ranges, this resource supplied to the market basic merchandise whose simplicity appealed immediately to a wide segment ranging from teen-agers to career women. The Fair merchandiser described the resource and his experience in obtaining it: "This resource stood for a distinct level—in price, in look, in quality. In 1960 I wanted to put this line into the store. But 'upstairs' blocked it. I had to fight for two years. Finally, in 1962, we put the Villager line in the store. It has been one of the best profit-makers in the entire division."[47]

This statement conflicted, however, with previous assertions that merchandise managers were kings in their own domain. Two explanations were offered. One was that the line required a considerable investment and the management viewed such a single, large commitment with disfavor. This is a polite way, it may be concluded, of

denying the risk always involved in bringing a complete new line
into the inventory. Another explanation was that the Villager required as a condition of entry that the store set aside a specific amount
of floor and rack space to be devoted exclusively to this line of
merchandise. The Villager also required that merchandise from other
resources could not be mixed with Villager goods nor could its goods
be mixed with any other line.

It is obvious from the startling success of the resource that many
retail firms met these conditions. But The Fair general-merchandise
manager or his associates delayed for two years a positive decision to
incur such risk and allocate the required floorspace.

In selecting from a resource offering, the retailer must align both
fashion and price level. One merchant cited an example where The
Fair failed to do this: "Over the years the Lees carpet line increased
its assortment and increased its price-range upward. But we went
down two price-lines to get prices we thought the public wanted. Lees
knew what it was doing and why and was right. We thought we
knew what we were doing and why but we were wrong."[48]

Merchandising Strategy Changes After 1963

By 1963, there were some indications that United States Department Stores was not pleased with its Keelim operation. A trade
press report on the total corporate performance noted that "with the
possible exception of The Fair, other United purchases have been
first-grade and have usually reflected favorably upon the profit and
growth pattern this preeminent mercantile company has developed."[49]
Moreover, as Table IV-1 shows, The Fair sales had not kept pace with
Keelim retail acceleration or with nationwide trends.

Early in 1964, United announced the retirement of the incumbent
president of The Fair and the appointment of Mark Sanders as
president. His career included major merchandising assignments in
the Southeast, Midwest, and West Coast regions for one of America's
largest retail firms.

I asked Sanders why he left his former association to affiliate with
United. His response also provided an answer to how he assayed the
Keelim demography of demand:

There was a great opportunity here to favorably alter the merchandising
and at the same time join the "Yankees" of retailing. There are more than

one million people in this market, many with a very high level of income. Samuelson's-Schmidt's does not provide what certain segments of this market want. It is a cargo operation and this market is already full of discounters. People simply must respond to exciting new ideas. Maybe they haven't been exposed to them. A good department store shouldn't have to expend time and money to prove it offers value. Your name should symbolize that– Dayton Company, Rich's, others have proven this is true. The customer has a right to assume you provide value. Our job is to offer and give something more than that. I've seen enough markets to know that Keelim is not as different as some people claim. If we can bring more attractive goods to Keelim than other stores show, I am sure we can increase our sales profitably.[50]

Asked to appraise the previous administration, Sanders pointed out that basically the previous management attempted to shape the market to what it had to offer because that was its method or style of adapting to change. Successful management of change requires, he said, adaptability by management to the marketplace change, not the other way around. But "the previous management knew only one way to respond and to adjust to change and that was to pound your way through."[51]

Whose view of this market was right? Were consumers interested in price only? In quality? In service? Consumer behavior in the food industry, the largest and most frequently patronized segment in retailing, offers some evidence. Investigation disclosed that in this one market, at least, an individualistic strategy could achieve victory. A & P commanded a massive 33.4 percent of the Keelim food market in 1960 but had declined to a meager 10.9 percent share in 1965. The sales volume leadership during this period was gained by Roadway Stores, a local chain, which had grown from 15.4 percent of the market in 1960 to 24.4 percent in 1965, and whose total number of stores in 1965 was just slightly more than one-half the number of stores operated by A & P. A trade press summarized this remarkable change:

The Roadway's success story is attributed to a hardworking management which sees service and atmosphere as two keys to unlock the grip the major chains had here. Its business is based on the theory of giving the customer what she wants and needs and not what management decides she should have. It offers a great variety of items. Women here say that "if you can't find it at Roadway's, stop looking, because you won't find it anywhere in Keelim." Although Keelim has been quite receptive to stamps and giveaways this chain has stayed away from this trend, offering only couponed in-and-out non-food promotions.[52]

New management appraisal of The Fair: assortments. The new president recognized that "customers have been ahead of us but we are now catching up with our customers." He asserted that The Fair was then (in early 1966) leading the community in ready-to-wear and in home furnishings, and that these two divisions had already been solving problems concerning sales volume, gross margin, and expenses before the administration changeover. The menswear division, he suggested, was oriented slightly lower in its price-lining than the market warranted. However, he pointed out that this division had developed a good basic stock business.

Personnel. The new management believed there was a need to tell employees at all levels what the firm was trying to accomplish and what their tasks were. And there was also a need by executives, especially, to convey these ideas of a new Fair to the public. They were encouraged to become very active in highly visible civic and public affairs; one objective was to be seen and publicized. Another objective was to overcome a certain stigma attached to the store arising from the poor branch operations and a "foreign" ownership.

At the executive level, the president organized a "Committee of Eleven," including four officials engaged in the operating, non-merchandising divisions and seven officials from merchandising divisions. They formed a quasi-policy board for The Fair, meeting to review and appraise those functions and activities that influenced or determined both the gross margin and the expenses, including determination of a strategy for main and branch stores. Further, management issued a monthly operating statement of profit and loss so that an individual executive, down to the buyer level, would know of his progress in controlling those factors for which he was responsible.

A gradual delegation of personal responsibility gave control of their sales staffs to the buyers. Merchandisers stated that in 1964 and 1965 the store had decreased the relatively high turnover rate among sales personnel. These executives offered three explanations. First, the executives themselves became responsible for the on-the-job training. For example, one buyer responsible for fourteen saleswomen working in his departments spoke of "his personal responsibility to train and educate these women, to motivate them."[53] Second, the store conducted a regular, planned training program throughout the year for all salespeople, on both a store-wide and a departmental basis. For example, both the personnel director and the fashion coordinator held individual and group meetings on subjects ranging from personal grooming to developments in fashions, which were not necessarily concerned with the particular saleswomen's departments. At the divisional level, the merchandise managers claimed they conducted meetings concerned with their own merchandise classifications, dramatizing the merits of the goods by demonstration and display. Salespeople's working hours were arranged so that they reported fifteen minutes earlier to attend these meetings. One buyer summed up the process: "In our Bath Shop, for instance, we can show a customer how to change the appearance of her bathroom with $15.00 worth of new fashion ideas. But this requires motivated and trained salespeople. And that is the purpose of our program."[54]

The third explanation for decreased personnel turnover pertained to branch store operations. The changeover from self-selection to personal service and selling, starting in 1964, offered an opportunity for mobility within the organization and in several instances enabled employees to work at locations closer to their residences.

Branch stores. As indicated, the new management reversed the operation of the branch stores from check-out, self-selection, supermarket orientation to traditional department store service and selling. All executives gave the "stepchildren" branches full-family status and were advised to remake the branches in the image of The Fair's main store. The fundamental premise was that customers generalize about the total retail firm from their experiences in a branch store or in the main store. The new president observed that "the budget stores, as branches, operated as cheapies and failed to take advantage of their affiliation, their being a part of The Fair downtown."

More specifically, at The Fair Village store, the new management hastened to build a floor-to-ceiling decorative wall separating itself from the adjacent supermarket. It also eliminated checkout lanes as initial steps in a major remodeling and redesign program. In a polite and positive statement justifying the changeover, Mr. Sanders stated publicly that:

We see clearly that our customers are looking for something more than convenience shopping in a suburban store. What they want is a full service store as nearly like the downtown as space will permit. We did not feel The Fair Village store adequately reflected the image The Fair has built up in this community over 60 years and which is projected in our advertising and in our downtown store.[55]

Six months later, The Fair eliminated shopping carts and other supermarket accoutrements at its Northgate branch. And by the beginning of the second year, in the spring of 1965, the Basement Store of the downtown location had been returned to full service operations.

Merchandising mix changes. Strategy changes under the new administration affected stock composition and presentation as well as market target definition and upgrading of branch stores. Because so many changes were made simultaneously, it is difficult to order them chronologically. It should be emphasized that the new president acknowledged several changes that had been proposed previously. Further, the evidence in Table IV-5, strongly suggests that despite some interview data, The Fair had already initiated a trade-up process and, in some instances, the advertising index of price zones had reached higher levels than shown for 9-city averages.

Physical changes. The branch stores were changed physically to resemble traditional department stores, as explained. In the downtown store, management realigned the fashion floors to highlight the merchandising purposes of the various departments. For example, it established a separate budget apparel shop called The Northstate Avenue Shop, because the name connoted a bargain to Keelim residents. Then, on the same floor, it constructed a Miss Keelim Shop to cater to the career girl market. Another shop, The Circle, a collection of better apparel, was opened on the same floor but distinctly separated physically from the others. This concept of the shop or the boutique, which, incidentally, was reminiscent of the earliest department stores, had already been instituted in many leading department stores in the nation. This was an instance of a store catching up with the trend.

Assortments. While individual merchants were encouraged to trade up, management emphasis was on finding the new, the different, the unusual looks and fashions. The store fashion coordinator remarked:

We didn't always buy what we thought the customers were sure to buy. It wasn't always a case of trading up; rather, one of being sensitive to the taste level, trying to buy and cater to the customer who is aware and sensitive to new ideas. There are people here willing and able to pay for it. One of our jobs is to sense this demand before customers actually express it.[56]

TABLE IV-5

Summary of 1960 Total Advertising Indexes for 9-City Group, Freeport and Mayfield's, Monroeville and Staplinger's, and The Fair

Neustadt Number	Classification Name	9-Cities 1960	Monroe-ville 1960	Staplinger's 1960	Free-port 1960	May-field's 1960	The Fair 1960	*TFAI / 9-CAI
10	Women's & misses' dresses	342	332	316	379	361	319	93.2
15	Junior dresses	408	432	424	446	471	355	87.0
32	Untrimmed cloth coats	352	360	388	379	513	361	102.5
22	Women's & misses' sweaters	368	391	420	409	480	397	107.9
21	Ladies skirts	372	370	464	427	519	379	101.9
23	Blouses	336	329	82	406	452	259	77.1
130	Men's dress shirts	414	444	434	421	447	391	94.4
80	Men's suits	347	376	377	371	443	313	90.2
132	Men's slacks	345	392	464	360	538	395	114.5
133	Men's sports coats	358	354	269	...	...	329	91.9
240	Mattresses	381	369	373	404	415	411	107.9
232	Sofas	431	459	443	468	520	459	106.5
220	Bedroom suites	399	392	492	468	540	416	104.3
184	Drapes	363	437	494	440	469	290	79.9
230	Occasional living room chairs	344	...	...	390	557	391	113.6
165	Towels	404	426	504	450	583	416	102.9
168	Blankets	323	326	403	362	433	321	99.4
167	Bedspreads	401	412	581	441	541	495	123.4

* The Fair Adv. Index .

9-City Adv. Index

SOURCE: Neustadt Statistical Organization, New York.

101

At the time of the interviews at The Fair, some twenty mannequins on the Fashion Floor displayed the pantsuits that were currently a fashion favorite. This same executive said:

For two years we alerted our buyers that this item is on the threshold of volume purchasing. Sources such as fabric houses, designers, publication editors, have been touting it for that length of time. Earlier this spring we advised our staff that this idea or item would be good and probably in prints because the market has predicted a print explosion. We were ready. Our buyers worked very closely with resources who developed the idea. Our display department, obviously, was ready and our sales staff knew all about the idea. We have been very successful with this and the merchandise is being sold at a desirable markup.[57]

Later in the season the trade press featured a review of the market development of this idea, the tremendous success, continuing demand, and concurrent shortage. Apparently only those who had sensed the trend were in a position to capitalize on the consumer demand that developed.[58]

Sales promotion. During the first eighteen months after the management changeover, The Fair tried three different styles of newspaper advertising layouts. One objective was to inform Keelim customers of the new Fair store. Another was to distinguish the advertising from The Samuelson-Schmidt massive advertising, estimated to consist of two and one-half times as much linage as published by The Fair. The third was to institutionalize the merchandise and the store rather than aim solely at producing results the next day. In response to the fact that they were continually outspaced, officials experimented with both television and radio advertising. Taking a lesson from the experiences of many national advertisers, The Fair attempted to increase the number of impressions it made on customers by means of both sound and sight.

The publicity department developed four electronic programs: a sustaining "talk show"; a format for use of spot radio to provide massive support for an event or to sell a particular item; a radio program written expressly for the station with the largest teenage listening audience; and a program consisting of a thrice-weekly television news show, which the store increased shortly thereafter to four telecasts per week. In order to reduce expenses, the advertising department produced its own commercials in the store, using the store as the background and store personnel and merchandise, of course, to communicate the commercial message. The Fair executives claimed that the show had been successful and had elicited many favorable customer comments.

Pricing. Generally, The Fair decreased its emphasis and number of offerings at lower price-lines. Most interviewees stated that in their departments they had extended the price-lining upward. The elimination of lower price-lines depended upon the particular department, what the trend had been, and what the resource markets, in turn, offered. In towels, for example, the buyer stated that in 1961 the ensemble groups included twenty different selections. Of these, he recalled, twelve were in the $1.00 range. In 1965, the inventory had been increased and invested as follows: one number at $1.00; two at $2.00; five at $3.00; two at $6.00; two at $7.50; and one at $10.00.[59] Another buyer compared differences in pricing: "Before, we almost always marked $15.75 per dozen goods at $1.98 each, or even less, depending upon competition. Now, I think we have a tendency to mark the goods at what we think it is worth to the customer. The other way, you let the manufacturer or the competition price your invoices."[60]

When the store stages a sale, everyone is expected to offer superior money-saving specials, which will establish in the customer's mind an unquestioning acceptance of The Fair's advertising and merchandising integrity. For example, during a store-wide Anniversary Sale conducted two weeks prior to the interview, the linen department offered seconds of a basic, always-in-stock national-brand towel regularly priced at $2.00 each, for 99 cents. The buyer explained that he purchased 150 dozen at $8.50 per dozen and sold out in four days. "Customers believe our ads and we deliver the value," he stated.

Results. The strategy after 1963 was to bring about a turnaround, and to do this quickly. Reliable estimates of sales volume trends could not be obtained. The president stated that the Basement Store now accounted for 7 percent of the total volume, a decline from 18 percent, but that the total store, including branches, had increased in absolute terms. The new branch, which opened in 1967 is a complete, full-service, traditional department store, resembling the downtown establishment.

Several of those merchandising executives who tried to upgrade the store during the 1949-1963 period continued their retail careers with The Fair. Others who also contributed during that period have recently accepted more attractive positions. One of America's largest

department store chains induced the fashion coordinator to leave
The Fair and accept a corporate-wide assignment involving essentially
the same technique that she used at The Fair. The sales promotion
director has been promoted to the United States Department Store
headquarters staff. According to trade press articles, the president is
to be rewarded with the presidency of a much larger and more significant United States Department Stores unit; one in which two past
presidents of the corporation itself served. It can only be assumed
from this that the mission at The Fair was accomplished.

Questionnaire and Price-Lining Analysis

Analysis of corroborative data is somewhat different in The Fair
case than in the Staplinger case. A limited number of questionnaire
responses was received from executives. Also, because Neustadt discontinued measurement of advertising in Keelim after 1960, it was not
possible to secure comparable data for 1965. However, the combination of questionnaire responses and the Neustadt data provides for a
significant albeit limited analysis.

A comparison of the advertising indexes of eighteen commodities
in 1960 between The Fair and the other units studied—the 9-city
group, Monroeville and Staplinger's, and Freeport and Mayfield's—is
summarized in Table IV-5.

With the exception of statements about decorative home furnishings
by both the merchandise manager and some buyers and also in some
ready-to-wear departments, particularly in ladies coats, it seemed
reasonable to expect to find that The Fair advertising indexes were
substantially below the 9-city averages and certainly less than the indexes for the other two cities and the other two stores for which data
could be obtained. The oft-repeated statements that The Fair had
become a "very promotional" store, that "advertising was always centered at or below volume price-points" would lead one to the aforementioned conclusion. Further, since the management was changed at
the end of 1963, and since reputedly these decisions in United Department Stores were not impetuously but deliberately made, one could
expect, again, that The Fair indexes would be below industry average
within two or three years of this management change.

However, for ten of the eighteen commodities, The Fair index in
1960 was greater than that for the 9-city group. More particularly, six
of these ten were in home furnishings (Table IV-5, Neustadt Numbers

240, 232, 220, 230, 165, and 167). In two of these classifications, mattresses and occasional living room chairs, The Fair index was higher than all except Mayfield's. These favorable comparisons substantiate claims by the merchandiser and several colleagues, and acknowledgment by Mark Sanders, that this division had begun the trade-up process.

The four other classifications in which The Fair advertising index exceeded the 9-city average were untrimmed cloth coats, women's sweaters, ladies' skirts and men's slacks (Table IV-5, Neustadt Numbers 32, 22, 21, and 132). The first of these supports the merchandiser's claim that he succeeded in upgrading women's coats.

Of the eight commodities whose advertising index was less than the 9-city index, only three were less than 90 percent of that standard. That is to say, of the eighteen compared, fifteen were at least 90 percent or more of the 9-city index. These are also shown in Table IV-4.

Merchandisers in women's apparel classifications had stated that "by necessity we had to put our advertising dollars behind the volume price-points. In the budget dresses (upstairs departments) the 'meat' price-lines were between $11.00 and $18.00. We were expected to emphasize these prices in our advertising."[61]

On the basis of interview data, it appeared that women's sportswear classifications would, as in dresses, be less than the 9-city averages. However, the advertising indexes for sweaters and skirts were above that standard and the one for blouses was below.

It is impossible to explain why certain of these sportswear classifications compared more favorably than others. Close examination of all The Fair price-lining data seems to support the "Big Item" or even the "Classification Merchandising by Customer Preference" merchandising programs. In several cases, there is abnormal concentration of linage in one or two price-zones when compared with 9-cities. However, the latter is an aggregate figure. The reader will note later in the Mayfield case that this "high concentration" occurs again at higher price-points. To the extent that a fundamental assumption of this study is reasonable, namely, that advertising strategy reflects the overall merchandising strategy, one must conclude that interviewees, in many instances, underestimated their own stores' trading-up process.

After review of interview data and by reference to the other cases, two explanations seem to be valid for this discrepancy and for the general underestimation which prevailed. The first is that one can assume that many of the positive merchandising forces had actually begun to take hold by 1960 but were abandoned in the wake of the "discount mania," which presumably overtook management at that time. It is entirely possible that The Fair was about to achieve a merchandising victory but mistook it as a sign to change direction. That is to say, if, as claimed, one management can shape a turnaround in two years, why could not another management have reversed this in another two-year period? There was considerable evidence that the former regime was capable of radical or extreme decisions.

A second explanation is that the interviewees have arbitrarily divided The Fair history into before-1964 and after-1964 periods, the former a "bad" time, the latter a "good" time. In such perspectives the prevailing tendency is to overlook until a later time, if ever, those accomplishments or steps taken that may not be regarded as constructive.

The price-lining data tend to support claims about The Fair merchandising after 1964. But because price-lining appears to be higher than suggested by interview data, some doubt is thereby cast upon the testimony concerning the strategy before 1964.

Summary

The Fair began in one classic form of the department store tradition, a confederation of leased or rented departments. Eventually, three of these tenants owned the store, and it became one of the outstanding retail enterprises in Keelim. The Fair led in fashion merchandising and remained competitive in a very price-promotion oriented community. Its affiliation with a strong buying syndicate aided in sustaining both strategies and attested to the management's keen awareness of its position as a trading agent between both consumer and resource markets.

From 1946 to 1949, the year when United acquired The Fair, changes in demographic and economic conditions favored retailing in Keelim. Since United was interested only in acquiring a store that potentially could dominate a market and also become a fashion leader, the purchase of The Fair in 1949 supports the claim that it was a fashion-minded store as well as an aggressive volume-seeker.

As demographic and economic changes from 1949 to 1966 again favored retailers, competition by both traditional and discount department stores increased. The Fair, in response, attempted a two-directional merchandising strategy.

In one direction it emphasized lower-priced goods, and opened its branch stores as department store supermarkets. In another direction, The Fair sought better-quality business in the downtown store, aimed at higher mark-ons, and invested considerable sums to display fashion merchandise, to provide more pleasant shopping, and to fortify its merchandising by a consumer-oriented classification intensification program.

The two-directional strategy did not succeed. A new management in 1964 redirected the merchandising toward consumer demand and consumer buying capacity for fashion and quality and service.

This case dramatically illustrates the marketing challenge and the necessity of correctly reading the market and then consistently pursuing a strategy befitting that interpretation. The Neustadt price-lining analysis confirms a great amount of the interview data. But it also provides a basis for questioning whether interviewees correctly assayed The Fair's own merchandising in 1960. Conceivably, The Fair was succeeding but didn't realize it or believe it and defensively adopted the rivals' strategy instead of continuing the development of its own.

The following conclusions are based upon data derived from interviews, publications, research agencies, and Neustadt analysis:

In response to an upward shift in demography of demand and increasing low-margin (discount) store competition, The Fair traded down during the 1949-1963 period. This strategic change was most pronounced in the branch stores and in the Basement Store of the central unit downtown. During the 1964-1965 period, The Fair succeeded in trading up and in achieving fashion leadership in both the main and branch stores.

The advertising price-lining apparently did not always follow the merchandise price-lining. In 1960, the only year for which meaningful data could be secured, The Fair emphasized low-margin merchandising. Yet the advertising price-lining in some divisions equalled or exceeded levels recorded for the 9-city group and the other stores measured. Apparently, the advertising price-lining was subjected to the same conflicting strategy as was the merchandise price-lining. Therefore, the hypothesis with regard to this factor is indeterminate.

In response to its traditional rivals, Samuelson's and Schmidt's, The Fair continued to compete on a promotional price basis until 1964. Thereafter, The Fair traded up as it merchandised for different and more specific market targets.

V

Mayfield Brothers

History of the Firm to 1945

In 1872, Joseph Mayfield opened a dry goods store in the Newtown section of Freeport, one of the largest cities in the East. His wide assortments appealed to families already established in that region and also to the large number of immigrants then settling there. He guided himself by a three-point credo: "Have what the people want and give them a good value; let the public know what you have and avoid misrepresentation; render good service."[1] Within five years the firm exceeded $2 million in sales, a spectacular merchandising achievement.

After 1905, immigrants and members of lower-income groups occupied the major residential areas of Newtown replacing many well-to-do Mayfield customers who had moved to the Bayhill section of Freeport. Despite these changes, Mayfield's continued its dynamic growth; by 1917 it had quadrupled its revenues. Throughout the World War I period and during the 1920s, the firm increased its share of the total Freeport market. In 1927, Harry Mayfield, who succeeded his father as president, sold the controlling interest in the firm to the American Mercantile Company. He remained as active president for the next ten years.

Interviewees frequently suggested that the post-World War II management found it necessary and desirable to alter the merchandising direction from the one taken during the previous fifteen years.

Further, interview data suggest that the present management executives at Mayfield's claim that their practices and policies were innovative. However, a historical review of the company indicates that the management of change in the 1925 to 1945 period affords a closer parallel to that of the 1945 to 1965 period than the interviewees realized.

Profitability. Throughout its ninety-three year history, Mayfield Brothers has always produced a profit. During the 1920s, when several mercantile firms merged in a pattern similar to current industry trends, the Mayfield net profits exceeded industry averages. It was this performance that induced the American Mercantile Company to purchase control of Mayfield's. During the 1930s, despite depression conditions, the firm earned a profit. The performance in 1936, for example, when measured as a percentage of sales, approximated the profits of 1946, as shown in Table IV-3.[2] This profit habit was to have profound effects upon the successive management after 1945.

Adjustment for volume. The Mayfield family management believed that the road to profitability was called Volume Avenue. They adopted diverse merchandising tactics in order to remain on this road. At one moment the firm sponsored innovative ideas in merchandising by means of institutional sales promotion events. At another moment Mayfield's engaged in the most intensive of price promotions to induce immediate response. It never lost its zest for new and exciting merchandising ideas.

For example, in 1930 Mayfield's advertised cigarettes at the lowest price in Freeport. Thousands of people tramped through the store to reach an obscure location. During the 1930s the store was frequently sued for its price-cutting practices, especially on such classifications as liquor and electrical appliances. In 1932, to stimulate sales, the store conducted a campaign to sell men's shirts outside of business hours. It paid its employees on a piece basis to sell the Mayfield brand of shirts at $1.00 each to friends, neighbors, and relatives. From one Sunday newspaper advertisement the company sold 5,000 comforters. Throughout this period customers continued to believe in Mayfield's integrity.

In addition to the use of price-competitive tactics, Mayfield's also sponsored a number of institutional events. In 1934, Charles Bletter and Company, a nationally-known converter and stylist of piece goods and home furnishings merchandise, selected Mayfield's as the pilot store to test a program of advertising, displaying, and selling a series of confined prints destined to be distributed on a selective basis. The store also sponsored a "Made in America" store-wide promotion. Mayfield's also managed to stay in the public eye and earn press plaudits in 1937 for its exhibition of modern American-designed home furnishings in model room settings within the store.

Mayfield's had established a paternal relationship with its employees. When union overtures were first made to Mayfield workers during the 1930s, the management had no objections: "Happy employees make it easier to secure volume." Later, the company vigorously opposed the union selected by these employees. Personnel costs resulting from unionization were to have a profound effect on merchandising strategy.

As a result of these tumultous merchandising and personnel policies, always stemming from a basic quest for sales volume, the public regarded Mayfield's as a "bargain, promotional, exciting store." A veteran buyer, James Reba, commenting on a branch store opening in 1952, summarized how the public viewed Mayfield's:

> There will always be many customers who remember you as you were. When we opened our branch in suburban Middletown, in 1952, the people there remembered us as a circus-tent, promotional store and they expected balloons, and popcorn, and door-busters. It took six months in Middletown before the customers realized we were a changed store. For a while we wondered if we had made a mistake. But now they like us because we have what they want and we have educated quite a few customers who weren't accustomed to our kind of merchandise.[3]

Adjustment for changes in demography of demand. Chapter I refers to the NICB finding that the escalation of quality of demand constituted the major change during the 1950-1960 period. A nationally-known sales promotion director, Kenneth Collins, reached a similar conclusion about the entire 1910-1960 period. Commenting on the sweeping reversal of attitude toward standards of taste, he wrote:

> The stores of 1910 sold an astonishing amount of junk and simply reflected an appalling level of popular culture. Merchants didn't conceive it might be profitable to educate people to want something better. They finally set out to train the public to buy better-styled merchandise because competition was extremely fierce and the way to beat competition was to show something better, something different, and incidentally, something higher priced.[4]

The merchandising of housewares during the first two decades of this century illustrated Mayfield's attempt to trade up and to elevate taste levels. In commenting on the retirement of a veteran merchant, a 1928 trade journal reported:

During his 41-year Mayfield association, Alexander Lewis was a keen student of changing economic conditions and a close observer of the demands of the ever-changing clientele which, as the surrounding residential territory became more exclusive, the Mayfield store attracted. In fact, it is to the anticipation of these changing demands, and the continuous maintenance of complete stocks of style and quality merchandise to meet these demands, even more than rightly priced merchandise, that Mr. Lewis attributes the success which he has been able to attain. Much of the stocks comprised imports from widely scattered regions of the world, representing selections made by Mr. Lewis himself.[5]

The drive for fashion distinction also has historic roots at Mayfield's. In 1928, the management appointed Winthrop Berner, a well-known advertising agency executive, as publicity director to increase emphasis on style and to focus public attention on the store's activities, including the ten-store addition to the main building scheduled for a 1930 opening.[6] One of his first steps was to publish a full-page advertisement informing the public about the store and indicating what the Mayfield mission was: "In this day and age of 'new styles' we have a responsibility to offer styles based on carefully planned, advance studies. We thereby provide you with 'style insurance.' "[7]

Berner organized a bureau of experienced stylists to coordinate and develop fashion awareness among sales and display personnel in the ready-to-wear, lingerie, accessories, home furnishings, and piece goods departments. The trade press, in August, 1929, commented on this campaign for fashion leadership to which the firm had allotted 10 percent of its total advertising expenditures: "This store is seeking 100,000 style-wise patrons of comfortable means, the type concerned with fine discriminations of taste and quality and equally interested in shopping convenience and sensible economies. This seems to be the store's aim during the present trading-up movement."[8]

Other events as well exemplify a strategy stressing trade up and merchandise alertness. When the Prohibition Amendment was repealed, the store was one of the first to offer bar accessories, featuring exclusively designed furniture and glassware. When television was first introduced in 1939, Mayfield's hailed it as a practical adjunct to selling and experimented with it as a sales promotion medium. It also advertised sets ranging in price from $189.90 to $540.00.

To assist customers in selecting home furnishings, the management appointed five departmental home advisors to increase its Customer Counseling service. Each department established a private office where the customer could discuss with a specialist, her needs from kitchen shelving to slip covers.[9]

In April, 1941, the store opened its All-In-One Deb Shop, one of the first shops in the country aimed at a specific age and life-cycle group. The new division, a series of shops within one department, included all outer apparel, intimate apparel, shoes, millinery, and sportswear. Store policy required that all merchandise be purchased from junior merchandise makers only.[10]

In 1942, Mayfield's introduced the gallery display technique to publicize and sell home furnishings. A group of beautiful wallpapers and fabrics, table linens and fashion accessories, all designed by a famous contemporary artist, keynoted the exhibition. The fabrics and wallpapers used in room settings complemented a new group of modern furniture in bleached birch and dark mahogany veneers, all presented for the first time at this show.

Throughout its history, Mayfield's never refrained from continuously innovating and adopting new methods and ideas in both operations and merchandising. It was the first Freeport department store to install a passenger elevator or an escalator, or to use automobile delivery service; it was also the first to try a double-page newspaper advertisement. In cooperation with the city's Department of Education, it established a continuation school for junior employees.

In retrospect, these merchandising ideas and programs are seen to have been significant; they illustrate the innovative character and dynamic posture of this firm. During a later period of elegance they were to be repeated by Mayfield's and to be eagerly imitated by other stores throughout the nation.

External Environmental Changes:
1945-1965

What were the conditions of demography of demand and of competition that management encountered from 1945 to 1965? The purpose of this section is threefold: to describe these changes in the environment external to Mayfield's, to explore how management evaluated these changes, and to explain those decisions of management that altered the Mayfield merchandising strategy.

― **Changes in demography of demand.** Tables A, 1-5, Appendix, summarize population and income changes in Freeport from 1945 to 1965. Although a great portion of the Mayfield analysis concerns the Newtown section, the data for metropolitan Freeport were used as a comparison base because Mayfield's continues to draw a significant share of its business from the total area.[11]

Freeport population increased proportionately less than any of the four areas studied, as can be seen in Appendix Table A-1. This is partially due to the large absolute population base in 1946. Also, great numbers of people who moved to suburban and other metropolitan areas are not included in the statistical definition. During the twenty postwar years, large numbers of people moved from Freeport. However, many immigrants and residents from other sections of the nation continued to settle in Freeport.

This latter fact undoubtedly accounts for data revealed in Appendix Tables A-2 and A-5. These show that total net effective buying income in the Freeport trading area increased proportionately less than in the others throughout the twenty years. Appendix Table A-5 shows the bi-modal nature of the income distribution changes. This fact bears significantly on the Mayfield merchandising strategy. As noted, both the "poverty range" and the "moderate-to-wealthy range" increased proportionately more in Freeport than elsewhere, including the United States as a whole. The number of households reporting an income of less than $2,500 in 1965 was 76.8 percent of the number with similar incomes in 1955, whereas 252.8 percent of the number with incomes of $7,000 and over in 1955 had that amount in 1965.

Appendix Tables A-3 and A-4 show that Freeport total retail and general merchandise sales did not increase proportionately as much as in other cities or in the United States. A Mayfield executive commented on the significance of both the retail sales and income increases shown in these tables: "There was and is and will be for a long time a very large market which such people (the more sophisticated and/or higher income customer) provide and of which we at best can get only a share."[12]

Changes in competition. It is quite obvious from the foregoing that an upward escalation in the quality of goods demanded did occur in Freeport. Furthermore, from the widespread population dispersion as well as the extremities of change in income distribution, it is clear that both traditional and discount department stores could flourish.

Changes in traditional department stores. Within Freeport two important changes had to do with the number of stores in Newtown and the development of branch stores. As to the first, three large department stores and three traditional specialty stores in the New-town section of Freeport went out of business. Regarding the second change, the remaining nine major department stores opened forty branch stores throughout the Freeport trading area. However, it was not until late 1965 that any retail firm challenged the supremacy of Mayfield's in its main store geographic trading area within Newtown. And then the challenger was Kleevering's, a Freeport promotional department store never before located in the Newtown section.

Changes in discount department stores. Freeport supported several low-margin department and specialty stores at all times. By virtue of its geographical location, Freeport was invaded by discount department stores soon after their start and immediate boom in the East. During the next twenty years, virtually every member of "The One Hundred Million Dollar Club" among discount retailers had opened at least one store in Freeport.[13] By 1965, one of these transacted more than $50 million worth of business in Freeport alone. An industry source estimated that in 1964 the seventy-eight discount department stores in Freeport accounted for 2.78 percent of total retail sales.[14]

Changes in Merchandising Strategy: 1945-1965

In 1945, the American Mercantile Company announced a change in management of the Mayfield store. To replace the president, who retired after a long and successful career with the store, the parent organization hired Adam Rudderham, a veteran merchant who had begun his career under the tutelage of a Mayfield competitor, had then transferred his skills to the Middle West, and now returned to his native area. While relating the objectives of the firm to the afore-mentioned changes in the external environment, Rudderham recalled the first years after he assumed the presidency:

We sought first to define what the job was. By that we meant to find out what were the manageable variables—the conditions about which we could act; who the customers were, what were their tastes, their jobs, the prices they were willing to pay. Given these, we next asked ourselves how to present what we had. Finally, of course, we had to ask: would these policies succeed?[15]

The management believed a successful store must serve and fit its community, have a recognizable character for an increasing number of its customers, be dynamic and steadily improve its position, build for the future, and earn a good profit, particularly so that it could provide for investment needs. The new management challenged four basic assumptions upon which the previous strategy rested. In effect, these challenges posed alternative strategies for the new management.

The first assumption it questioned was whether increased sales volume was the only avenue to increased profits. What happens, it asked, when revenues fail to outdistance rapidly-increasing expenses?

Second, management wondered if Mayfield's should continue to seek patronage from all income groups in all of Freeport. Was it worth all the costs required to secure business from the entire Freeport market? One veteran merchandiser, who joined Mayfield's in 1950 after a career with other retailers in Freeport, commented on the economic and demographic changes as well as the policies adopted since 1945. He said:

After the war, Mayfield's had to decide whether to return to the 1930s and try to slug it out on a volume basis and attempt to attract customers from the entire metropolitan area or whether to curry the favor of the market which surrounded its store in the Newtown section. To generalize in very broad terms, our neighborhood had changed from a slum center to a luxury area. The simple fact is that the changing customer could not find a changing Mayfield's.[16]

Third, the management questioned whether Mayfield's offered a consistent assortment of merchandise to the market it presumably served. One issue was whether it could profitably continue to be both a promotional store and a fashion store. A corollary issue was whether it could offer wide assortments of goods, including basic stocks and fashion and unusual merchandise, and simultaneously continue store-wide sales and other price-oriented promotion events.

The fourth basic assumption the new management questioned was that low price necessarily constituted value. They asked: does value always or only mean price, and the cheapest price at that? Aren't all customers interested in value? Perhaps, the management reasoned, value includes the excitement of shopping in a well-lighted, pleasant store which dramatically displays merchandise of superior design. Perhaps sophisticated merchandise in good taste is as meaningful to some customers as price might be to others. Interviewees at Mayfield's insisted that "value" is the paramount word, whether in Freeport, Monroeville, Keelim, or any community, large or small. "The key," they said, "was to find out what value means to the market you intend to serve."[17]

Throughout the interviews, the executives voluntarily compared the current administration with the preceding one. When asked why these merchants found it necessary to question these assumptions at such lengths, one official elaborated:

Both customers and the trade considered Mayfield's as a "me too" store which shouted it had everything, and competed with Freeport's two largest department stores primarily on a price basis. By such actions the store forced itself to follow their merchandising leadership. Throughout the 1930s and early 1940s the financial statements were not outstanding. The store was not geared to its community. One day it was a Macy's, the next a Goldblatt's, and the following week it tried to look like Neiman-Marcus. In terms of the profit and loss statement, the gross margin was low, the expenses high, and profit less than the board felt possible under the circumstances.[18]

During interviews several comments were made that suggested the firm had not been profitable. Yet, through examining records from various sources, it was proved, as seen in Table V-1, that Mayfield's had been profitable.

Several executives indicated that the firm had not been as profitable as possible, and others suggested that its performance was only average or mediocre. The board of directors believed that management had not seized all the opportunities inherent in a changing demography of demand (the resurgence of Newtown, the World War II conditions), nor had it prepared as well as it might for the postwar opportunities and competition. Also, it had failed to upgrade merchandise and to update physical assets, to heighten employee morale, and to prepare for its own succession.

The enthusiastic members of the present management tended to point with pride to what has been accomplished since 1945. It was claimed there had been many mistakes in the administration of expenses as well as in the judgment about expense appropriations. For example, merit increases for wage-earning employees had been withheld unreasonably. Maintenance budgets had been reduced in the face of a declining capital replacement program. The present management rectified these past mistakes. However, in their explanation of these events, they tended to overlook some of the accomplishments prior to

TABLE V-1

**Comparison of Mayfield Sales and Profits with
Selected Industry Performances
(fiscal 1946 = 100)**

Year Ending January 31	Mayfield Sales Fiscal 1946 = 100	Mayfield Net Profit Percent to Sales Fiscal 1946 = 100	Federated Department Stores Sales	Industry Net Profit Percent to Sales
1936	43.9	96.3	38.9	71.4
1938	44.8	75.1	40.5	47.2
1939	43.4	55.6	39.9	73.6
1940	45.0	76.8	41.5	80.2
1941	46.0	74.5	43.2	91.1
1942	51.1	71.8	49.5	80.2
1943	52.5	66.7	53.6	82.2
1944	59.5	63.8	61.5	80.0
1945	78.0	74.9	68.6	80.0
1946	77.9	79.0	75.6	131.1
1947	100.0	100.0	100.0	100.0
1948	115.9	76.3	130.0	101.1
1949	122.6	105.4	148.0	69.2
1966	244.3	124.9	568.5	84.0

SOURCES: Mayfield data extracted from Moody's public documents, and *Freeport Times.* Company did not publish financial details after 1929. Federated Department Stores data from published records. Industry net profit based on Harvard data and 16-Store group records.

1945, including the uninterrupted profit performance during the 1930s.

The Board of Directors estimated that the organization and strategy would not sufficiently meet the demands that retailing would require in the future. The board expected a projection based upon a clearly defined set of objectives, which, in turn, would be related to forces changing internally and externally. The board also questioned whether increased sales volume alone could provide an increasing profit performance.

To define clearly what objectives it intended to pursue and by what means it proposed to execute a merchandising program, the new management initiated an information-gathering system, which it continues to employ currently. For the purpose of this study, store executives made available certain customer records for the past fifteen years. Management used three methods to gather information by which it could evaluate the store's market position.

First, executives sought opinions of all within and outside the store: the customer at the counter or the acquaintance at a social affair. Second, executives constantly examined credit sales records. They related the kinds, quantities, and price-ranges of purchases to the place of residence of these customers. They also related these variables to presumed income and occupational data. The word "presumed" is used advisedly. The firm did not carry out formal research to ascertain the data for all of these variables. Rather, it attempted to alert the executive group to the significance of each variable and to the way all were related. The third method was to conduct a biennial survey of customers actually shopping in the store. Using a simplified questionnaire, members of the executive training squad interviewed customers in both the Upstairs and Basement stores. Executives reasoned they could increase profitable volume if they could only merchandise more effectively to those who already were their customers.

Residence of Customers

To find out where its customers resided, the store divided the total Freeport trading area into eight sections. One of these was Newtown, which, in turn, was divided into eight zones. The store interviewer asked the customer in which section or zone he lived and where the customer or family head worked. The store then related such data to newspaper circulation and merchandise delivery range.

The initial survey revealed that 50 percent of the Upstairs' customers resided in the Newtown section of Freeport. In the latest (1964) survey, 57 percent reported they resided in the Newtown section. Management was impressed from the beginning by the fact that the majority (70 percent) of the Newtown customers lived in just four of the eight arbitrary divisions into which the management had divided Newtown; this meant that of one hundred customers in Mayfield's

Upstairs Store, fifty resided in Newtown and that, of these, thirty-five lived in four zones. The most recent survey (1964) shows that the same proportion of Newtown customers live in these same four zones.

The trends are similar among customers in Mayfield's Basement Store. Whereas in the initial survey 40 percent of the Basement Store customers reported they lived in Newtown, the latest survey shows 44 percent as living there. Again, these same four zones in Newtown accounted for 28 percent of total Basement Store customers initially. Now, 31 percent report residence in these same four zones.

It is true, of course, that a current evaluation must include the impact of branches on parent stores as well as on competitors. However, as will be shown, some 68 percent of Mayfield's total current volume is generated in the Main Store even though it has opened an additional three branches since the initial survey. Also, both the population increase and the mounting economic affluence have enabled more citizens to live in the high-rent districts located in the four zones from which such a large percentage of Mayfield's customers come.

There has been a remarkably consistent relationship between Mayfield's customers and their work addresses. Approximately 70 percent of the customers either live in or work in the Newtown section of Freeport, and this proportion has persisted since the surveys began. In the latest interviews, for example, of all the customers surveyed in both the Upstairs and Basement Stores, 52 percent said they lived in the Newtown section, and 18 percent reported they worked in Newtown but lived elsewhere in Freeport.

Although customers report they use various methods of transportation to arrive at Mayfield's, one fact seems to correlate with many of the foregoing disclosures about the demography of Mayfield's clientele. Since the surveys began, approximately 25 percent of the customers have said that they walk to the store, an unusual circumstance for a metropolitan area. This provides a basis, of course, for understanding the exceedingly large percentage of total business generated from a relatively small geographic area such as the four zones of the Newtown section.

The store also learned from its research that customers living in the Newtown section were shopping for many of their home furnishings, apparel, and children's and menswear in other sections of the city. By analyzing where those customers shopped for particular merchandise, Mayfield's learned of its own merchandise deficiencies.

These findings influenced the ultimate Mayfield strategy for the next twenty years: to become and to call itself a Neighborhood Store. It is interesting to note that, except during the 1930 to 1944 period, when it attempted to compete on a city-wide basis for sales volume, Mayfield's always had been a neighborhood store.

Mayfield's surveys did not provide economic data. Management explained that real estate values, taken as a barometer, indicated that relatively high-income or wealthy families resided in zones surrounding the store.

The customer surveys revealed data concerning internal variables. One of these was that customers, as previously noted, shopped at Mayfield's only for certain classifications but travelled to other stores, often at greater distances, to search for other classifications. Mayfield's stocked many of these classifications, but obviously did not offer what the customer wanted.

The second variable was publicity. The Newtown section accounted for approximately 10 percent of the total Freeport trading area population. As already explained, 50 percent of Mayfield's customers lived within the Newtown section. Since newspaper advertising rates were based on area-wide circulation, management realized its publicity reached many who were not or probably would not be customers. The publicity director explained:

An important revelation was that our newspaper advertising was very wasteful and therefore very expensive. We paid 100 percent rate to reach a very small percentage of those whom we regarded as our customers. Several meanings were clear. First, we would have to drastically limit our advertising. We would have to find other methods to obtain business without newspaper expenditures comparable to other stores. Second, we had to use limited advertising to accomplish goals other than securing tomorrow's business. Third, we needed to find goods which would appeal to those whom we found by our survey to be our potential customers.[19]

The surveys also revealed customer complaints about poor service and inattention by salespeople and nonselling employees. Management concluded it must immediately institute a retraining program for all personnel. Two reasons were cited. The combined payrolls were the largest item of expense. Also, it was necessary that the employees, whether in selling or in delivery service, exemplify the new Mayfield's and provide a level of service befitting the contemplated level of merchandise quality.

Faced with the revealing data obtained from customer research and the need to devise a more profitable strategy, management perceived it would be necessary to formulate policies bearing upon three questions: what was Mayfield's target market to be? what kinds of assortments should it offer? and on what basis should the company price these offerings? Interviewees expatiated on the alternatives perceived by management concerning each issue.

The management decision regarding the target market differed from Joseph Mayfield's original credo. The founder intended to reach a very wide spectrum of the market—in terms of income groups, merchandise price-ranges, and taste levels. The new strategy was to reach a very narrow spectrum of the market. The vice-president in charge of research, Gerald Adams, summarized this objective:

We set a long-range trading-up goal for ourselves (which was completely independent of outside conditions and was in no way deflected by outside conditions). Neither population changes or income changes or discount department store competition affected our course. Naturally, we did go along with increasing resource cost changes.

In other words, we were aiming to get more and more business from the more sophisticated and/or higher income customer. Incidentally, not all customers who like our better taste and more sophisticated style merchandise necessarily have higher incomes, and not all families with higher incomes necessarily like our sophisticated merchandise. We wanted a larger share of this market, not because it was increasing, but because it was large enough as it already existed. And, of course, we wanted to create a store to serve this market, because if we did our job well we would be outside the price-competitive area. A few percentage points downward or upward in income or population or blue collar vs. white collar does not make us jump through a new hoop.[20]

This generalization must be tempered, however. Surely the successful strategy devised by Mayfield's rested on a very accurate analysis of its external environment and a reallocation of resources and manpower in order to seize the opportunity to fill a void in the marketplace.

Merchandise assortments. The store also had to decide whether it would offer the same variety of goods, and also whether to increase or decrease the assortments. In turn, these decisions required some estimate of the effects upon profitability as well as upon customer satisfaction. To avoid competition, which could delay its march on the new profit path, and to adjust to a changing demography of demand, Mayfield's decided to trade up and to alter its variety and assortments so that eventually it could stock, department by department, what customers would want tomorrow. This policy required emphasis on quality rather than on price. One buyer recalled: "During the next ten years (1946-1956) we traded up, sought exclusive and better goods. Even when we ran a promotion, a close-out, the goods had to be the best quality available. Fifteen years ago (1950) I would have used price as the primary ingredient of value."[21]

In establishing a policy by which its merchants could plan for the store's inventory assortments, the management decided that profit factors must become the basis for adding, subtracting, or modifying a classification. Expenses differed with each classification. Large bulky merchandise, such as furniture, required considerable internal handling and delivery to the customer. Certain domestics and soft home furnishings classifications, as then merchandised, required or depended upon extensive newspaper advertising support in order to create demand. In the face of limited physical space, the merchandising of these kinds of classifications tended to diminish the gross margin contribution per square foot. Also, these goods inhibited the merchandising of higher gross margin goods, which often required more room for dramatic display. On the basis of criteria formulated from this kind of analysis, Mayfield's eventually eliminated from the inventory many classifications, or modified the assortment selection within the classifications. One of the first tactical moves by the new management was to jettison millions of dollars worth of unprofitable volume.

Pricing policies. Could or should Mayfield's continue to price its merchandise solely on a competitive basis, that is, in accordance with policies set by rivals? The management decided it could not, especially at the lower ranges, because to do so would preclude a greater gross margin. The president elaborated:

Necessities dictated by community characteristics forced us to adopt certain policies which either cut down our volume of business or made it difficult to increase the volume. But these were negative defensive moves. The constructive steps were to get more and more customers to prefer our store to our competitors. Some of the ways others did it successfully would be suicide for us. We needed to build a particular character, one which said, "fashion, quality, good taste," one which would satisfy community needs while it provided us with an opportunity to build a profit. Certainly, we knew that a highly promotional store built on buying the next day's business with low-margin merchandise had neither met community desires nor satisfied profit requirements.[22]

Implementation of Merchandising Strategy

The first step in changing the target market was to reorganize the people and the functions in the company. The second step was to reduce expenses, and diminish the number of merchandising events, and eliminate some classifications of goods. In the third step, Mayfield's capitalized on strengths or advantages it already possessed. The second and third steps illustrated defensive and offensive strategies, respectively, as defined in Chapter I.

To improve profit performance, management reorganized the talents and resources of the firm, especially in the three functional areas that affected merchandising strategy: management, personnel, and personal selling.

Management. Because earnings result from the differences between gross margin and total expense, the new president divided the merchandising and expense responsibilities between a two-man leadership. He assumed the title of general manager in addition to the presidency and directed all activities relevant to personnel, operations, and control. His new associate assumed the titles of chairman of the board and merchandise manager, and directed all buying, promotion, and selling functions.

Within the merchandising function they placed profit responsibility closer to the selling situation. The president commented:

The solution lay in increasing the strength of buyers and placing merchandise men as divisional heads at the vice-presidential level. We believed buyers were *the* people for two reasons: they constantly interpret what the customer wants as well as what and who in the market can satisfy that want; and the buyer is the logical executive to help us lick the expense problem. Both the merchandise manager and the buyer, by their decisions and activities, create a great many of the expenses a department store incurs. We hoped to organize the functions so that both the merchandising vice-president and the buyer could act as product managers.[23]

The firm eliminated the traditional role of divisional merchandise managers. Buyers reported directly to vice-presidents responsible for merchandising five groups: women's ready-to-wear, men's and boys', children's wear, hard home furnishings, and soft home furnishings. The objectives were to delegate profit responsibility and to expedite and assure communications from the top two executives to the floor level, where sales were generated and expenses controlled.

Constrained only by store objectives, buyers were to control their own open-to-buy and expense budgets. Management apportioned advertising budgets to the merchandising vice-presidents rather than to the publicity division.

Management also reorganized the staff functions to provide capable specialists who understood retailing and who could provide assistance so that top management and buyers could accelerate sales and profit performance. The way in which this change assisted management to move toward its objective can be illustrated by the changes in the personnel function and, in turn, in the personal selling function.

Personnel. Although confronted in 1945 with a militant union, the management fundamentally believed it could improve the relationship between employer and employee. The president sought and found an outstanding director of personnel whose previous career and reputation in retailing eminently prepared him for this particular challenge. The instructions to him were simple: find some basis of rapport with the union leadership; attempt each day to close the gap between management and the employee by one inch; and through leadership training, motivate the individual employee, particularly the salesclerk, to improve her performance.

This new director of personnel reorganized the function in two directions. He combined employment (recruitment and hiring) and training functions under one administrative official. He delegated direct supervision of salesclerk activities to the buyer, thus consistently following a previous reorganization of merchandising responsibilities. The basic assumption was that the buyer, responsible for the controllable salesclerk payroll expense, could most efficiently manage the function if the personnel department acted only as a supporting arm. Further, since the buyer was the closest to the salesperson, both physically and in common interest, he could best counter union attempts to enforce tight seniority provisions in the union contract, which enabled some incompetent employees to retain their jobs.

Commencing in 1953, members of the executive training squad attended executive round-table discussions on good leadership. The objectives were two-fold: to help develop skilled conference leaders, and to expose potential executives to realistic business conditions. These discussions employed the case method of study. Each participant, including the executive trainee, brought into the session an actual case that he was currently handling.

Personal selling. Buyers and assistants conducted both formal and informal meetings to inform salesclerks about all merchandise classifications. They emphasized quality rather than price. One buyer commented:

> For years we taught the customer to buy towels during the annual events—Anniversary Sales, White Sales, Department Promotions, Store-Wide Sales—now we had to convince them to buy towels and sheets and curtains on the merits of fashion and quality. But first we had to retrain our salesclerks to sell on that basis. In addition we were attracting a service-conscious, service-demanding customer for these better goods. We think the very presence of these customers helped to raise the standards of performance.[24]

The store provided special training classes in diction, grooming, and general salesmanship for those who desired them. In addition, many employees responded favorably to a gradually changing internal environment—improved and redecorated store interiors that were cleaner and brighter; merchandise of superior quality and fashion; customers who acted as if they came from a "gold-coast" area, which they did. In short, these employees improved their performance by virtue of expectation and aspiration.

To assist buyers in their managerial roles, the store continually shopped employees by means of outside professional service agencies. Complete reports were filed with the personnel department whose officials, after review, conferred with buyers about how to encourage employee self-improvement. Personnel and buying staffs were admonished to laud and criticize employees as warranted by individual shopping reports.

Merchandising Changes: "Defensive" Moves

To solidify its position, to establish a firmer basis of trading up, and to appeal to a newly-defined market segment, Mayfield management executed a series of "defensive" moves. Three of these were reductions in expenses, reductions in the number of merchandising events, and changes in classifications and departments.

Expense reductions. No longer obsessed with a self-demand to attract traffic from all of Freeport, convinced that advertising had been expended on wrong items to the wrong audience, management drastically limited its publicity expenses. It reduced the newspaper budget by 50 percent. Monies were allocated on a two-fold criterion: Is the item in good taste and distinctive? Will it help to enhance the total

Mayfield Company? Allocations based on sales volume or on past performance were discontinued.

The delivery expense, as noted, was unusually burdensome, amounting to 1 percent of sales during the 1940s.[25] In its desire to secure volume, the firm readily delivered advertised specials, whether they were groceries or furniture. Usually these specials were merchandised at low gross margins, thereby depressing profits. After 1946, the company decided to curtail advertising expenditures for such merchandise and to simultaneously campaign vigorously to encourage customers to carry their own parcels rather than request store delivery service, a distinguishing feature of department stores.

Thus, throughout the organization, and especially at the buyer level, Mayfield's educated all personnel to think of the expense implication of every decision concerning procurement, potential gross margin, cost of handling and selling, and final delivery of merchandise to the customer. At the present time, there is posted in every buyer's office a diagram showing the exact cost of various-size packages and wrappings used for delivery to customers. Every two weeks a detailed profit and loss statement based on controllable expenses is given to each buyer.

Special events. Special events such as store-wide sales require large advertising expenditures and usually some added inventory investment. Executives claimed that the store discontinued most of these events in order to carry out the new merchandising strategy. By 1952, a trade journal authority confirmed that Mayfield's had gradually diminished the amount and frequency of these store-wide promotions. He wrote:

As a result of these policies the store is consistently beating Federal Reserve figures for its trading area and in place of a middle-of-the-road type of trade and below, Mayfield's enjoys a more profitable moderate-to-better business. But it should also be remembered that its location in the Newtown section of Freeport enabled it to obtain a bigger portion of the "upper-crust" business available. These conditions, coupled with its expense-cutting drive, which is increasingly effective, explain why this store is performing better than most in the area.[26]

Merchandise classification and departmental changes. After 1945, Mayfield's attempted to eliminate or minimize troublesome departments, regardless of kinds of merchandise under consideration. The primary criterion was whether an executive could find a way to merchandise the classification profitably. As total profit increased, the firm augmented its criteria to include taste, that is to say, merchandise was added, retained, or dropped on the basis of whether it could profitably meet the Mayfield standards of good taste.

Because of the prevailing expense structure, as noted, it was difficult to merchandise some hard goods classifications profitably. The store decided it would no longer be enslaved to volume and percentage of volume increases. Rather, it would select merchandise that enabled the merchant to secure both higher dollar unit sales and higher gross margins. Mayfield's also decided "to follow simple storekeeping methods and not to buy phony sales merchandise for big promotions."

A chronological enumeration of some classification changes and the elimination of whole departments illustrate how the firm implemented these policies. In 1947, the store announced it would discontinue basement men's dress and work clothing, floor coverings, and furniture at the year end. When asked if sales for these categories had been unsatisfactory, the store president responded:

Not necessarily. It is just that we can utilize the space to expand other departments which are more essential to a basement operation. We will give up more than a million dollars in volume. But by utilizing this space we will be able to expand our ready-to-wear and related departments and we expect to increase our total basement profits as well as build a steadier business.[27]

In 1959, Mayfield's decided to abandon major appliance categories but continue to sell and service such electronics as television and radio. The president stated it did not make much sense to continue the big appliances since the store didn't run a promotional business.

Adjusting to a recent competitive change, the firm hewed to its own standards and objectives. Klevering's, a strong, local price-promotional group of stores, opened a branch near Mayfield's main store. It sought dominance in children's wear by competing with Mayfield's Basement Store children's departments. Upon reviewing its customer surveys, census data, and its own performance in children's wear, Mayfield's learned that an increasing proportion of residents in the immediate Newtown section were childless or had already raised families. Executives reasoned they could not profitably sell basement price-ranges competitively with Klevering's but could meet the demand for style distinction and quality merchandise in its Upstairs Store departments. Mayfield's decided to eliminate children's wear in the basement and to divert a portion of that inventory to the upstairs departments. It reallocated the abandoned basement space to a newly coordinated women's fashion division comprising intimate fashion departments, currently one of the strongest classifications for coordination and profit.

Mayfield's merchandising of electrical housewares exemplified a policy that shifted from de-emphasis to emphasis as the buyers found a method of competing on a profitable basis. In the annual spring white goods and housewares sale in 1956, the buyer deleted electrical housewares from the thirty-six-page newspaper supplement. The reason given was that this classification was vulnerable to low-margin competitors. There was no gain, he pointed out, in spending good money to achieve unprofitable volume. However, in the spring, 1966, supplement, the buyer devoted three pages to this classification. The offerings, very competitively priced at profitable gross margins, represented the purchase of a nationally-branded manufacturer's entire inventory at close-out prices, or consisted of electrical merchandise produced only for Mayfield's. (Klevering's also provided keen competition in electrical housewares.) Again, as in 1956, Mayfield's buyers avoided brands that might be found elsewhere at lower prices. When it was deemed necessary to stock items such as the electric knife as soon as it first appeared on the market, the merchandising decision simply was to meet the competitive price on identical merchandise.

Through group buying, Mayfield's could have obtained most favorable prices on many nationally-branded proprietary drugs and cosmetics. But it did not stock certain of these classifications because when competitively priced they did not yield sufficient gross margin to cover concomitant expenses. Instead, the company emphasized those national brands and its own exclusive brands of merchandise where it obtained adequate gross margin. Repeatedly it secured one of the largest cosmetic volumes in the nation on a satisfactorily profitable basis.

The Basement Store paralleled the Upstairs' pattern. It partially absorbed some of the lower price-lines dropped by the Upstairs Store. A recent trade press report commented on this procedure:

In a unique move Mayfield's will merchandise its basement division as a part of the upstairs store. This move culminates the long-range plan to trade up downstairs store merchandise to price-levels often far above those of the average store's upstairs budget price-levels. . . . Spokesmen feel it will make possible further merchandise upgrading throughout the store, better allocation of price-lines, better advertising coverage and professional buying abroad—where in some cases departments have been too small to do this efficiently.[28]

Two additional examples illustrate Mayfield's decision to merchandise only those departments that could yield a profit, or to modify a department so it could earn a profit. In its food operation, Mayfield's substituted one kind of offering for another. It deliberately abandoned a million-dollar grocery business and thereby jettisoned a profitless department. In its place, Mayfield's gradually built a worldwide reputation for gourmet foods. This shop now outdistances the previous food operation in profit and prestige and is consistent with the store image.

After analyzing the unpainted furniture department, store executives convinced the buyer to discontinue certain kinds of merchandise that required expensive advertising and handling and which, when priced competitively, yielded a loss for the department. In their place, the buyer offered custom-designed unpainted furniture. The customer could finish it herself or have it finished by the store's own craftsmen. In a smaller space the firm now generates more profit and prestige than before.

Merchandising Changes: "Offensive" Moves

Even as it compensated for and corrected weaknesses of organization and high expenses, Mayfield's also formulated plans to capitalize on its relative strengths. One of these was its locational advantage, which had not been exploited. Also, the management seized an opportunity to assert fashion leadership and to differentiate the store and its merchandise by distinctive displays.

Fashion leadership. Mayfield's has relentlessly pursued the goal of fashion leadership on a store-wide basis since 1953. "Fashion means good styling, good taste, and includes a bit of snob appeal." Fashion leadership depends, one executive pointed out, on resource development, coordination, and authority. Buyers were trained to seek distinctive merchandise for people who desired the unusual. For example, one official commented:

It is not merely a question of going into the next higher, standardized, fixed price-line. We do not provide just the next better grade of white shirt. It could very well be the same grade, but a new and exclusive and more attractive style, color, or fabric brings the shirt we introduce into a new price-line. This is a process that is done not by science but by merchandising direction beginning at the top level and taught and permeated throughout our buying organization.[29]

Resource development. Many resources were reluctant to sell to Mayfield's, especially during the period from 1945 to 1952. Some famous-brand resources in both apparel and home furnishings markets, including Seventh Avenue manufacturers and better china and glass producers, for example, would not accept an order from this store. Branded furniture makers anticipated price-cutting or unconfirmed orders or discontinued buying. There was fear among all these resources that Mayfield competitors would discontinue their buying if the resource sold merchandise to Mayfield's.

To increase fashion emphasis, buyers began to search for ideas and resources outside the domestic market. They found European craftsmen who could adapt Old World designs for the American consumer, thereby establishing new and individual trends. They could price this merchandise on a noncompetitive basis and thus increase gross margins. The merchandising of imports has become a significant part of Mayfield's and of other stores' assortments. Ironically, this movement arose partially as a result of domestic resource refusal to sell to Mayfield's. In the president's words, "It took ten long years of struggle to achieve our present standing in the market."

It is interesting to observe that Alexander's of New York is currently engaged in a similar struggle to obtain merchandise for its new Manhattan store. A successful metropolitan price-cutter, Alexander's has invaded a wealthy area of New York and hopes to establish itself as a purveyor of quality as well as price. In early 1966, the trade press reported that this aggressive firm, which had always reached projected sales goals in other metropolitan areas, had thus far fallen short of its planned goal. One reason offered was that pressure from Fifth Avenue stores upon local and national resources had precluded any possibility that Alexander's could obtain apparel and other soft lines of merchandise from those sources.[30]

As Mayfield's fashion reputation grew with customers and as domestic makers learned that Mayfield's buyers could unhesitatingly contract for merchandise and would work unstintingly with the resource, doors previously shut began to open. Resources wanted to sell to Mayfield's because of the prestige that accrued to them. One supplier said: "I know that my business with the May Company, Gimbel, Allied, and Federated stores has improved because I do a big job with Mayfield's."[31]

Fashion coordination. Management strengthened its merchandising organization by adding a specialized person called a fashion coordinator, who usually was an individual trained in the fine arts, with a business background including some merchandising experience. She developed fashion ideas, for instance, the use of color so that an item could be coordinated with a variety of other merchandise in a particular theme. These fashion coordinators were trained to work with a merchandising staff, to provide a fashion touch and feel, and to help the buyer find the unusual and unique, thereby increasing the customer's choice. As a result, "the customer believed one person, not five buyers, had selected the assortment of towels and soaps, draperies and floor coverings, and had coordinated them in the bath shop."[32]

Although Mayfield's was one of the first major stores to develop foreign resources, it did not stage an import fair until the late 1950s. The publicity director described the event:

This became a total store-wide production. We printed special boxes, wrapping paper, even a shopping bag without our name on it. The bag became a status symbol. Somehow thousands of people found out whose bag it was and the demand by shoppers from one end of the city to the other was unprecedented. Judging from both traffic and sales they stayed to see the Import Fair. When someone asked when we began to plan for this the president told them "fourteen years ago." It epitomized our point of view about a store: excitement, unusual merchandise in good taste, and of such quality that it will sell.[33]

In the home furnishings divisions, the store set up completely new semiannual exhibitions of decorative ideas displayed in room models. In the ready-to-wear division, repeating its 1941 innovation, it created a coordinated shop for a specific customer group. For example, for the junior-sized customer who was also a working and career woman, it coordinated such items as coats, suits, dresses, and sportswear in design features of color, silhouette, and fabrics. The intention was to provide accelerated service and easier shopping for the young career woman by collecting this fashion presentation in one location.[34]

Interviewee descriptions of buying effectiveness were corroborated by fashion press reports:

A visit to Mayfield's is almost as good as taking a capsule tour of Europe. Imports from France, Italy, Spain, Bavaria, and England range from home furnishings to food and are displayed on virtually every floor of the store. It is a highly commendable collection, representing the combined efforts of forty buyers from thirty-five different departments who covered more than 400,000 miles in Europe to make the show possible. The biggest display is on the eighth floor. Helen Delaney, Mayfield's interior designer, has created room settings which, while designed for contemporary living, are inspired by ideas from the fifteenth·to the nineteenth century. They include everything from a study in a villa in Tuscany to a Viennese sitting room furnished in the Biedermeier manner. Some of the furnishings on display are antiques. Most were made expressly for Mayfield's in Europe. Those in the latter category are either line-for-line copies or so skillfully adapted that the change in scale is not noticeable.[35]

Fashion authority. Mayfield's attempted to establish itself as a fashion authority in all divisions, including the Basement Store. As recounted previously, as early as 1947 it replaced unprofitable, albeit large volume, departments with women's ready-to-wear and apparel classifications. By 1952, the merchandising management of the Basement Store had programmed seventeen fashion promotions, each a week-long event from seventeen different departments. One year the basement division developd an Italian-inspired "Capri" event. A merchandiser stated: "We are seeking new ways to do business in our basement store. We have now made two Atlantic crossings, one to England, and one to Italy, to find appeal for the customer on some basis other than typical downstairs store stress on price."[36]

Mayfield merchandisers view fashion authority as a means to obtain improved markup. They regard this as one of the creative functions of their jobs. A fashion coordinator who had returned from an Asian buying trip just prior to the interview described this portion of Mayfield merchandising:

We recently developed a whole new, exciting business in emerald, sapphire, and ruby fine jewelry. By buying the gems direct from a cutter and providing beautiful designs to skilled Hong Kong craftsmen, we end up with beautiful jewelry pieces on which we can take a much better markup than we could if we bought these items in the regular channels, for example, in the French and Italian jewel market. And we still can retail the items at considerably below the current retail market. Incidentally, in this price operation we added considerable new volume in high-priced merchandise, which is the equivalent to adding higher price-lines. By such means, we improve our markup and add to our reputation so that more customers interested in this kind of merchandise come to our store. This is an art and not a science.[37]

The publicity director reiterated in an interview that the store reallocated its newspaper advertising to emphasize its fashion authority:

We try to make our aims clearer by the items we promote. We do this by judgment, not by percentage. We will not promote the kind of item we are trying to drop regardless of the immediate sales potential. There is, surely, the side pressure of trying to sell enough to justify the cost of a particular ad. Yes, we review our ads for a past season to see how well we have done regarding what we are aiming at. But as we shifted from the defensive to the offensive during these twenty years we diminished the sale and clearance ads.[38]

Fashion display. Whenever they refer to "promotion of merchandise," department store executives usually emphasize publicity, notably newspaper advertising. Display is mentioned but seldom emphasized. At Mayfield's, a completely different program and utilization of display is used to carry out the merchandising strategy. The statement "taste in merchandising also means how you set it before the customer" epitomizes the Mayfield belief and practice. As noted, the management determined in 1946 to reallocate monies from advertising to interior improvement.

Management demonstrated its fashion leadership by skillfully integrating display into the total merchandising effort. Executives were trained to look for, create, insist upon an environment in which they could show off merchandise to the best advantage. The research director reviewed the progress in this effort:

We maintained a constant program of rebuilding and refixturing the store as well as providing the necessary lighting to make it match the merchandise character we tried to create. To make this a practical reality, we set up a department of design which participated in every physical change involving both fixtures and display. We have rebuilt almost every department in the main store, and this is a constant process. We also paid great attention to display, and color and design coordination. Exciting presentations enhanced our fashion reputation. It is in this area that we spent some of the money we saved in advertising.[39]

One objective of coordinated merchandising and display was to create a gift department within each department. Each of the five merchandising groups had a fashion coordinator who worked as a staff specialist with buyers, publicity, and display departments to create merchandise gift ideas. These displays sold merchandise, enhanced the appearance of the total area by skilled use of colors of the merchandise itself, and achieved the publicity objectives for which they were designed.

A fashion report published in the *Freeport News* pertaining to shops with unusual fashion interest specifically referred to "Modern Place," a shop on Mayfield's fourth floor. It said:

Modern Place is one of those fashion cases where a woman of moderate means can find clothes of distinction that are not on store racks all over the city. Anita Posener, the shop's buyer, has worked with manufacturers in New York to develop exclusive styles and fabrics. The result is a spring and summer collection of simply-designed, well-cut dresses and costumes.[40]

Mayfield's merchandising strategy in the housewares division illustrates the store's adjustment to external change, particularly to discounting, and to changing customer taste and income. As noted in the account of Mayfield's in the 1920s, the housewares division had always been a volume and profit producer, partially responsible for its reputation as a dominant "pots and pans" store. Resource distribution in housewares classifications had changed, partially as a result of increased production since 1945. Further, court decisions removed price protection and prohibited discriminatory practices such as discounts, advertising, and freight allowances, which had enabled some retailers to increase their gross margins or reduce their retail prices.

Nor was price-cutting the competitive tool of discounters only. In New York, for example, three leading traditional department stores, Macy's, Gimbel's, and Abraham and Straus engaged in a price war in 1951 in which they used housewares, particularly nationally-advertised products, as the main ammunition. Merchants in other communities, including Freeport, soon imitated their New York counterparts. Mayfield's reluctantly joined in the battle.

Already committed to trading up and to fashion emphasis, Mayfield's either had to transform its merchandising and selling policies or delete completely or partially many of these housewares categories in order to pursue the primary objective, increased profits. The combined decision was to pursue the trading-up policy even more vigorously, seeking new resources, deleting the most price-competitive ranges within a given classification, and altering selling methods. The basic innovation was to sell housewares from sample items displayed in full view of the customer.

To assist the customer, the store provided sign cards with simple information whereby she could compare and select from the complete departmental assortment. Signing also included coded information that advised the clerk of availability and location of merchandise on display.

Mayfield's approach aroused considerable attention from other retailers. A trade journal reported:

It is not self-service. It is fully staffed by clerks who assist the customer. It was designed to give customers service at a minimum of selling costs. For practical purposes the housewares department is a three-dimensional catalogue which displays a complete line of items for sale. Plans began in the warehouse because it was there that the mechanics and hence the costs of housekeeping originate. After remerchandising every category on the basis of costs of handling and potential markup, the store redesigned the selling floor fixtures and layout.[41]

The store has retained this basic layout and central merchandising idea since its inception. It has met with customer approval and patronage and has advanced the department toward its profit objective.

The question of branch store operations was considered during interviews. Mayfield's opened its first branch store in 1951 and subsequently opened three additional stores. The largest branch accounts for 10 percent of the company sales. Remarkably, however, Mayfield's produced $110 a square foot in its flagship store in 1965. The main store accounted for 67.7 percent of the total business. Interviewees stated the branches are operated in the same manner, guided by the same merchandising strategy as the main store. They also stated that if and when Mayfield's opens additional branches, they foresaw some operational problems, such as coordination and supervision, but did not anticipate any change in the policy of duplicating the main store in the branches.

Corroboration of Interview Data

Three methods were employed to verify interview data. The first comprised search of local and trade press and other publication files, as well as the literature, to learn what reports had been printed over time. These have been noted earlier.

Second, interviewees and other Mayfield executives were asked to answer a questionnaire on merchandise and advertising price-lining for two years, 1960 and 1965. The research director stated that although they would like to cooperate as they did during the interviews, they would be unable to answer the questionnaires because they do not keep price-lining figures as far back as 1960. Further, he reiterated the essential point that "our method is one which a determined store with a clear idea of what it wants to do has devised to take advantage of the market opportunity as we saw it."[42]

The third method used to verify the interview data was to secure Neustadt measurements of Mayfield's advertising by price-line and to compare expenditures of 1960 and 1965. Based upon interview data, it appeared that several distinct characteristics should be found in Mayfield advertising.

First, it seemed reasonable to assume that a majority of advertising price-lining would be in the upper three zones and a relatively smaller percentage in zones 1-3. The expectation was based on repeated statements that the firm had diminished the number of sale, clearance, and special purchase events. Also, since advertising presumably was used to institutionalize by virtue of items promoted, it seemed reasonable to expect an emphasis on higher-priced items which would bear a larger percentage and dollar gross margin. While this is not necessarily so in all cases, it can be presumed to be so in the Mayfield case.

Second, by reason of the foregoing, Mayfield's advertising indexes would be expected to be higher than those of other stores in Freeport. Also, they would certainly rank favorably with other stores in the 9-city group.

Third, when comparing the relative changes from 1960 to 1965, among three groups—Mayfield's, Freeport, and 9-cities—it was anticipated that Mayfield's would still show a relatively higher index change, since interviewees reported no abatement in the constant drive to trade up and to maintain fashion leadership.

The results of examining the Neustadt data on advertising price-lining are summarized in Table V-2. As was the case in Chapter II, and again in Chapter III, the merchandise classification of Women's and Misses' Dresses was selected to exemplify the use of Neustadt data in the Mayfield case. Table V-3 reflects these comparisons. Analysis of advertising linage by price-zone for each of the seventeen classifications shows that in all but one of these the Mayfield Company expended a majority, if not a plurality, of its linage in zones 4-6. Mayfield's advertising frequently was about at the opposite end of the price-range from the other Freeport stores and from the 9-cities. In eleven of the seventeen classifications, it did not advertise at all in price-zones 1-3, and in four of the seventeen instances expended 5 percent or less in the lower three zones. These findings confirm interview statements on how Mayfield's budgeted its advertising within the price-zone range.

An array of total advertising indexes for each of the seventeen

TABLE V-2

Summary of Responses to Questions Concerning Data in Table V-3

Commodity	Question 1 Yes	Question 1 No	Question 2 Yes	Question 2 No	Question 3 Yes	Question 3 No	Question 4 Yes	Question 4 No	Question 5 Yes	Question 5 No	Question 6 Yes	Question 6 No	Totals Yes	Totals No
Women's & misses' dresses	x		x		x		x		x		x		6	0
Junior dresses	x		x		x		x		x		x		6	0
Women's & misses' cloth coats	x		x			x		x		x	x		3	3
Women's & misses' sweaters	x		x		x		x		x		x		6	0
Women's & misses' skirts	x			x	x		x			x		x	3	3
Blouses		x	x		x		x		x		x		5	1
Men's dress shirts	x			x	x		x		x		x		5	1
Men's wool suits	x		x		x		x		x		x		6	0
Men's slacks		x	x			x		x		x		x	1	5
Mattresses	x		x		x		x		x		x		6	0
Sofas	x		x		x		x		x		x		6	0
Bedroom suites	x		x			x		x		x		x	2	4
Occasional living room chairs	x		x		x			x		x	x		4	2
Drapes	x			x		x		x		x		x	1	5
Towels		x	x			x		x		x		x	1	5
Blankets	x		x		x		x			x	x		5	1
Bedspreads	x			x	x		x			x		x	3	3
Totals	14	3	13	4	12	5	11	6	8	9	11	6	69	33

137

TABLE V-3

Analyis of Advertising Price-lining in 1960 and 1965
Women's and Misses' Dresses, 9-Cities, Freeport, and Mayfield's

Name of Mdse. Class. Women's and Misses' Dresses   NRMA Dept. No. 42-11

Neustadt Code No. 10. Neustadt Description: Silk Dresses, Rayon and other   DSIPI Group: IX
Synthetics, Woolens in Women's and Misses' Sizes, Dresses for street wear,   DSIPI Index, 1960: 185.9 (1941 = 100)
afternoon, and evening wear included. Junior Sizes excluded.   DSIPI Index, 1965: 192.5 (1941 = 100)
DSIPI Description: Women's Wear–Dresses.

Relative Change in Index, 1965/1960: 102.8

Price Zone No.	Price Zone Range	Analysis: 9-Cities				Analysis: Freeport				Analysis: Mayfield's			
		1960		1965		1960		1965		1960		1965	
		Percent of Adv./Zone	Index of Adv.	Percent of Adv./Zone	Index of Adv.	Percent of Adv./Zone	Index of Adv.	Percent of Adv./Zone	Index of Adv.	Percent of Adv./Zone	Index of Adv.	Percent of Adv./Zone	Index of Adv.
(1)	Under $10.00	13	13	14	14	12	12	13	13	1	1	0	0
(2)	$10.01 to $18.00	28	56	22	44	24	48	14	28	35	70	13	26
(3)	$18.01 to $28.00	15	45	14	42	13	39	11	33	16	48	42	126
(4)	$28.01 to $38.00	12	48	12	48	12	60	12	48	15	60	6	24
(5)	$38.01 to $50.00	12	60	14	70	14	70	9	95	16	80	19	95
(6)	Over $50.00	20	120	24	144	25	150	31	186	17	102	20	120
	TOTALS	100	342	100	362	100	379	100	403	100	361	100	395
	1965/1960 Index:	105.8				106.3				109.4			
	Price Center:	$ 24.00		$ 28.00		Above		Above		Above		Below	

Freeport P.C. higher than 9-Cities both years; proportionately higher in 1965. In 1960 Mayfield P.C. more than 9-Cities but lower than Freeport. Mayfield P.C. in 1965 less than both Freeport and 9-Cities. Despite lower P.C. Mayfield index higher due to decided shift from zone 2 to zone 3 in 1965.

1. Comp. their own adv. indexes, did 9-City group trade up? x Yes; ___ No.
2. Comp. its own adv. indexes, did Freeport trade up? x Yes; ___ No.
3. Comp. its own adv. indexes, did Mayfield's trade up? x Yes; ___ No.
4. Comp. with Freeport did Mayfield's trade up, relatively? x Yes; ___ No.
5. Comp. with 9-Cities, did Mayfield's trade up, relatively? x Yes; ___ No.
6. Comp. relative changes in DSIPI and its own adv. indexes, did Mayfield's trade up? x Yes; ___ No.
   Its change was (greater) than DSIPI change by 6.6 percent.
7. Other comments: Store index change proportionately greater than either Freeport or 9-Cities. However, in both years absolute index less than Freeport though more than 9-Cities. Interview data suggested that in dresses Mayfield would score higher.

138

TABLE V-4

Summary of Total Advertising Indexes for 9-City Group, Freeport, and Mayfield's, 1960 and 1965 for Selected Classifications

Neustadt Number	*Classification Name*	*9-Cities*		*Freeport*		*Mayfield's*	
		1960	*1965*	*1960*	*1965*	*1960*	*1965*
10	Women's & misses' dresses	342	362	379	403	361	395
15	Junior dresses	408	421	446	474	471	535
32	Cloth coats	352	374	379	410	513	491
22	Women's & misses' sweaters	368	384	409	423	480	526
21	Women's & misses' skirts	372	388	427	416	519	538
23	Women's blouses	336	336	406	414	452	497
130	Men's dress shirts	414	424	421	417	447	485
80	Men's wool suits	347	418	371	450	443	593
132	Men's slacks	345	326	360	379	538	500
240	Mattresses	381	430	404	457	415	533
232	Sofas	431	441	468	482	520	565
220	Bedroom suites	399	425	468	496	540	545
230	Occasional living room chairs	344	443	390	478	557	600
184	Drapes	363	405	440	418	469	440
165	Towels	404	384	450	454	583	540
168	Blankets	323	407	362	453	433	552
167	Bedspreads	401	424	441	421	541	572

SOURCE: Neustadt Statistical Organization, New York.

classifications for 1960 and 1965 for all groups examined is shown in Table V-4. In both 1960 and 1965, the Mayfield index is exceeded in only one instance, that of Women's and Misses' Dresses, and then only by the Freeport index. In all other classifications the Mayfield indexes exceeded those of Freeport and the 9-cities. In 1965, the Mayfield index is 500 or more in twelve of the seventeen classifications, while there is not one index in either Freeport or the 9-cities which exceeds 500.

The Neustadt organization also constructs a composite advertising index for all 77 classifications. These are measured in the same manner as were the seventeen used in this study. In both 1960 and 1965, Mayfield's ranked among the first ten department stores in the nation. The total indexes show that Mayfield's moved upward within the first ten during the 1960 to 1965 span. More specifically, the total composite index for Mayfield's in 1960 was 452 when the highest index was 552; and in 1965, 503 compared with the highest department store index of 578. Again, such a comparison supports the Mayfield interview claims of trading up in advertising price-lining; and to the extent that this reflects the merchandising, one can assume that the store also traded up in merchandising as well.

These calculations confirm the Mayfield interview statements that the store had traded up higher than other stores in Freeport. Obviously, the same data support the claim that the firm had traded up more than most metropolitan department stores.

Mayfield's has exemplified an individualistic and consumer-oriented posture during the past ten years. Analysis of some classifications supports this claim. For example, although stores in the 9-city group and in Freeport tended to place as much as 50 percent of their linage in price zones 1-3 for the Blouse classification, Mayfield's has concentrated in zones 4-6, as seen in Table V-5. The significance, as pointed out in the Staplinger case, is that this classification is one of the most desirable trade-up classifications in apparel, particularly for increased gross margin potential. Table V-5 reveals that Mayfield's advertised very little in the lower price zones in both 1960 and 1965.

Summary

Until 1945, Mayfield Brothers pursued a simple strategy of constant promotion, whether by price emphasis or special events, in order to secure a profit believed obtainable only by increasing its volume. In changing its merchandising strategy after 1945, Mayfield's responded to a pronounced change in demographic and economic conditions in the trading area immediately surrounding its store. Although com-

TABLE V-5

Summary of Percentages of Advertising Expended in Price Zones 1-3 by 9-Cities, Freeport, and Mayfield's, in 1960 and 1965

Neustadt Number	Classification Name	9-Cities		Freeport		Mayfield's	
		1960	1965	1960	1965	1960	1965
10	Women's & misses' dresses	56	50	49	38	52	55
15	Junior dresses	32	30	23	19	4	0
32	Cloth coats	50	42	43	30	9	5
22	Women's & misses' sweaters	48	40	34	35	3	3
21	Women's & misses' skirts	38	36	27	31	0	0
23	Women's blouses	48	50	27	29	3	3
130	Men's dress shirts	31	29	29	30	0	0
80	Men's wool suits	50	34	45	24	26	0
132	Men's slacks	59	61	48	46	0	0
240	Mattresses	38	25	24	10	11	0
232	Sofas	18	18	13	9	1	0
220	Bedroom suites	36	27	19	26	0	0
230	Occasional living room chairs	52	29	41	19	5	0
184	Drapes	51	40	33	39	24	27
165	Towels	33	42	22	25	1	3
168	Blankets	49	30	39	21	27	0
167	Bedspreads	40	33	33	27	12	0

SOURCE: Neustadt Statistical Organization, New York.

petitive conditions also changed, the Mayfield management was more influenced by changes in those variables and conditions that have been summarized under the concept of demography of demand.

Management redefined its market target and reaffirmed its fashion authority and leadership. To implement the strategy, the Mayfield management reorganized itself, reassigning the executives, and redefining their functions and responsibilities. The management also assumed the risk inherent in both the defensive and offensive strategies formulated, including the development of new resources.

Interviewees claimed that the company charted and successfully followed a new path to profits, carved out a unique niche in the Freeport market for itself, and joined the community leadership in fashion merchandising. Analysis of newspaper price-lining tends to substantiate these statements and to corroborate the general claim that in response to external changes, Mayfield's altered its merchandising strategy by trading up. Again, it should be pointed out that internal stresses—demand for greater profit, managerial evaluation of these external forces, and management philosophy of merchandising —also account for the changes made. Comparison of advertising price-lining for 1960 and 1965 tends to support the hypothesis that the advertising strategy paralleled the merchandising strategy.

VI

The L. H. Kane Company

History of the Firm to 1945

The L. H. Kane Company, like many other traditional department stores that have survived more than fifty years, began as a dry goods store. Founded in Haverford, Centerstate, in 1884, as the Johnson Dry Goods House, the firm was purchased on contract by Leonard H. Kane, a local carpet salesman, in 1896. When Kane completed his payments for the stock and store in 1908, he changed the name to reflect his sole ownership.

Throughout the history of this firm, Haverford has remained the largest city in a three-county area; the 1900 tri-county population was 93,000; by 1940, it was over 180,000. Approximately 45 percent of the total population then resided in Haverford, which benefited from an unusual and expanding economic base of business, education, and government activities.

After L. H. Kane died in 1927, his heirs managed the business for two years and then sold it to the Ingham Trust, a private investment organization whose major interests were in Centerstate. Perceiving additional opportunities in 1937, the owners constructed a modern 90,000-square-foot department store at a different downtown location.

A veteran merchant described Kane's as "a promotional store seeking volume, giving good value, always making a profit, very careful

143

about good customer relations." It did not attempt to be a "prestige" department store until after 1945.

Kane's catered to the working-to-middle class groups. Indeed, upon opening the new store in 1937 (incidentally, it contained a considerable number of "dummy" boxes on the shelves), a few executives feared the modern decor, the brightness and the newness might offend or discourage many customers. One veteran at the store reminisced: "We had quite a job to convince many of our customers that we were still the same value-giving Kane's. Some thought we had gone too high-class and that our prices would also be high."[1]

Kane's has remained a privately-owned firm. As such, it does not disclose publicly any records of sales or earnings. In response to requests for research data, however, executives cooperated during interviews by providing certain vital sales and gross margin figures pertinent to the post-1945 period. The officials pointed out that Kane's had earned a profit during the decade prior to World War II and in every subsequent year and that the expansions had been financed out of earnings.

As compared with other traditional department stores in Haverford, the subject store ranked third in sales volume, at least until 1937. The Agnew Company, regarded as both the quality store and the sales volume leader, was the oldest department store in the community. It vended many nationally-branded merchandise lines and enjoyed continued patronage from middle-to-better income groups.

The second major competitor was the Haverford Dry Goods Company, a very price-conscious promotional store catering to "the working class." Despite the designation, this same firm also enjoyed a large trade in its fabrics, domestics, and linens divisions from all income groups.

One additional observation is important. After 1937, in keeping with its new "house," the Kane Company gradually increased the number of quality lines of merchandise. This narrowed the customer choice between Kane's and Agnew's regarding shopping environment, assortments, price-ranges, and merchandise quality.

Several of the major executives at Kane's have worked together for twenty years or more, witnessing a changing external environment. As they advanced in responsibility at the firm, they increasingly influenced its merchandising strategy in response to those changes. The president of the L. H. Kane Company, Lester Henshaw, joined the company in 1931 in the accounting department and eventually transferred into the merchandising division, where he served in the capacities of buyer, merchandise manager, and then as general manager prior to assuming his current office.

Changes in the Haverford Environment:
1945-1965

Demographic and economic changes in Haverford and in the tri-county trading area it dominated were exceedingly favorable for the retail industry during the two decades studied. Therefore, as might be expected, there were a number of significant competitive changes, which affected Kane's merchandising strategy.

Changes in demography of demand. As seen in Appendix Table A-1, Haverford enjoyed a population increase proportionately greater than that in the other four cities studied, as well as that of the United States. All three sectors of Haverford's economy—manufacturing and distribution, government (both federal and Centerstate), and education—offered increasing numbers of jobs and a wider diversity of employment over this twenty-year span.

The foregoing conditions account for the positive changes in total net effective income seen in Appendix Table A-2. Although one of Centerstate's depressed areas during the 1930-1939 period, Haverford became a huge supplier of war material after 1939. During World War II, the manufacturing sector of the Haverford economy expanded while the other two sectors—government and education—remained relatively stable. At the end of World War II, however, all three sectors attracted thousands of new residents who found employment in the widely diversified opportunities.

Appendix Table A-3 reflects these conditions, since (as is usually accepted) retail sales over time are a positive function of income. Despite the encouraging increase in Haverford retail sales between 1950 and 1955, the discount stores did not invade the community until 1959. The largest relative increase of retail sales was recorded during the next period, 1960 to 1965. By that time both traditional and discount department stores had expanded or announced plans to open stores in Haverford.

General merchandise sales include department store sales. Appendix Table A-4 shows that Haverford's increases in this classification ex-

ceeded those of general retailing. Income distribution, set forth in
Appendix Table A-5, again reflects the favorable environment for
retailing. The relative increase in the percentage of households in
the $00.00-$2,499 group in Haverford was less than that in the other
cities and less than the U.S. total. Its relative increase in the $7,000
and over group was the second highest. At the top end of the group
incomes, those households with incomes of $10,000 and over, Haver-
ford's percentage change from 1955 to 1965 was, relatively, the most
favorable among the four cities compared. Coupled with the population increases noted in Appendix Table A-1, these conditions provided a most favorable change in demography of demand for merchants in this community.

The relative increase in the percentage of families receiving incomes of $10,000 and more can be traced to three conditions. First,
the number and size of educational and governmental institutions
and organizations increased rapidly. Those segments of the population which derived incomes from such sources expanded rapidly as
the compensation scale for such employment accelerated. For instance,
salaries paid to teachers and college faculties underwent a great relative rise as did those paid to the technically or professionally trained
personnel required to provide services by governmental agencies.
Second, diversification as well as increase of size of existing firms
characterized industrial expansion during this period. Hence there
was increased demand for specialized personnel in headquarters staffs
of established firms as well as in newly-formed firms. Third, all of
these kinds of economic units employed an unusually large number of
women, thereby affording a second income for many families.

The percentage increase of families with incomes under $4,000 can
be traced to the influx of nonwhite population and to the relatively
large number of married students. Both of the latter groups presumably would welcome entrance of low-margin retail stores.

Economic opportunities in goverment and industry, as well as rapid
growth of educational institutions in Haverford County, undoubtedly
account for the positive change in educational attainment. According
to the 1960 Census, the median school years completed by persons
twenty-five years old and over in Haverford had increased from 10.1
years in 1940 to 12.1 years. This compares with 8.8 and 10.8 years,
respectively, for all of Centerstate.[2]

Changes in Competition

Although Haverford was the smallest community studied, the same major competitive changes that occurred in the other cities significantly affected Kane's merchandising strategy. Table VI-1 summarizes the competitive changes among traditional department store and discount store firms, and those brought about by the opening of a shopping center.

Traditional department stores. The first significant change occurred in 1949, when the long-established Haverford Dry Goods Company went out of business. This store had retained considerable patronage in the dry goods classifications but failed to keep pace in apparel for the family. Both Kane's and Agnew's eagerly sought certain lines of merchandise that had been confined to this company. Another beneficiary of this departure was Kane's Basement Store, where many bargain-minded customers sought their needs.

From 1945 to 1952, Agnew's, the long-established "better store in town," declined in competitive vigor and in sales volume. Interviewees and observers attributed this to the retirement of Walter Agnew, son of the founder, who had competently managed this enterprise until 1945. At that time he turned the active direction over to his son, James. His lack of interest led, after the father's death in 1952, to the second major change in this rivalry.

In 1954, Lincoln Department Stores, a national retail chain, purchased Agnew's. The Kane executives anticipated a revived, intensive rivalry. They also hoped this store's resurgence would attract old and new customers to the downtown shopping district.

The new Agnew ownership initiated a three-pronged competitive thrust within the first year. It embarked upon a major reconstruction and renovation of the store building. To rebuild the strong resource relationships the store once enjoyed, the management succeeded in persuading several major manufacturers of nationally-branded merchandise to distribute their products through Agnew's exclusively rather than through Kane's or, at least, to share the distribution with Kane's. This kind of competition for resources was, however, not a new phenomenon among Haverford retailers. Indeed, during the period of Agnew's decline, the Kane Company had induced these same resources to forsake Agnew's. The third prong of this drive consisted of a prolonged series of sales promotion events relying primarily upon price appeal. The objective was a swift presentation

TABLE VI-1
Major Competitive Changes Among Department Stores in Haverford as Indicated by Gross Space Occupied, 1954-1965

Date	Firm	Action Taken	Gross Space (sq. ft.)
1954	Agnew's	purchased by Lincoln Investment Trust	no immediate additions; major renovations
1954	Sears	abandons 15,000 sq. ft. downtown Haverford building, opens at Eastgate Shopping Center	200,000
1954	Union Mercantile Company	opens at Eastgate Shopping Center	75,000
1955	L. H. Kane Company	installs escalators, remodels	loses 3,000 sq. ft. of space
1954	L. H. Kane Company	buys nearby warehouse building for workshops	adds 5,000
1959	L. H. Kane Company	purchases property for East Haverford branch	32,000
1959	Biff's	national discount department store chain opens in abandoned factory; 52 departments	100,000
1961	L. H. Kane Company	opens branch store, East Haverford	32,000
1961	L. H. Kane Company	opens Western Avenue store across alley from main store	31,000
1962	Bargain Fair	national discount department store chain opens next to Eastgate	65,000
1963	Enterprise Stores	national discount department store chain opens at south end of Haverford; 60 departments	75,000
1962	Adolph's	national discount department store chain opens at west end of Haverford; 62 departments	89,000

TABLE VI-1—Continued

Date	Firm	Action Taken	Gross Space (sq. ft.)
1962	Foremost Discount Stores	national discount department store chain opens in Haverford; 100 departments	65,000
1963	Patriot Discount Stores	regional discount department store chain opens at south end of Haverford; 57 departments	80,000
1963	Sears	adds "Seasonal Sales Center" at Eastgate	12,000
1964	L. H. Kane Company	opens Corner Shop, downtown	4,800
1964	Patriot Discount Stores	opens second store, in East Haverford	45,000
1965	L. H. Kane	opens Campus Shop in East Haverford, across street from Branch Store	4,600

SOURCE: Interviews and files of the *Haverford News* for respective stores.

of the revitalized Agnew's to an increasing number of Haverford customers. A Kane official recalled: "Make no mistake about it. They hurt us at first. They drew crowds. Their claims were exaggerated. This local store became a dumping ground for the markdowns of some other stores owned by this national company. Consequently their Bargain Basement soared in volume."[3]

Shopping centers. The second competitive change was the 1954 opening of Eastgate, the major shopping center in the Fulton County trading area. Several attractions favored Eastgate merchants. The shopping center was located between Haverford and the adjacent East Haverford, which had quadrupled in size from 1930 to 1950. It was expected that future growth would continue in that direction.

As Haverford central shopping district retailers and their respective city government representatives worried over the perennial problem of customer parking, Eastgate invited 2,000 customers to park free of charge. The announcement that Sears would build a 200,000 square-foot full-line department store in Eastgate meant that a significant competitor would attract customers from downtown to a new area. A home furnishings merchandiser at Kane's summarized the effects of this change. "We lost volume and customers as the entire downtown suffered. Previously, when a customer shopped Sears for some hardware item they might come to us for ready-to-wear or at least use us as a comparative basis for a final decision on home furnishings."[4]

Another change is directly related to the Sears move. Its large store attracted other retailers as well as customers to the shopping center. Soon, tenants occupied all 500,000 square feet of retail selling area in the center. Among these was the Union Mercantile Company, a regional department store chain. Its branch opened in a 75,000 square-foot one-story building, offering medium-to-budget-priced merchandise and evening shopping hours. Haverford customers had become familiar with the Union name through the large amount of advertising placed in metropolitan newspapers circulated in the community. A merchandiser at Kane's observed:

Had this regional chain opened its store downtown it would not have posed a serious threat to our business. They were a depression baby who built a tremendous image on price. After the war they couldn't make up their mind who they wanted to be. One minute they featured national-brand shirts and the next day they were pounding price again. But when they opened in the same shopping center with Sears, they gained from the traffic and offered a basis of comparison. They certainly compounded the reasons for customers to stop at the shopping center first.[5]

Discount department stores. The third major competitive change began in 1959, when large-scale discount department stores invaded Haverford. It should be explained that three smaller stores attempted to merchandise at low margins at earlier dates. Typical of these was a locally-owned, locally-managed store opened in the former Haverford Dry Goods location. It did not attract a great number of shoppers. It established a local reputation as a "cheap store" rather than as a discount store.

Biff's was the first major discount store to open, occupying 100,000 square feet in an old manufacturing plant. Despite the fact that large-scale discount stores had already adopted many practices of traditional department stores (such as personal selling, adequate and convenient parking, machine-made signs, low-level displays), Biff's heaped goods on card tables, used hand-painted signs, and provided meager parking facilities. Large numbers of customers responded enthusiastically to the new outlet. This new competition affected Kane's Basement Store more than any other division.

The overwhelming success of Biff's coincided with plans announced by national and regional discount chains to open stores in Haverford. Within three years, by the end of 1962, shoppers could choose from the wares of five nationally-operated discount department stores. One year later a sixth firm, a regional "promotional discount department store" established its first branch in Haverford and in the subsequent year followed with its second. Table VI-1 shows that from August, 1959, through November, 1964, discount department stores added 519,000 square feet to the supply of retail selling area.

Changes in Merchandising Strategies: 1945-1965

Kane's merchandising strategy until 1945 can be summarized in a five-point plan: (1) to obtain at a profit an increasingly larger share of the Haverford retail business, (2) to meet and thwart all competitive efforts to undersell Kane's, (3) to resist competitive attempts to secure any nationally-famous brand distributed by Kane's, (4) to feature the theme of value in all sales promotion techniques to the working class through the middle-class markets, and (5) to stress quality of service as well as quality of merchandise. Interviewees pointed out that service meant and included a vigorous adherence to basic stock merchandising and referred to this as the "Filene Basic Stock Plan."

Table VI-2 shows that from fiscal 1946 through fiscal 1954 the company increased sales volume in all but two years. Even though the company did not disclose profit performance, the relative changes in gross margin expressed as a percentage of owned department sales suggest that the company earned relatively favorable profits.[6]

Retrospectively, we can gain some viewpoint of that period from the remarks of the Kane general manager, Sherman Aamondt, who joined the company initially as controller:

There were five major department stores downtown (Kane's, Agnew's, Haverford Dry Goods, Sears, and Penney's), all competing differently for sales. This attracted a wide segment from the entire trading area. Then, after we achieved the volume leadership, a number of competitors disappeared from downtown only to transplant their attractions elsewhere. Haverford Dry Goods went out of business. As a result, we had to depend upon our-

TABLE VI-2

Selected Operating Ratios of the L. H. Kane Company

Year Fiscal Ending 1/31	L. H. Kane Co. Sales Fiscal 1946=100	16-Store Aggregate Sales Index: Fiscal 1946=100	L. H. Kane Co. Gross Margin Percent of Owned Department Sales: Fiscal 1946=100
1947	100.0	100.0	100.0
1948	108.6	100.7	94.8
1949	103.4	N.A.	95.9
1950	108.6	N.A.	95.1
1951	108.6	N.A.	94.5
1952	110.4	125.5	91.6
1953	120.6	130.0	93.7
1954	129.3	131.7	94.0
1955	127.6	136.3	93.5
1956	132.9	144.4	93.5
1957	127.6	159.9	94.0
1958	130.2	165.4	92.7
1959	127.6	169.3	92.7
1960	139.7	183.9	92.4
1961	144.2	185.9	94.8
1962	162.4	198.7	94.5
1963	177.1	208.9	93.7
1964	191.9	238.5	92.4
1965	226.5	248.7	93.2
1966	258.4	266.7	93.2

SOURCE: L. H. Kane Company, company records. For 16-store aggregate, see Table III-3, Staplinger Case.

selves more than ever to draw traffic downtown and to satisfy even a wider range of needs in order to sustain and increase our volume.[7]

Kane's, of course, was not the sole source of attraction downtown. Beginning in 1954, the new Agnew management campaigned to draw shoppers to the central business district and from Kane's as well. Initially, as shown in Tables VI-3 and VI-4, Agnew's increased its share of traffic compared with Kane's.

Both national and regional discount department stores had opened units in other major Centerstate cities. Hence, by 1956, the Kane Company witnessed these changes: on the favorable side, a total increase in population and income, fewer downtown rivals, increasing acceptance of Kane's as a quality and famous-brand store; on the unfavorable side, a disturbing diversion of traffic, both vehicular and pedestrian, to Eastgate Shopping Center; a powerful rival (Agnew's) threatening price warfare and resource raids; eventual entry of discount stores in locations outside the central shopping district; and a general reliance by retailers in Haverford upon sale and bazaar merchandising, more reminiscent of depression than prosperity.

In determining whether to undertake any departures in merchandising strategy, the Kane executives considered several alternatives. The interview data yield the following summaries.

TABLE VI-3

Comparison of Agnew and Kane Customer Traffic Count, 1954-1965
(index: 1954 = 100)

Year	L. H. Kane Co.	Agnew's
1954	100	100
1955	96	119
1956	90	102
1957	96	99
1958	97	103
1959	102	106
1960	106	112
1961	102	108
1962	102	102
1963	101	91
1964	112	92
1965	112	77

SOURCE: L. H. Kane Company records.

TABLE VI-4

Traffic Count of Agnew's Expressed as Percentage of L. H. Kane Company Traffic Count, 1954-1965

| Year | 13-Week Periods Ending Approximately | | | | Total Year |
	4-30	7-31	10-31	1-31	
1954	47	52	60	65	57
1955	68	68	72	73	71
1956	64	64	65	65	65
1957	55	55	58	63	59
1958	58	60	62	61	60
1959	51	59	61	64	59
1960	60	62	61	59	60
1961	59	64	68	56	61
1962	57	59	64	52	57
1963	53	47	58	49	51
1964	47	55	47	41	47
1965	36	40	42	39	39

SOURCE: L. H. Kane Company records.

Alternatives

Should Kane's emphasize the quality and famous-brand and style characteristics of its store and merchandise, or should it increasingly emphasize its value (price-competitive) characteristics? Should Kane's meet and try to beat competitive promotional tactics, or should it chart an individual sales promotion course? Should it increase the number of classifications carried so as to fill a void for downtown shoppers left by the Sears relocation, or should it widen the selection within the classifications already carried and increase its price-ranges upward to appeal to additional market segments? In anticipation of discount stores and shrinking gross margins due to increased price competition, should Kane's increase or decrease personal selling and services? Finally, should Kane's remain downtown, in the same size building, enlarge downtown, or open branch stores?

The L. H. Kane Company

Lester Henshaw emphasized that a successful retail firm
a philosophy, or, as he stated, "the top must know its own n
garding the alternatives set forth, he said:

We saw no need to change objectives. But we had to change the means to
remain a volume leader and a profit producer and to represent something to
our customers. I think I made the most difficult and important business
decisions in my business career during those years, from 1954 to 1957. Some
of our own people wanted to fight fire with fire, to merchandise the same
kind of goods competitors carried. We tried to consider what was good for
the store and also what would be good for our customers.[8]

How did these officials relate profit to the costs of these various alternatives? Sherman Aamondt recalled:

We decided that if we competed on a basis and pattern established by
these other firms our profits would be adversely affected. There were four
conditions we regarded negatively. First, we would have to continue to buy
tomorrow's business, which would require increased advertising cost. Second,
we would then have to spend an increasingly greater proportion of our advertising on merchandise which bore a lower gross margin. Third, this in
turn presented a problem: How to finance an inventory which on the one
hand emphasized basic stocks and fashion goods in order to achieve relia-
bility and quality, and on the other hand, an inventory of promotional
goods in order to demonstrate value. A fourth compounding problem was
that you couldn't keep good, branded resources unless you were a steady
user. But if you flood your stocks with promotional and price goods you
find yourself squeezing the basics and fashions and you end up holding back
or diminishing the size of orders from your best resources.[9]

Decisions

The fundamental decision during the twenty-year period was to
increasingly emphasize Kane's as both a quality store and a value
store. From 1945 to 1955, for instance, the firm perceived that its
opportunity lay in capitalizing on its traditional rival's declining
managerial strengths, and therefore Kane's assiduously cultivated and
increased the store's family of nationally-famous branded resources.
From 1955 to 1960, L. H. Kane shifted to the value emphasis. The
1960 to 1965 period was one of physical expansion to thwart competition, to extend the store to enlarged residential areas, and to broad-
en the range of merchandise classifications offered.

Brandwagon program: 1945-1955. During this period the store campaigned in advertisements and window displays, featured the appearances of manufacturer's representatives, and staged exclusive showings of merchandise offerings to dramatize Kane's as the "Brandwagon Store," as the store for dependable quality and "style-right" merchandise. In many promotional events the exclusive distribution provided Kane's with a pricing advantage or additional gross margin.

1955-1960 period. During this period the management was beset by a barrage of "sale," "savings," "value" events in which all the aforementioned rivals competed on a comparative-price basis. In response, Kane's shifted to what the president termed "a plan to demonstrate that we were a value as well as a quality store." Commenting on this period, he said:

This was the period of the "big lie." Everyone, and we must be included, engaged in an exaggeration contest. The only certainty was that one of these competitors would use a larger comparative price than the next. Everyone "saled" the town to death. The result was that customers simply didn't respond unless you ran a sale.[10]

In 1956, Kane's radically changed the sales promotion program. Essentially, it abandoned use of comparative prices, totally and absolutely. Sales promotion personnel could not quote or use comparative prices in newspaper advertising or display messages.

The management expected the store would lose some volume. Table VI-2 shows a decline in sales volume during fiscal 1956. Despite this pressure and the disagreement voiced by some Kane executives, the president insisted that the program continue. A national news bulletin published an admiring comment at a later date:

Two years ago the president of a store in a smaller city dared to throw his crutches away. He dropped comparative prices. This store is developing a new character and is winning a position of public confidence. A new spirit permeates the organization from the boss man down . . . but this decision was only the trigger. . . . When store people could no longer depend on cut prices and sales as crutches they had to do a better merchandising job . . . buyers became better advertising people.[11]

This decision affected the buying function as well. It turned the efforts of all toward nonprice features of the total retail mix. Buyers were constrained to demonstrate value without resort to comparative prices. Executives claimed the public response demonstrated greater confidence in Kane's advertisements. Based on the sales decline, which

coincidentally followed this decision, one might question the preceding judgment. However, as seen in Table VI-2, the company, by
fiscal 1959, regained and surpassed its previous record of sales volume
and also managed to arrest a decline in its gross margin performance.

During this interim period when sales declined, the company improved its basic stock composition. The general merchandise manager
noted that "while this is indeed prosaic, and everyone says they do
a good basic stock job, not everyone adds more inventory in face
of a declining sales picture. But we did. We reiterated our 'never out'
program to sell down to and not through the stock levels required
in the program."

When these sales promotion and merchandising policies had been
integrated into the daily operation, there arose "a desire to do something to put an additional punch into the sales promotion program."
The objective was to build a sales campaign whose cumulative effect,
month after month, would increase customer traffic to Kane's. The
sales promotion manager described this planning: "We gave a great
deal of thought to what it would take to do this. Finally, it occurred
to us that rarely is the quality store the value store. Our question
became: what could be done to make the quality store the value
store? And could we do this within our advertising rules?"[12]

In August, 1958, Kane's embarked upon a promotional merchandising plan to achieve the aforementioned objective. The president explained:

A store seldom obtains anywhere near the total percentage it should get
on any one item. And there's a reason for that. The budget is rarely sufficient to permit a department to realize the maximum potential on an
item. And even if the budget were sufficient, the average buyer does not
attempt to do this. The risk would be too great. Also, he's caught in the
middle. Here I am, on the one hand constantly harping on basic stocks,
always aware of the inventory levels, and then asking the buyer to commit
himself on a promotion which the weather, alone, could kill.[13]

The store decided to overcome such objections by adopting the
following guidelines. First, a department would take certain items
and operate on a dollar gross margin basis rather than a markup
basis. They hoped that most of the competition would not challenge
these special offerings. This proved true even though the campaign
was coordinated in 1958, just prior to the discount store invasion of
the community. Second, no departmental open-to-buy was to be

affected by any special promotion purchase. That is to say, a buyer would not have to diminish his planned purchases, especially for basic stocks, in order to fulfill the plan. Third, no basic store inventory was to be penalized due to investment in heavy inventories for these so-called super-feature items. Fourth, as long as the item represented a true, unusual value for the customer and yet met Kane's quality standards, the department would receive ample newspaper advertising and in-store display support.

To encourage public interest in the forthcoming campaign, Kane's sponsored an essay contest, offering a $1,000 first prize for the best answer to the question: "What is a value?" In announcing the contest the company pointed out that the widespread use of deceptive pricing and misleading advertising practices threatened America's standards of value. Since the subject of value was of vital concern to the public as well as to Kane's, the firm wanted to know what the public concept of value was.

The contest drew nearly 5,000 entries from persons fifteen years of age and older. Kane's announced the names of 68 prize winners in a full-page advertisement and simultaneously urged the public to look for the following Thursday's advertisements, which would demonstrate what Kane's considered a value to be.

Subsequently, Kane's advertised a series of forty-two "super-feature" items. Each advertisement featured a clear, identifiable picture of the merchandise, an institutional message about what constituted a super feature, and a simple statement of the reason for the sale. The deliberate understatement was part of the appeal. This gave the ads an impact that overstating could not provide.

Customers demonstrated increasing confidence in the promotion. Some items were oversold within thirty to fifty minutes after the store opened. In all, the forty-two promotions generated more than 3 percent of the 1958 sales volume.

Encouraged by the stimulation to traffic and sales and profit (when measured in gross margin dollars and direct costs), the store repeated this program in 1959 under the title "Kane's Certified Values." Through its close and steady working relationships with many of the nation's branded resources, the store procured necessary values and was able to boast to the public that it was indeed a quality as well as a value store. The timing proved propitious, since Kane's was already aware that the first major discount store was about to open. Kane's also paid heed to the forecast that during the latter half of

1959, Fulton County would face turbulent economic weather, as proved to be the case.

In 1960, however, the firm did not repeat this program. It had served the purpose for which it was designed, to reestablish Kane's as a value and quality store, to anticipate new competition, and to heighten public confidence.

We might note that while Kane's frequently reverted to what it deemed the fundamentals of merchandising, such as its branded resource or basic stock programs, it also abandoned traditional concepts and practices when necessary. For example, it did not hesitate to adopt a basic tenet of discount merchandising, namely, to price merchandise on the basis of potential gross margin dollars rather than on a basis of mark-on percentage. The suggestion here is that Kane's was not so much unique as adaptive in its merchandising strategy.

Increase of resource brandwagon program. As Kane's drew away from the need or desire to "buy tomorrow's business," it reiterated the theme that nationally-known brands of merchandise represent both quality and value in which the customer could place confidence. Kane's entered its merchandising and sales promotion program in a national name-brand contest in 1959. Favorable comments encouraged continued participation, and in 1960 it received a certificate from the Brand Names Foundation as one of the ten best name-brand stores in the nation. More recently, competing with 278 other finalists in the national contest, the Kane Company was awarded a certificate of distinction in the department store category.

Kane's cooperated with a national magazine in the promotion of a coordinated teen-age merchandise wardrobe and grooming program. Due to the Kane success in Haverford the magazine urged the store to enter its plan and report of operation in the nationwide contest for department stores sponsored by the National Retail Merchants Association. This effort earned an honorable mention for the store.

Both external and internal conditions influenced these decisions. One representative of management stated: "We recognize the need to go after the great moderate market, to go after the affluent society, for people are not as price-minded as they were five years ago."[14] In effect, the merchandising was adjusted to a demand already existing. Furthermore, he added: "Although such a program increased the risk, we believed we had to step up to where we thought our customers were going and where we would be able to offer something different."[15]

Internally, the limited space in one store downtown inhibited some expansion plans related to the brand-resource merchandising program. Further, this lack of space precluded expansion of the number of classifications as well as adding to price-lines within existing classifications. How Kane's resolved the space problems is discussed next.

Physical Expansion

Both alteration of existing space and expansion of downtown and outlying areas enabled Kane's to alter the merchandising strategy from 1945 to 1965. The major physical alteration of the main store building occurred in 1950 when the company completed a remodeling program costing in excess of $500,000. Installation of escalators and air conditioning enabled the company to "offer the public the most modern shopping environment in Haverford."

In 1954, the company compensated for the loss of space involved in this remodeling by acquiring an adjacent building of 5,000 square feet in which it placed workshops for the drapery, slipcover, and upholstery departments. As a result, it could more adequately stock and display home furnishings merchandise in the main building. In response to the Eastgate opening, Kane's, in 1955, acquired a dairy plant one block from the main store, intending to use this site for a private parking ramp. Eventually it sold this property to the city for a parking lot but thereby assured nearby parking for its customers.

1961-1965. Although the first actual physical expansion after 1955 did not occur until 1961, the research, land purchase, and general planning began in 1958. The expansion took place in four stages between 1961 and 1965.

Stage one: branch store. A change in demography of demand and in competition resulted in the first expansion, a branch store in East Haverford, which was not only the fastest growing community in the trading area but also included the Eastgate shopping center. Residents in this city of homes were employed primarily by government agencies, a nearby educational institution, and a huge producer of consumer durable goods. The population also included a fast-growing sector of faculty and students, who of necessity were interested in price as well as quality merchandise. By locating its branch in East Haverford the company could appeal to these groups as well as offer a shopping alternative to Eastgate.

A store official remarked, "The branch store will be a quality center representing what our downtown store stands for and the branch emphasis will be upon apparel for the entire family and furnishings for the home."[16]

This first branch provided an inexpensive lesson for store officials. Successful market segmentation requires an accurate reading of the market, of the particular desires and life-styles of a particular portion of the market. Kane's estimated that 70 percent of its customers would prefer merchandise similar to that stocked in the downtown main store, and that 30 percent would prefer the younger, more collegiate types of apparel and furnishings. Sales, customer comments, and salespeople's want-slips demonstrated that demand was just the reverse. Fortunately, proximity to the main store enabled the branch store to rectify the deficiencies in stock assortments. Three months after the opening, the store offered an array of merchandise more closely approximating demand. By the end of the first year the store earned the profit projected for that period.

There were several reasons for this desirable performance. One was, of course, the fact that the store stocked relatively higher markup and higher priced merchandise; the response to style emphasis, once the initial mistake was rectified, was most positive.

Customers wanted and were pleased to find competent sales help offered in this full-service store. Moreover, the advantage of the Kane name accrued to the branch store, the largest in East Haverford. Customers found at the branch all of the main store's facilities and conveniences, such as credit and delivery. One final comment is in order. The branch manager reported the store received very few calls for the lower-priced lines carried in some of the main store departments or for the price-lines carried in Kane's Basement Store. Apparently, this store did not appeal to lower-income or married student patronage. It did, as indicated, appeal to those who desired quality and fashion.

Stage two: Western Avenue store. Sears' departure from downtown created a merchandising problem for Kane's: many customers seeking goods in hard home furnishings, sporting goods, housewares, hardware, and automotive classifications went to Eastgate, thereby decreasing the total downtown demand. The problem was complicated by the fact that Kane's lacked sufficient physical space to feature and display assortments consistent with the other merchandising criteria the firm had established.

In 1959, the first major discount store opened its doors and drew thousands of shoppers to the very departments in which Kane's was weak. In addition, Sears announced an expansion to handle a burgeoning business. Finally, as if to make the handicap greater, the local city council failed to reach a decision on parking for downtown shoppers.

Despite these changes, the Kane Company did not solve its downtown merchandising problem. It had to concentrate upon the branch opening early in 1961. But a final precipitating circumstance occurred almost simultaneously with the branch store opening; an automobile agency vacated its building at the rear of the main Kane store. This remained vacant for approximately two months.

Lester Henshaw, the Kane president, learned that a national discount chain intended to establish a downtown Haverford store in the vacant automobile agency building. Kane's commenced negotiations at once and soon leased the site for forty years. Ninety-five days later, the doors opened to a completely remodeled, redecorated, and departmentalized store. It included 40,000 square feet of selling and storage space and housed nine new departments and five others transferred from the main Kane building.

The present merchandiser and manager of this Western Avenue store recalled the first planning meeting:

Mr. Henshaw believed the city was ready for a store which would feature price and promotion, quality and service, and which would also supply certain kinds of goods downtown. The general idea was to turn the entire Kane operation into a downtown shopping center. We would take out of the main store and place into the Western Avenue store all kinds of goods vulnerable to discount merchandising. We would promote as if we were running a three-ring circus most of the time, staging a major event once a month. But the format would be different from the main store. While competing promotionally with discount stores and Sears, we would meet Kane quality standards. We would have to stand for both quality and value.[17]

The Western Avenue store included departments for hardware, custom kitchens, home improvements, paints, auto accessories, sewing machines, occasional furniture items, housewares, and toys. Transferred from the main store were departments for sporting goods, appliances, vacuum cleaners, and appliance services.

These transfers enabled the better furniture and bedding departments to expand and to display more effectively the better lines of merchandise from branded resources. Kane's constructed model rooms in the added space and assembled in separate shops the various classifications of furniture.

The Western Avenue manager attributes the store's success partially to resource relationships. By narrowing the number of resources to a few nationally-branded lines and featuring broad assortments within those lines, the store always had on hand a quality assortment competitively priced. The store offered its customers adequate service on whatever it sold. By assuring its resources of continuity and adequate representation, the store negotiated for larger gross margins.

Kane's was particularly sensitive to the market segment attracted to the Western Avenue store. The manager commented:

We knew we were hitting right. Customers told us so. Of course the real sign is the amount of their purchases and that we could measure every day. But we were drawing a different kind of customer, one we judged did not usually come to a department store for these kinds of goods. Also, the layout was better than the main store for those customers. Perhaps they felt more at home. Now fortunately they use the main store.[18]

The data presented in Table VI-2 reveal that the impact of the Western Avenue store must have been favorable, and the data tend to support the claims expressed by that store's general manager. By the end of its second full year of operation, the Western Avenue store contributed approximately 18 percent of the total Kane sales volume, which included the East Haverford branch store. The reader will note that the gross margin percentage of owned department sales declined in the three fiscal years ending January 31, 1962, 1963, and 1964. These declines can be attributed to the Western Avenue store, which had been merchandised on a gross margin dollar rather than a percentage basis. By the end of fiscal 1965 (seen in Table VI-2 as ending January 31, 1966), when it was estimated that Western Avenue accounted for approximately 23 percent of total corporate sales volume, the gross margin percentage decline had been arrested. The unusual consideration is that the percentage had declined so very little! The sales index rise, also seen in Table VI-2, suggests that Western Avenue sales increased both absolutely and relatively more than any other division. The inference is clear: Western Avenue must have generated its volume at a very high gross margin percentage when measured against industry standards. But the significant result for Kane's is that it achieved its objectives: immediate acceleration of a large sales volume, formidable competition in the selected classifications, and attraction for and retention of customers whom Kane's might otherwise have lost.

Stage three: The Corner Shop. During the decade from 1950 to 1960, women's and misses' sportswear as well as junior sportswear expanded relatively faster than many other department store merchandise classifications. This encouraged development of "a store within a store," that is, a shop featuring a particular kind of fashion, such as knitted suits or dresses, or devoted to a particular age group, such as a Young Modern Miss Shop.

Although Kane's rearranged stocks to match these specialized demands, it was not until early in 1964 that additional space became available. Approximately 4,800 square feet of ground floor space downtown, located in the northwest corner of the block housing its main building, had been leased to a group of small specialty shops. When the leases expired in 1964, Kane's arranged to join this area with the main building. After considerable renovation the Corner Shop opened in August, 1964. Kane's merchandise manager appraised the results thus far:

We regard this expansion rather hopefully. With a street door entry and its proximity to the parking lot, we aimed this primarily at the career women who work in various downtown buildings and who need to shop in a hurry. It has attracted many from this particular group of customers and has produced volume which exceeds national averages on the basis of dollars per square foot and gross margin. It has not hindered the growth of our regular sportswear departments.[19]

Stage four: The Campus Corner. Again in response to a changing demography of demand, Kane's recently carried out its fourth expansion since 1961. During the years subsequent to the branch opening, two groups of customers within the East Haverford area changed. Increasing co-ed enrollment at the educational institution increased the demand for sportswear and casual ready-to-wear. Management had to decide whether to expand the casual ready-to-wear departments. From another group of East Haverford customers, the store received requests for wider assortments of "styled home furnishings." These would supplement the basic stock assortments constituting the greater part of the branch store inventories in such classifications.

The problem was how to satisfy both groups without sacrificing display and stock space for either group of merchandise classifications. The problem was further complicated by the general merchandising strategy that the store must always maintain adequate stocks of whatever was deemed to be a basic in any given classification.

Through its many resource contacts, the Kane management learned that a corner dress shop located across the street from its branch store, containing 4,200 square feet of selling space, had not developed the volume of business the owner anticipated or needed to sustain his investment. Upon hearing that other mercantile firms, including three national chains, were interested in acquiring the leasehold rights in return for purchase of the business, the Kane management outbid all others and acquired both the stock and leasehold. This separate shop, renamed The Campus Corner, currently features popular clothes and shoes for university and teen-age groups. As a result, Kane's main branch store now has adequate room to display and merchandise its better styled lines of soft home furnishings in the vacated space.

Sales Promotion

The sales promotion function at Kane's encompasses the planning and execution of advertising and display programs and those customer relations activities that serve to bring the customer and the store together on an informal, personal, and more intimate basis. Five aspects of its sales promotion activity warrant attention here.

Newspapers. Kane's, until 1955, had been the largest newspaper advertiser in Haverford, as measured by the linage published. The management wished to retain this position, if at all possible, in order to combat the Sears relocation and the Agnew resurgence. Both rivals, it was surmised, would increase substantially their outlays for this medium. In addition, the population increases and dispersion encouraged Kane's to sustain or increase its budget. The foregoing is stated to indicate how much importance the firm attached to newspaper advertising and partially explains why the campaigns pertaining to comparative pricing merited so much attention from the management.

Table VI-5, however, shows that Sears exceeded Kane's advertising from 1955 to 1958, exclusive. Since its total linage decreased until 1962 and since Kane's had devoted considerable linage to value demonstrations, it can be assumed that the store expended proportionately more of the total linage on lower price zones.

Subsequent to the value demonstration program and particularly after the first expansions in 1961, the store adopted as a criterion for

TABLE VI-5

Trend in Advertising Linage of L. H. Kane Company and Advertising Linage of Sears and Agnew Company Expressed as Percentage of L. H. Kane Company, 1955-1965

Year	L. H. Kane Co. Linage Changes 1955=100	Agnew Co. Advertising Linage as Percent of L. H. Kane Co. Linage	Sears Advertising Linage as Percent of L. H. Kane Co. Linage
1955	100.0	79.1	107.0
1956	96.0	67.7	100.7
1957	86.6	57.9	102.4
1958	85.1	59.5	104.1
1959	86.9	59.8	98.5
1960	80.3	66.9	92.3
1961	90.3	62.6	72.4
1962	105.0	50.7	69.9
1963	106.9	48.8	73.8
1964	114.5	41.6	69.2
1965	127.2	33.7	66.3

SOURCE: *Haverford News* Advertising Department.

newspaper advertising what is known as the *ABC* scale. The sales promotion director explained:

We prefer to use the Hudson scheme, where an item is classified as *A* if the intent of the advertisement is to secure immediate sales; *B*, if for the purpose of departmental institutional value; and *C*, if for store-wide institutional value. We are not there yet. We are leading into that, recognizing that on the one hand we must help to build sales, as in the Western Avenue Store, for example, and that on the other hand we must build the store as well as sales. Currently we are allocating about 55 percent for *A*, about 35 percent for *B*, and 10 percent for *C*. Some indication of what such a program can mean to a store is attested by what happened to Hudson's during a recent newspaper strike. That store was affected less than others because without newspaper guidance to persuade or influence the customer the tremendous institutional investment paid off for Hudson's.[20]

Kane's style emphasis. During the 1959-1965 period, Kane's increased its total merchandising emphasis on style in all divisions by means of sales promotion methods other than by newspaper advertising. To project Kane's as the style leader in the community, the store conducted shows and special events for the general public both inside and outside the store. For example, Kane's highlighted thirty-three different room exhibits at the Civic Center to demonstrate "gracious living for 1960." Each display presented a portion or area of a room as the starting point or idea base for the entire room's decor. The project featured items seldom offered for sale or exhibited in the Haverford area.

Kane's had staged a bridal fashion show at irregular intervals throughout the period from 1945 to 1961. In the latter year, the merchandise manager coordinated store efforts with *Brides Magazine* and staged the event at the Civic Center. By securing the co-sponsorship of a local junior women's organization, to which it donated the proceeds, the store attracted a capacity audience of 6,000 and gained wide publicity. This event has been repeated each year.

A third type of event illustrating Kane's emphasis on style was an international Festival of Fashion, which featured imports selected by the store's resident buying office staff. Although this type of event had become commonplace in large metropolitan areas, very few smaller independent stores could afford either the cost of procurement or the risk in inventory investment attendant upon such a merchandising program.

Kane's management initiated a program within its New York buying office syndicate to share the costs and risks of purchasing abroad groups of merchandise especially suitable for members of the syndicate. Buyers were sent to the European market to select items that would be likely to sell in communities such as Haverford and in such stores as Kane's. The success of the total program more than met the expectations of the stores that underwrote the initial costs; as a result, both the buying office and Kane's have repeated the promotion several times.

Youth theme. Kane's encouraged youth group activities. The personnel director reported on a typical episode:

We formed a Young American Board made up of girls who were juniors and seniors in high school. It was really their idea, organized by themselves in a series of parties. They asked to use our auditorium as a meeting place. Of

course, we obliged. Now they are planning a school-wide program of participation for hundreds of girls at Haverford High School. The purpose is to
help unfortunate children in the community. Our cost is my time and the
auditorium maintenance. We are happy because we truly see this as one of
our roles. And, of course, I need not tell you the value of this kind of institutional publicity.[21]

Local home economics and sewing classes, 4-H groups, and Girl
Scouts have accustomed themselves to count on Kane's for use of
their auditorium for exhibitions or meetings. Twice a year, the store-
sponsored charm school for pre-teen girls fills the auditorium to capacity for five weeks. Parents are drawn to the store for registration and
for the grand finale, a fashion show.

Kane's has identified itself with youth in several sales promotion
activities. The director explained that "today, youth is an idea, not
an age, a Ponce de León image, one all customer segments seek." The
store developed slogans: "The Wonderful World of Kane's," and
"The Wonderful World of Youth at Kane's." It used these themes in
all media and commissioned music for them; it published the score
in a newspaper advertisement and broadcast the music over the local
radio stations. While it is difficult to trace any change in sales to such
efforts, still they do exemplify the methods Kane's used to implement
its merchandising strategy.

Kane's civic orientation. Kane's, especially during the past ten years,
has established itself as the community-minded, civic-oriented store
in the trading area. The management has pursued this as vigorously
as its program on comparative pricing, physical expansion, and merchandising of basics. Nor has the firm overlooked the publicity value
as attested by the following descriptions extracted from local press
publications:

Sightless students from the State School for the Blind expressed a desire
to model in a fashion show. When asked to participate, the officials at
Kane's immediately offered to outfit the boys and girls and to provide
instruction. The program drew a large audience in the auditorium of the
local Lions Club and the store received a very generous amount of publicity.
Kane's sponsors and stages style shows at the civic auditorium in con-
junction with some large, local women's organizations. Further, it cooper-
ates with both of the large community hospitals by offering on a day set
aside for each, a percentage of all sales attributed to the "saleslady hos-
tesses," members of the various hospital auxiliary groups.[22]

Big-city look. Local real estate agents reported in 1963 and 1964 to the Kane management that a regional department store giant planned to open a store in downtown Haverford, or perhaps in an outlying area. In either event the structure purportedly would be the largest retail building in the trading area. During this same period the Centerstate highway department completed a freeway enabling Haverford customers to travel in seventy-five minutes to one of the nation's largest shopping centers.

Always attuned to competitive possibilities, the Kane management decided to act as if the rumors had become reality. Sales promotion director Westin recounted the story of the decision:

We decided that we needed to present an image of ourselves as a "big-city" store with the big-city look and particularly an image of wide assortments and fashion-right goods. Our objective was to create a series of impacts in publicity to make people aware of Kane's. If we used the cooperative contributions from resources in the usual way, we would end up with a series of smaller ads and these would not be as distinctive as we believed our advertising should be. Consequently we planned five double-truck advertisements during the Christmas season, 1964, using original art work. Actually we combined several smaller ads on the same classifications of goods. But through the integration of outstanding art work and a common theme we created the image and impression of bigness. It represented a tremendous investment for us in art work. But there is no question in our mind that it set us apart not only from the local competition but, judging from customer reaction and sales results, ready to take on whatever metropolitan store might construct here.[23]

During the Christmas season of 1965, the firm enlarged upon this theme, increasing the number of impacts to ten, two of which were published in color. Again, the sales promotion director commented: "We began to think that it was wrong to say we're a little store. We aspired to be big. By letting people know, by planning for six months rather than deciding on a day-to-day basis we could become big-city in looks and results."[24]

Summary

Analysis of the L. H. Kane merchandising strategy reveals that this company was more oriented toward competitive than toward consumer behavior. Although the management was aware of increased consumer affluence and suburban development, the primary and compelling reasons for change were impending or actual competitive activity. In altering its merchandising strategy, Kane's discovered some inner and outward strengths. The no-comparative price policy brought several benefits to the company: one, it demonstrated that a bold program persistently carried out could secure an objective; and, two, that public response manifested a large reservoir of consumer confidence.

Kane's attempted to broaden rather than to segment its market. Through the Basement Store, the Western Avenue Store, and its store-wide events, it attracted the "value-customer"; through augmented fashion stress in apparel for the family and in home furnishings, and through its East Haverford expansion, it attracted the "quality-customer." And for the customer seeking dependability above all, Kane's offered basic stock and brand name merchandise.

Location and size were significant factors in merchandising strategy changes. Kane's turned the presumed liability of a downtown location into an asset by increasing its size so that it could then offer an expanded merchandise line. By opening a branch store in East Haverford, Kane's brought its wares closer to the customer. In both instances it was aided by keen market intelligence. Had the company not obtained these additional locations and increased its size in both, it is doubtful if it could have gained the volume of sales and been able to assume the big-city look the management believed necessary to either forestall or meet anticipated competition.

On the basis of interview data and available questionnaires, the following conclusions were reached:

1) In response to low-margin (discount) department store competition, Kane's altered its merchandising strategy by both trading up and trading down in its merchandise price-lining. It accomplished the former by escalating the price-zone range of basic stock and branded assortments. But it also substituted gross margin dollars for gross margin percentage concepts in order to effectively compete in certain classifications it elected to retain rather than eliminate. To compete, therefore, the firm had to trade down in both merchandising and advertising. Kane's was equally influenced by how its traditional rivals behaved, particularly until 1959. Regarding both kinds of competitors, Kane's repeatedly demonstrated a superior capacity for reaction rather than innovation.

2) In response to an upward shift in demography of demand, Kane's traded up, thus emphasizing its position as the Haverford quality

department store. The interview data strongly suggest, however, that this trading up occurred more within established ranges than in up-wardly-increased ranges.

VII
Conclusions

This research was undertaken to examine how and why traditional department stores adjusted merchandising strategies in response to changes in two external conditions: demography of demand and competition. In regard to the first condition, the study focused on the factors of population and income; in regard to the second, while it focused on discount department stores, the investigation also took account of the development of shopping centers and changes by traditional department store rivals.

It was hypothesized that, in response to changes in these conditions, the traditional department store would trade up in its merchandise price-lining and that the firm would act similarly with regard to its advertising price-lining. An intensive study of four department stores was conducted by means of personal interviews. In addition, trade journal and newspaper files were searched. To corroborate or contradict interview data, a second investigation was conducted among interviewees and their colleagues by means of a mail questionnaire.

Each company has passed its 65th birthday, the oldest being Mayfield's, which opened in 1872. Three of the firms—Staplinger's, Kane's, and Mayfield's—started as dry goods stores. The Fair was organized as a confederation of leased departments or "stores." Staplinger's is unique in two respects: it is the only one in which ownership remains with the founders' descendants, one of whom is an active

172

chairman of the board; and it is the only one that has sold in both wholesale and retail markets.

This closing chapter summarizes the nine principal conclusions based upon four intensive case investigations. As set forth initially, I hope the supporting data as well as the conclusions will assist the practitioner in his ever-present challenge to master change. Also, I trust this book adds to our understanding of change in the business community.

Magnitude of Changes in Demography of Demand and Competition

1) *Changes in demography of demand and in competition occurred in all four cases, but the magnitude of change for each external variable differed in each case.*

Demography of Demand

Table VII-1 ranks the four communities of this study—Monroeville, Haverford, Keelim, and Freeport—in terms of the five variables considered in Appendix Tables A-1 through A-5: population, net effective income, retail sales, general merchandise sales, and income distribution.

Although population increased in all instances, the relative changes in Monroeville and Freeport were less than the relative population change in the entire United States. Total net effective buying income and total retail sales increased in all four communities as well as in the total United States. The relative change for both variables was greater in the nation than in three of the four communities, the exception being Haverford.

In relative terms, the general merchandise sales increased more in both Haverford and Keelim than in the total nation. Again, in relative terms, the impact of the change in the percentage of households with annual incomes of less than $2,500 was less in Haverford than in the other cities. On the same comparative basis, Haverford is to be singled out as the city where the percentage of households with incomes of $10,000 and over increased the most. Further study of the data summarized in Table VII-1 shows that the most favorable changes in demography of demand, relatively, were in Haverford; the least favorable, in Freeport.

TABLE VII-1

Comparison of Selected External Variables in Four Cities in 1965 as Shown in Tables A1-5, Appendix C

Item	Monroeville		Keelim		Freeport		Haverford	
	Index	Rank	Index	Rank	Index	Rank	Index	Rank
Table 1—population (index: 1946 = 100)	127.5	*3	137.6	2	107.4	*4	153.9	1
Table 2—net effect income (index: 1946 = 100)	289.5	*2	252.5	*3	227.7	*4	334.8	1
Table 3—retail sales (index: 1946 = 100)	246.7	*2	217.5	*3	205.3	*4	330.4	1
Table 4—general merchandise sales (index: 1946 = 100)	217.3	*3	309.7	2	188.6	*4	429.1	1
Table 5—income distribution 1955 = 100								
(1955 = 100) $7,000 and over	211.7	*4	222.1	*3	252.8	1	249.4	2
(1960 = 100) $10,000 and over	168.6	3	175.9	2	144.6	4	176.8	1
(1955 = 100) $0.00 to $2,499	61.0	3	60.2	2	76.8	4	49.4	1

*Indicates that the index figure shown was less than the index figure for the total United States.

SOURCE: Tables A1-5, Appendix C.

174

Competition

Three kinds of change in competition developed in each community. The magnitude of change for each kind differed in each case.

Discount competition. National, regional, and local discount department stores developed and flourished in three of the four markets. In Haverford, however, only national and regional firms succeeded; no local discount department store succeeded in Haverford. Discount stores appeared earliest in Freeport and latest in Haverford. The most numerous as well as largest-sized of the discount stores were found in Freeport.

Shopping center competition. The shopping center development constituted a second kind of competition in the four cities. The largest number of, and the largest-sized shopping centers were constructed in Freeport, and they preceded similar developments in the other three cities. In Haverford, the first shopping center, and the only one in excess of 500,000 square feet, opened in 1955.

In all cases, major department store rivals occupied shopping center sites before the subject stores expanded to these new locations. Thus competition intensified not only because rivals acted sooner but also because the shopping centers themselves proved to be such powerful forces of attraction for all customers.

Traditional department stores. Competition among traditional department stores also changed during this twenty-year period. In Monroeville, two traditional department store firms floundered during the first decade but then successfully redirected their merchandising strategies during the second. Several stores that opened branch stores in suburbs prior to 1945 eventually entered shopping centers. Only one major firm in this market, Smith and Company, appears to have continued the same strategy throughout the period studied.

In Keelim, competition from traditional department stores increased when two long-time rivals expanded into shopping centers and then merged. Another change occurred when a traditional store from another community opened Keelim's largest retail store. In Freeport, several traditional stores went out of business. Many others, however, expanded as they opened branches in burgeoning suburban communities and in shopping centers. In Haverford, one traditional rival went out of business and a second became a vigorous competitor after being acquired by a national distributing firm.

The conclusion in regard to changes in competition is the converse of that for demography of demand. The most intense changes in all three kinds of competition—discount department stores, shopping centers, and traditional department stores—occurred in Freeport; the least intensive, in Haverford.

Two caveats are necessary regarding this last conclusion, however. The first is that Haverford, as noted, is the smallest of the cities compared; this may account for the fact that it was the last to attract both discount firms and shopping center developers. Further, the major competitive changes in Haverford occurred after 1954 when the Sears store moved from downtown to the shopping center and when a financially strong company purchased Agnew's, the only traditional department store remaining in Haverford.

The second limitation is that the changes in demography of demand were compared on a relative and not on an absolute basis. On the other hand, comparison of changes in competition was based on absolute, although admittedly incomplete, data.

Stores' Attitudes Toward Changes

2) *Stores did not regard changes in demography of demand and changes in competition as being equally significant.*

The significance placed by each store on the changes in these external variables did not vary in accordance with either the direction or the magnitude of change.

For example, although relative changes in the demography of demand in Freeport were less than in the other three communities, Mayfield's was more influenced than the others by the changes in this variable. On the other hand, in Haverford, where relative changes in demography of demand were the most favorable, the Kane Company moved with greater alacrity and creativity in response to competitive changes than to changes in demand.

In the first instance, Mayfield's perceived an opportunity existing in its "old neighborhood," which had changed demographically and economically. As a result it paid least attention to competition, although the changes among both traditional and discount stores as well as in the shopping centers were very intense and rapid in Freeport. By such behavior it altered a strategy that historically had been oriented toward competitive behavior.

In the second instance, Kane's dramatic abandonment of comparative pricing, for example, was traced more to reaction to competition than to awareness of change in demand. Its physical expansion occurred as a result of competitive changes, or such impending changes, rather than as a result of any changes in demand. However, it should be noted that in merchandising for these additional spaces, in both the Western Avenue store and in the branch units, Kane's was influenced by changes in demand as well as those in competition.

At The Fair, executives, although sensitive to these conditions, did not agree either about the magnitude of change or about which of these was more significant. For example, the conflict in merchandising strategy was traced to the ambivalence about changes in income distribution and the effect of this change upon demand. Until 1963, The Fair's strategy was influenced more by competition than by demand. After 1963, a different interpretation of the same data resulted in a one-directional strategy, which utilized the firm's resources more successfully. The change in strategy was also traced to a reversed orientation toward these two variables.

Staplinger executives were aware of changes in demography of demand. They knew their customers were moving to the suburbs. They recognized the changes in income distribution and perceived that newly-formed demand resulting from this change offered the greatest opportunity for profitable merchandising. Nonetheless, Staplinger's reacted more to competition than to demand during the first decade of the period studied. Later, especially after 1955, this firm redefined its merchandising more toward a changing demand than in response to changing competition.

Regarding these factors of demography of demand, there is an interesting difference between the Staplinger and The Fair management of marketing intelligence. In both communities, the dominant newspaper conducts extensive research for retail clients and supplies a constant stream of data concerning both demand and competition. Staplinger's digested it, acted on it, and acknowledged that it influenced strategy. The Fair, on the other hand, ignored the data at its disposal. After 1963, the new management based its decision to change the merchandising strategy upon this same information.

Responses to Changes in Competition

Responses to discount competition were highly individual and cannot be traced to number of discount units or size of these units or timing of their entry. The largest number and largest-sized discount stores were established in Freeport earlier than in the other three cities. However, Mayfield's strategy centered on demand analysis arising from population and income changes. Further, the Mayfield executives had been through other retail revolutions and had decided they could not operate profitably if they competed on a low-margin basis. It is reasonable to conclude, therefore, that the store in the city with the most intense discount store competition seemed to be the least concerned with it.

Of the four cities studied, Haverford was the last to feel the impact of discount retailing. However, it has been shown that once these competitors entered that community, the L. H. Kane Company responded directly, in both merchandising and advertising. One of Kane's most significant expansions, the Western Avenue store, was attributed to the threat that a discount department store might occupy a downtown retail location. Kane's responded by seizing the location for itself and opening its own promotional store therein.

Staplinger's reacted to discount retailing initially by imitating it in the branch operations. This merchandising strategy appeared to be one way to increase volume rapidly in locations outside the Monroeville central business district. The strategy also bore promise of satisfying certain merchandising constraints, such as turnover and gross margin contribution per square foot, which fundamentally arose from financial conditions within the company.

Contrary to Mayfield's response, The Fair reacted to discounting by imitating its methods in branch stores and even in the Basement Store of the Main Store location. As long as The Fair considered one of its primary market targets to be those families whose incomes were in the lower ranges of the total Keelim income scale, the merchandising strategy paralleled that of discount retailers.

The competitive change to which all four stores responded similarly was the shopping center. However, in all four cases, the stores were late, very late, in responding to this external development. When the subject stores discovered that their customers had not only moved away physically but were disposed to patronize more convenient and, often, better-stocked stores located in shopping centers, all four firms opened in shopping centers. On the basis of assortments, personal service, and convenience, competition from traditional department stores and specialty stores located in shopping centers was often more intense than from discount stores.

The research disclosed that these stores were not always aware of the magnitude of the demographic trend that made shopping centers possible. Again, each reaction differed.

Staplinger's could not extricate itself from an inhibiting lease. But even if it could have obtained a release it is doubtful that management would have substituted shopping center locations for downtown: the older Staplinger management was tradition-bound in its belief that downtown would resurge as the primary center of retail activity. Staplinger's was also financially unable to participate in some shopping centers offered to it, notably to join Smith and Company as major tenants in what became the largest shopping center in Midstate. The Fair misinterpreted a parent company policy, and, like Staplinger's, settled for secondary locations. Mayfield's stubbornly clung to its main store location, believing it must perfect this unit first. The L. H. Kane Company, despite the lesson offered by the 1954 Sears' experience in Haverford, waited until 1962 to open its first branch store.

Monroeville illustrates the competitive vigor of traditional department stores as they, too, attempted to adjust to all of the foregoing conditions. The literature often concentrates on changes in demand and on discount retailing, but fails to consider what other traditional stores do, except to note, of course, their entry into or sponsorship of shopping centers.

Other traditional department stores also changed and offered competition, which must be considered in an analysis of merchandising strategy changes among the subject stores. These kinds of competitive changes in Freeport were not as significant to Mayfield's as they were to, say, Kane's in Haverford. In the former instance, the management decided to concentrate on a single market segment and to cease to compete on a city-wide basis for patronage from a broader income group.

In two of the four stores, particularly, executives imaginatively interpreted what would be the effects of these changes on their customers. Interviewees at Mayfield's reiterated that they attempted to upgrade their merchandise to what they deemed to be the taste level of their customers, or, again, to educate their customers to this taste level. At The Fair, it will be recalled, one major executive expressed the belief that the most profound change in retailing was not discounting, or scrambled merchandising, but what he called "the taste revolution." It was not until 1964, however, that a strategy based on these perceptions of external change was formulated.

In the other two stores, the executives were aware of the changing demands. Officials at Kane's acknowledged a demand for better-quality merchandise, while at Staplinger's the merchants knew that an increasing number of customers with much larger incomes also wanted better quality merchandise than they had purchased before.

Influence of Internal Conditions

3) *The changes in merchandising strategy were not due solely to external change; the changes were traced to internal conditions as well.*

To find out how and why a firm responded to external change it was necessary to analyze internal conditions, which influenced response. All four cases demonstrated that merchandising strategy decisions could be traced to managerial assumptions about how profits were to be achieved and also to how management perceived its market.

Managements' Role

Management in each case proposed a different means to achieve an ultimate end—profit. In the Staplinger case, the initial objective was to survive. This does not imply that it was a failing company. But it was not a profitable one. Financial variables significantly influenced those merchandising decisions that helped to restore the company's financial health. After Staplinger's realized it could not make profits by virtue of its venerableness, or goodness, that is to say, after it ceased to take profitability for granted, it began to formulate a strategy to survive and grow. When it no longer assumed it could generate profits by appealing to the upper-income class, it cast about for a market segment to which it could merchandise profitably.

The Fair assumed that the necessary and sufficient condition for sustained or increased profitability was to achieve market sales dominance. In the Mayfield case, however, management realized that pursuit of sales volume had not resulted in satisfactory profits. Mayfield's objective was to serve those customers who resided in the neighborhood and who, coincidentally, were financially able to purchase better-quality merchandise. Mayfield management assumed it could eventually increase profits by reducing sales of those classifications whose inherent transaction costs or vulnerability to competition made it unlikely that the firm might produce a profit for those kinds of merchandise.

Kane's objective was to secure an increasing share of the market and to become and remain the leading sales volume department store in Haverford. Its detailed record on store traffic and sales per capita indicates how significant Kane's considered this objective to be. In all endeavors, the merchandisers at Kane's were reminded of the profit-and-loss variables operating in every transaction. The willingness to alter the assumptions concerning gross margin at the Western Avenue store attests Kane's flexibility.

A second set of assumptions, which management made and which influenced merchandising strategy, concerned the composition of the store's market—who the customers were and how the store could find out about them. "Reading the market" was a decisive step in strategy formulation.

Staplinger's recognized that it had to cater to a new market segment, one far broader than ever before in its history. It knew this not only from general awareness of postwar circumstances but from the excellent research studies conducted by the *Monroeville Gazette*.

Even at first observation, it appears The Fair misread its market. There was and is a large Keelim market for popular-to-budget-priced merchandise. But the mistaken assumption was that this represented an opportunity for the kind of enterprise The Fair wanted to be. The Fair could not build a satisfactory profit by acting on this assumption. Further, from the evidence seen, it appears the management ignored or failed to analyze the statistical profiles and other economic and demographic data provided by the *Keelim News*. The management simply assumed Keelim was "still the same old Keelim."

Mayfield's obviously read its market correctly. It should be noted again that the company employed very simple, very inexpensive research to determine some basic facts upon which to build a strategy. The Mayfield case tends to confirm the statements in the literature, especially one by Alderson, that a department store, in order to survive, must "renounce the universal marketing task of matching all goods with all people."[1]

Kane's interpreted its market both successfully and unsuccessfully. As to the former, it correctly assumed, for example, that customers wanted and would respond to a Western Avenue type of store. (Of course, one could conjecture that this decision by Kane's resulted as much from reaction to competitive conditions as it did to recognition of merchandising opportunities.) Kane's initial merchandising of the

East Haverford branch store represented a false assumption about the market.

In order to understand these various reactions to change, it is necessary to understand the mind of management. Without knowledge of the financial orientation of Staplinger's management after 1949, its drive for sales volume is incomprehensible. Or, in The Fair case, it is essential to have some acquaintance with the background of the men who read the market one way, while simultaneously an outside firm, also a traditional store, perceived an entirely different opportunity.

Naturally, all managements agreed that the ultimate objective was profit. In view of the foregoing account of internal assumptions and perceptions, it would be most unlikely to find that the stores would rank the remaining objectives or subordinate means in the same order. And even if they did agree on the ranking, this study shows that it is unlikely that the implementation or behavior would be alike, due to the different backgrounds and perspectives of the different merchants.

Financial Factors

The emphasis on financial factors by the firms would seem to support several recent suggestions in the retailing literature, which stressed the significance of accounting or financial principles in formulating a successful merchandising strategy. Kibarian, as noted, urged adoption of a contributions-to-profits approach.[2] Entenberg emphasized the importance of return on investment.[3] Trade organizations have begun to use gross margin dollars generated per square foot of selling area as a standard for measuring merchandising performance. All of these are adding to or supplementing such traditional decision-rules as sales volume, per se, or gross margin percentage in developing a strategy.

These additional standards were adopted early by Mayfield's in its strategy formulation, and they were developed into precise guidelines for buyers, especially throughout the period studied. It is also interesting to note, again, that Kane's adopted the gross margin dollar contribution and abandoned the gross margin percentage as a standard in devising a strategy for the Western Avenue store. The financial perspective pervaded all of the Staplinger decisions. The Fair, until 1964, appeared to heed these suggestions the least of the stores studied. However, after 1963, these financial criteria became a prime concern of the executive policy board.

In Chapter II, three limitations to this study were set forth. One of these inhered in the subject, namely, a basic assumption that the external environment acted as the triggering agent, the cause, the reason for action to be taken. It was then pointed out that the firm could adjust, could change its merchandising strategy for other reasons. One of these might be internal necessities, such as demand for larger profits. Another might be a change in managerial perspective or interpretation of the same or similar set of external conditions.

Also, in Chapter II, it was pointed out that the degree of this first limitation could be ascertained only after conducting the research. This third finding, that the change in merchandising strategy could be traced to internal conditions, and the second finding, that managements differed in their perceptions of the external changes, suggest that the limitation was not an imposing one. Indeed, the awareness of this limitation undoubtedly influenced the investigation by intensifying the effort to ferret out evidence indicating the significance of internal causes.

It may be well to restate the third limitation mentioned in Chapter II: whether these very firms are special cases or whether they are representative of the industry. The justification was that limiting the scope of the research, it would be possible to secure and contribute more knowledge by means of a smaller number of intensive case studies. As noted previously, the degree of this limitation could be ascertained only after conducting the research.

The first finding, already cited, was that external conditions varied in each market and that the magnitude of change in the subject cities was both greater and smaller than that in the nation. The investigation considered competitive changes beyond the original scope, namely, that in addition to analysis of the impact of discount stores, the study also encompassed changes in shopping centers and in traditional department stores. However, a comparison between Haverford, a smaller-sized trading area, and the other three communities, each regarded as a metropolis, suggests that it would be difficult to generalize about the department store industry from this limited number of cases. Certain characteristics of external change—timing, extent, intensity—differed as between the three metropolitan areas and the smaller community of Haverford. Also, it should be noted that both of the external conditions—demography of demand and low-margin (discount) store competition—increased. The study did reveal that the percentage of households with lower-income groups increased and that other competitive institutions in retailing—traditional department store rivals and shopping centers—had to be considered in testing the hypothesis. Nonetheless, the study did not encompass any of the other three possible sets of conditions which conceivably might obtain: for example, an increase in demography of demand and a decrease in low-margin store competition. Hence it is doubtful if conclusions can be drawn about the whole industry from this study. On the other hand, limiting the range of the research did result in more knowledge about the how and the why of the behavior of these firms than if alternative means of investigation had been employed.

Adjustment of Merchandising Strategies

4) *By 1965, all firms had partially adjusted their merchandising strategies as hypothesized; throughout the twenty-year period, however, only one firm completely adjusted its merchandising strategy as hypothesized.*

Throughout the period studied one firm, Mayfield's consistently implemented a merchandising strategy that had been formulated in response to external environmental changes. The management of this firm segmented from its former total trading area a particular geographical portion in which it found sufficient demand so that a revised merchandise mix could be profitably offered there. Once the new strategy had been accepted, Mayfield's consistently traded up in the merchandise and advertising price-lining.

The Mayfield strategy confirms several statements from the literature, which were cited in Chapters I and II. The decision to formulate a strategy based upon patronage motives and market segmentation in response to a change in demography of demand is akin to Bucklin's proposals.[4] Also, Rich and Portis suggested that in response to discount store competition a traditional department store might trade up, drop some of the more competitive hard-goods lines, emphasize fashion, and offer more services.[5] Essentially, this is the strategem which Mayfield's devised. It succeeded.

The other three firms, however, did not respond initially as hypothesized. Staplinger's, from 1945 to 1955, traded down. In merchandise price-lining it sought sales volume in lower price-ranges, and it advertised these lower ranges to influence a market segment larger than it had cultivated heretofore. Later, as the firm realized it had traded down almost to discount-store ranges, Staplinger's traded up to the level originally defined, during the period from 1946 to 1950, as its target. Newspaper price-lining reflected these policies.

Again referring to Rich and Portis, it will be recalled that they pointed out, as one alternative to discount competition a traditional store might convert to self-service, drop other services, and feature discount prices. During those years when Staplinger's appeared to follow this strategy, the firm failed to progress. However, when Staplinger's followed the second alternative (as noted in the preceding comments on Mayfield's), the Monroeville store did improve.

The Fair, from 1949 to 1963, traded down in its branches and, at times, in its main store Basement, as it imitated the discount department store. Again, as pointed out in Chapter I, one of the alternative strategies suggested in the literature was that a store might convert to self-service, drop other services, and feature discount prices. The authors did not advocate this strategy either for a department store that already was a leading retailer in a community or for a store that aspired to be one. This study showed that one core of The Fair's dual-core strategic response was to execute such a strategy. This merchandising did not result in a satisfactory profit.

After 1963, The Fair reversed this strategy and emphasized traditional department store characteristics. During the period from 1949 to 1963, however, the advertising price-lining did not always reflect the merchandise price-lining.

The L. H. Kane Company responded to the external environmental changes by both trading up and trading down. It traded up in furniture, some home furnishings, and apparel groups, but traded down in appliances and hard home furnishings, as it sought to retain customers and sales volume leadership. The trend in newspaper advertising was indeterminate: the store at one time emphasized its brand-resource program and at another time stressed its competitive price position.

In formulating its merchandising strategy, especially after 1960, Kane's actions coincide with another suggestion found in the literature. This was to upgrade merchandise lines and emphasize fashion, but, at the same time, to add certain features of the discounters on a limited basis. When the L. H. Kane Company followed this pattern, it succeeded.

Physical Change

5) *Each firm expanded or modified the physical facilities of the downtown store and opened branch stores. However, execution of*

either or both of these physical changes did not always result in a
successful revision of merchandising strategy.

Staplinger's did not increase sales volume commensurate with external opportunities until it opened branch stores. But this did not
result in a profitable adjustment, because the strategy in the branches
was dissimilar to that of the main store, both historically and as proposed for the future. In the main store, Staplinger's did not rehabili-
tate for two reasons: it did not have the financial resources or the
profit performance to warrant such investment, and it was constrained
from such risk by a high-cost lease. Later, these conditions necessitated
Staplinger's diversification into real estate. In the period from 1959
to 1965, in order to assure itself of a market, Staplinger's developed a
real estate complex wherein people could live, work, and shop.

It should be recalled, too, that this firm developed branches later
than most stores. The reasons were primarily financial. After over-
coming that handicap, Staplinger's launched its major branch and
shopping center expansions and concentrated on those price-ranges
and kinds of assortments it sighted for itself during the 1945-1950
period.

The Fair initially used branches to "pump volume" because it
assumed the branch operations should be different from the main
store in their merchandising. Its late start in opening branches was
traced to guidelines issued by the parent company. When The Fair
did expand, it selected secondary locations, even though its parent
company certainly possessed the financial resources to compete with
Dean and Company or any other mercantile firm for prime locations.
Further, it constructed or leased small spaces because it conceived of
branches as "twigs," because of its primary assumption that "the downtown store must be the key to area dominance."

When The Fair altered these assumptions and acted on different
premises, it really modified a merchandising strategy that had been
unrealistic relative to the market. The proposed new shopping center
in 1967 attests this last statement.

Mayfield's formulated a strategy to exploit a unique opportunity of
location. One way to achieve success was to continually add to, and
refurbish, its old structures. Also, it concentrated on display and
dramatization of fashion-right merchandise in all classifications it believed would appeal to the particular market segment it decided to
capture.

Mayfield's also was late in establishing branches. Then it attempted to include the features of the "mother store," that is, a customer would find the same kind of atmosphere and assortment within a classification as in the Newtown store. Mayfield's was late because it believed that only by constantly perfecting the main store could it devise a pattern, a strategy, a reputation, strong enough to sustain the branches.

L. H. Kane was able to execute a revised strategy as a result of physical expansion and additional locations. It appears, however, that Kane's was late in all instances and this may account partially for the fact that Kane's, despite its volume spurt in the 1962 and 1965 period, did not increase its volume commensurate with market demand. In this case the size of location affected strategy implementation. To display and sell better-quality merchandise (and thus generate more gross margin dollars per square foot), the store required a certain minimum physical area. By opening the Western Avenue addition, for example, Kane's gained this additional area in the main store, which enabled it to feature displays of better-quality home furnishings.

Resource Relationships

6) *During the period studied all stores realigned resource relationships.*

In adjusting their merchandising strategies, all stores realigned resource relationships. This occurred regardless of which external variables influenced the firm. Changes in resource relationships did not occur only because of external variables, however. Again, changes in internal conditions, including management philosophy, also account for the resource relationship. Even when a firm correctly read the market, it then had to look at the other channel end—the supply side of the trade relationship—in order to adjust profitably.

Staplinger's required an alignment with a different set of resources in order to reach and appeal to the selected market target after 1945. The basic decision was to change the residential buying organization. There were other reasons for this decision. From the experiences, records, and research talents of department stores already affiliated in the buying organization, Staplinger's hoped to find the guidance it needed to change strategies. Another objective was to seek assistance in expense controls, which the management believed were necessary if the firm was to realize a profit. Staplinger's achieved both objectives.

The Fair also illustrates the significance of resource relationships. During the 1945 to 1965 period, despite a change in ownership, The

Fair maintained its affiliation with the same buying group. Prior to this change in ownership, many manufacturers regarded The Fair as the prestige outlet in Keelim. During the 1949 to 1963 turbulence, however, The Fair's own merchandisers fought among themselves for several of these sources. And there was a general tendency to purchase from among the lower price-ranges of these manufacturers. But the reason for this lay in lack of direction by top management in defining what particular task in a total strategy each department was to perform. Yet not all merchandisers at The Fair viewed resources in this manner: several placed great confidence in resource stability and capacity to innovate. Hence, while one group perceived manufacturers as sources for profits and ideas as well as goods, others regarded them as units in the bucket brigade of passing goods in a process from raw materials to consumers. After 1963, the management enforced a policy of seeking and cooperating with resources who could provide those goods and ideas by which The Fair could implement its altered strategy. Simultaneously, the management eliminated internal conflicts regarding resources.

Mayfield's developed its own sources of supply for many classifications in order to trade up and procure the merchandise it sensed was demanded, or for which it believed it could create a demand. Domestic manufacturers hesitated, soon after 1945, to deal with Mayfield's because they feared Mayfield's might either resume price-cutting practices or fail to confirm orders. In addition, these resources feared reprisals from Mayfield's competitors. As a result, buyers and merchandisers developed both foreign and domestic sources out of necessity as well as from a desire to offer a unique array of merchandise. Resources cooperated superbly, after a time, because dealing with Mayfield's meant confirmed, large orders, and work with creative, enthusiastic buyers. Once Mayfield's had become a prestige account, the affiliation was a means to secure new accounts and firmer relationships with other retailers. Mayfield's viewed resources as a key means to profits, not so much by price reductions as by creation of a new and unique offering of goods the store could merchandise at gross margins considerably greater than average.

Development of what the L. H. Kane Company called the "Brand-wagon Program" was fundamental to the Kane merchandising strategy. This assured stability and dependability to the customer. Alone, or even with its buying syndicate associates, Kane's could not actually launch a style, a design, a new product, or a new resource. Accordingly, Kane's depended on resources, especially manufacturers of nationally-advertised brands, for fashion guidance, and Kane's protected these affiliations. In turn, Kane's proved a dependable customer and this cooperation enabled Kane's to secure adequate supplies of merchandise whereby it could substitute several successful value events for comparative-price promotional sales.

The forces causing change for retailers were described in Chapter I. The experiences of these four stores tend to support Alderson's claim that "the retailer must adjust to his environment, few having the power to change it . . . and no matter how impressive innovations may be in such adaptation the retailer's operation continues to be that of moving merchandise which someone else has designed or invented."[6] However, Mayfield's experience suggests that, as a middleman, a retailer can decidedly influence the supply side of his market.

The Timing of Change

7) *In response to external change the stores tended to be late rather than early in altering their merchandising strategies.*

The importance of timing was described in Chapter I. Gross claimed that those who adopted a successful strategy in response to low-margin retailers did so early in the rivalry, anticipating the entry of innovators.[7] Similarly, the factor of timing can be used to compare the reactions of the four subject stores with regard to branch stores and shopping center occupancy.

Mayfield's abandoned the rivalry with low-margin competition early in the contest. Both Staplinger's and The Fair either failed to anticipate these competitors or ignored them until it was too late; both then finally tried to imitate the low-margin stores. L. H. Kane anticipated their advent, adopted a portion of their strategy to join issue with them, and later, in its Western Avenue store, succeeded in sharing a portion of the low-margin market.

Regarding branch stores, however, these four cases illustrate tardiness and error. All four were late in establishing branch store operations, and in developing shopping centers or locating branches in shopping centers.

Sales Promotion Tactics

8) *In changing their merchandising strategies two of the four firms modified the sales promotion tactics.*

To implement their strategies, Mayfield's and Kane's revised their sales promotion tactics. Mayfield's reallocated monies from newspaper advertising to display; Kane's eliminated comparative prices in both advertising and display. Both knowingly accepted the inherent risks of changing identities, an objective both achieved.

Mayfield's reduced newspaper advertising and increased display allocations because it found the former an inefficient expenditure, and it needed the latter to sell more goods to the traffic it already had. This store also reduced allocations for low-margin goods, sales, and clearances, because it decided to stress its best quality and value and not its markdowns. It is interesting to note that when Joseph Mayfield founded his store he selected a building that had the largest plate glass windows in all of Freeport, because he believed he could differentiate his offering by utilizing ample display space both "outside and inside" the store.

Kane's abandoned comparative pricing in advertising and display in order to differentiate itself from competition and to concentrate on the quality rather than on the price attributes of merchandise. While this decision could be judged a defensive measure against competitive pricing, the advantageous perspective of time proves that it also was an offensive measure in that it set Kane's apart from all other retailers in the area. As stated in Chapter II, an offensive strategy is that by which a firm capitalizes fully on the relative strengths or advantages it enjoys or can create.

One departure from the expected concentration of advertising in newspapers was the finding that three of the firms (Mayfield's is the exception) are experimenting with electronic media, particularly television, on a sustained basis. In order to reduce costs, two of these (The Fair and Kane's) are using their main store physical plants and store personnel in the production of televised advertising messages.

Lack of Information

9) *Stores do not have information pertaining to merchandise or advertising price-lining.*

There is a wide chasm between the literature and department store behavior concerning the significance of price-lining information. As noted in Chapters I and II, all textbooks on retailing include a section on price-lining and claim it to be a necessary technique for successful merchandising. The NRMA's recent study on classification merchandising leads one to believe a store (of the size included in this study) would maintain price-lining data.[8]

Although the subject stores record myriad details about many operating expenses and merchandising events, they did not maintain data by which price-lining for merchandising or advertising could be measured.

The literature repeats, trade associations reiterate, and interviwees stressed the merit of maintaining sound basic stocks. Since price is a crucial variable at all times, and since the DSIPI data indicated that department store prices from 1960 to 1965 were stable, it was expected, at least, to find in these stores price-lining information about basic stocks. However, even for such a classification as Men's Dress Shirts, it was impossible to secure either merchandise or advertising price-lining data for the period under study.

An effort was made to determine whether this paucity of information was peculiar only to these stores or whether it was prevalent throughout the industry. Inquiries were directed to large cooperative buying associations and to other individual stores.[9] Respondents offered two general answers. The first was that the expense required first to ferret out, then to record and analyze such data was not justified by the benefits that might be derived. The respondents did add, however, that electronic data processing might make price-lining investigation and analysis more feasible.[10] The second answer was that knowledge of "what we did five years ago will not help us for tomorrow. Styles, tastes, resource offerings change too fast. Price changes from one year to the next can make even last year's data obsolete."

One respondent did acknowledge that if the conditions underlying demand were to become less favorable, the knowledge about price-lining might become more valuable. When asked what the store would do if employment in the community declined, or if sales slackened, the buyer stated, "We would diminish some emphasis on fashion, watch the top price-lines, and go back to greater basic stock emphasis."[11]

The paradox about information is more apparent when one realizes that the NRMA has devoted considerable time and expense to develop a classification code in which price-lining, as noted in Chapter I, is a significant and necessary datum for increased merchandising efficiency. Indeed, the NRMA committee asseverates that "price-lining acts as the communications link between dollar and unit controls and helps to monitor consumer demand."[12] When queried about the finding of this research, a member of the NRMA committee commented: "As a marketing institution, department stores do not take advantage of available data, mechanization, and theory."[13]

In Chapter II, again, another limitation was cited. This pertained to the methodology of investigation, more specifically, the limitation of the "egocentric predicament" imposed by virtue of personal interviews. To diminish the effect of this limitation, a second investigation to seek corroborative evidence was conducted. One facet of this latter inquiry was to seek specific price-lining data for each of eighteen classifications. It was this effort to find corroborative evidence that brought to light the dearth of information stores possessed about merchandise and advertising price-lining. The limitation, it appears, does not arise so much from the method of investigation as it does from the failure of firms in this industry to generate and maintain records about major, if not primary, investment, the inventory, and, as well, about its second largest controllable expense, advertising.

Conclusions

1) To ascertain both how and why a firm alters its merchandising strategy in response to external change, it is also necessary to study the internal variables of the company.

2) To successfully alter a merchandising strategy in response to external change, it is necessary that the management of an intermediary institution (such as a department store) take account of its storehouse of knowledge about itself as well as the knowledge it possesses about the external environment.

Knowledge about itself includes awareness of those assumptions that underlie managerial selection of an overall plan or concept for carrying on the firm's business, including the guidelines or decision-rules employed to reach the goals. Knowledge about its external environment encompasses both the resource of supply side as well as the customer or demand side of the market.

3) To successfully alter a merchandising strategy, a firm need not necessarily respond to all external changes cited in this study. The response may be only to demography of demand or only to competition; or it may be to a newly perceived opportunity in the marketplace (which in turn may have resulted from a change in either or both of the aforementioned conditions).

4) Marketing theory suggests that advertising price-lining should

reflect merchandise price-lining. The lack of information about this relationship casts some doubt on the efficiency of industry-wide proposals such as the NRMA classification program.

5) Trading up is a relative term. Self-comparison rather than industry comparison was the only standard by which the hypothesis could be tested.

The Mayfield case demonstrated that where management secured knowledge about its market and about itself, where it closely aligned merchandise and advertising price-lining, for instance, it also clearly defined and designed a strategy which, when implemented, resulted in a satisfactory profit. This case also demonstrated that to alter a merchandising strategy successfully, the managerial conception of value must be congruent with that of the consumer.

In Chapter I, it was claimed that a merchant prince's skill may lie in his judgment of opportunities rather than in his origination of techniques. Also, a retailing executive was quoted to the effect that breakthroughs and innovations, as well as successful merchandising strategies, were generated by merchants who could foresee some great new trend in the future, who could more or less instinctively sense the need for change, and who could risk power to make those changes. The four case histories narrated in this book tend to confirm the foregoing propositions. In addition, each case reveals uniqueness rather than uniformity. The uniqueness stems from the management within the firm; management, being made up of individuals interacting with other individuals, in each case had a different response to the internal and external factors that demanded change. The response varied from action, when a firm seized the initiative, to reaction, when a firm changed only because of external pressures. Strategy varied from one formulated on the concept that merchandising embraces the management of "the three M's—men, money, and merchandise," to a strategy formulated solely in response to competitive rivalry.

The most important factor in merchandising is the understanding of value; the four firms were successful in direct relation to their knowledge of, and adjustment to, the customers' concept of value. In addition, it is apparent from this study that a successful merchandising strategy requires that management communicate its goals and its image to all concerned—to the firm's own organization and to the consumer.

Appendixes

APPENDIX A
Departments/Classifications for Which Questionnaires Were Dispatched

NRMA NO.	Merchandise Classification	Percent Volume Total Main Store	Percent Total Main Store Advertising
42–11	Women's & misses' dresses	3.3	3.6
42–12	Junior dresses	1.3	1.3
41–11	Women's & misses' untrimmed cloth coats	2.0	2.0
43–00	Women's skirts (including all sizes)		
43–00	Blouses (all sizes)	3.4	3.6
43–00	Women's sweaters (all sizes)		
51–11	Men's dress shirts	3.2	2.7
52–00	Men's suits		
52–00	Men's sport coats	2.3	2.7
53–11	Men's slacks		
61–11	Mattresses	1.1	1.8
61–22	Bedroom suites	1.3	2.2
61–21	Sofas	1.6	2.9
61–23	Occasional & living room chairs	0.5	0.9
15–11	Towels	1.3	1.6
15–12	Bedspreads		
15–12	Blankets	0.9	1.2
64–12	Made-up drapes	0.6	0.7
	Totals	22.8	27.2

SOURCE: *Operating Results of Department and Specialty Stores in 1964* (New York: Controllers' Congress, National Retail Merchants Association, 1965).

APPENDIX B: QUESTIONNAIRE

Explanation of Terms

Merchandise price-lining: refers to establishing a range of regularly stocked retail prices for a merchandise classification. For example, in price-lining women's dresses, a store could establish a range extending from $10.00 to $50.00.

Advertising price-lining: refers to the range of retail prices usually advertised in newspapers for that merchandise classification. It may or may not be as extensive as the merchandise price-lining.

For Charts I-IV, which follow, each price range is divided into six, continuous zones. *Price zones* for each classification have been derived from national research on price-lining for 1960 and 1965. For example, within the aforementioned women's dress classification, the total range is divided as follows: zone (1): under $10.00; zone (2): $10.01-$18.00; zone (3): $18.01-$28.00; zone (4): $28.01-$38.00; zone (5): $38.01-$50.00; zone (6): over $50.00. More specifically, the retail price of $14.95 would be in price-zone (2), $10.01-$18.00.

In Charts I and II the *Percentage of Total Dollar Sales* for the particular classification has been divided into multiples of ten. In Charts III and IV the *Percentage of Total Newspaper Advertising* (either by dollars expended or by linage used) has also been divided into multiples of ten.

For all charts the percentages are continuous. Thus 10 percent includes any ratio from zero to 10 percent; 20 percent includes any ratio from 10.01 percent to 20 percent; 30 percent includes any ratio from 20.01 percent to 30 percent, etc. More specifically, a ratio of 14.8 percent would be placed in the 20 percent column.

What You Are Requested to Do for Charts I and II:

1) For the two years, 1960 and 1965, please state the percentage of total dollar sales secured at the various price-zones.

2) If you do not have records, or if you were not associated with the store at the time periods for which inquiry is made, please do the following: inquire from your associates in your division or within the organization who may be able to reflect upon the trends within the department, or, estimate what you believe might have been the case.

3) Please indicate source of information at the bottom of the chart.

For Charts III and IV:

1)   State the percentage of total newspaper advertising expended for each of the applicable price-points for 1960 and 1965. NOTE: If your percentage figures represent *linage* rather than dollar measurements, use the former. Please note this change, however.

2)   Please see directions for Charts I–II, number 2, above.

3)   Please indicate source of information at the bottom of the chart.

CHART I: *Analysis of Total Dollar Sales by Price-Range*

Name of Merchandise Classification:_____
Your Dept. Number:_____ NRMA Equivalent_____
Information for year *1965*.

Price Zone No.	Price Zone Range	Percentage of Total Dollar Sales									
		10	20	30	40	50	60	70	80	90	100
(1)	Under $_____										
(2)	$_____ to $_____										
(3)	$_____ to $_____										
(4)	$_____ to $_____										
(5)	$_____ to $_____										
(6)	Over $_____										

Source: (Check)   Store Records_____   Other Execs. _____
                            Estimate_____
Do percentages checked total 100 percent?_____ .   Thank You.

CHART II: *Analysis of Total Dollar Sales by Price-Range*

Name of Merchandise Classification:_____
Your Dept. Number:_____ NRMA Equivalent_____
Information for year *1960*.

Price Zone No.	Price Zone Range	Percentage of Total Dollar Sales									
		10	20	30	40	50	60	70	80	90	100
(1)	Under $_____										
(2)	$_____ to $_____										
(3)	$_____ to $_____										
(4)	$_____ to $_____										
(5)	$_____ to $_____										
(6)	Over $_____										

Source: (Check)   Store Records_____   Other Execs. _____
                            Estimate_____
Do percentages checked total 100 percent?_____ .   Thank You.

Chart III. *Analysis of Total Newspaper Advertising by Price-Range*

Name of Merchandise Classification:_____
Your Dept. Number:_____ NRMA Equivalent_____
Information for year *1965*.

Price Zone No.	Price Zone Range	Percentage of Total Newspaper Advertising									
		10	20	30	40	50	60	70	80	90	100
(1)	Under $_____										
(2)	$_____ to $_____										
(3)	$_____ to $_____										
(4)	$_____ to $_____										
(5)	$_____ to $_____										
(6)	Over $_____										

Source: (Check) Store Records_____   Other Execs. _____
                        Estimate_____
Do percentages checked total 100 percent?_____ .   Thank You.

CHART IV. *Analysis of Total Newspaper Advertising by Price-Range*

Name of Merchandise Classification:_____
Your Dept. Number:_____ NRMA Equivalent_____
Information for year *1960*.

Price Zone No.	Price Zone Range	Percentage of Total Newspaper Advertising									
		10	20	30	40	50	60	70	80	90	100
(1)	Under $_____										
(2)	$_____ to $_____										
(3)	$_____ to $_____										
(4)	$_____ to $_____										
(5)	$_____ to $_____										
(6)	Over $_____										

Source: (Check) Store Records_____   Other Execs. _____
                        Estimate_____
Do percentages checked total 100 percent?_____ .   Thank You.

Effect of Environmental Events Upon Merchandising Decisions in Your Trading Area from 1960 to 1965

(Please check appropriate answer and comment when applicable)

Ques No.	Environmental Event	Stay Same	Increase	Decrease	Do You Attribute Any Differences Between Charts I-II to This Environmental Event? — Yes	No	Comment	Do You Attribute Any Differences Between Charts III-IV to This Environmental Event? — Yes	No	Comment
	Population-geography									
1										
a	Did population?						Comment:			Comment:
b	Did geographical trading area for your firm?						Comment:			Comment:
	Household incomes									
2										
a	Did average household income?						Comment:			Comment:
b	Did percent of household income under $3,000						Comment:			Comment:
c	Did percent of household income from $3,000-6,999						Comment:			Comment:
d	Did percent of household income from $7,000-9,999						Comment:			Comment:
e	Did percent of household income over $10,000						Comment:			Comment:
	Occupations									
3										
a	Did percent of white collar workers?*						Comment:			Comment:
b	Did percent of service workers?**						Comment:			Comment:
c	Did percent of manual workers?***						Comment:			Comment:

*Professional, managerial, clerical, and sales.
**Private household and other service.
***Craftsmen, and foremen, operatives and laborers except farm and mine laborers.

Effect of Environmental Events (Continued)

Ques. No.	Environmental Event	Stay Same	Increase	Decrease	Do You Attribute Any Differences Between Charts I-II to This Environmental Event? Yes / No	Do You Attribute Any Differences Between Charts III-IV to This Environmental Event? Yes / No
d	Did percent of farm workers?*****				Comment:___	Comment:___
e	Did percent of women in work force?				Comment:___	Comment:___
f	Did percent of married women in work force?				Comment:___	Comment:___
4	*Resource Prices*					
a	Did resource (market-wholesale) prices for comparable quality merchandise?				Comment:___	Comment:___
b	Did retail prices for comparable quality merchandise?				Comment:___	Comment:___
c	Did the cumulative mark-on percent for comparable quality mdse. in your classification?				Comment:___	Comment:___

Other Events

In addition to the Environmental Events suggested as reasons for differences between Charts I and II and between Charts III and IV, perhaps there are others which occur to you. Please indicate these below.

Event: _____   Comment:___   Comment:___

Event: _____   Comment:___   Comment:___

*****Farmers, farm managers, laborers.

200

Effect of Competitive Events Upon Merchandising Decisions in Your Trading Area from 1960 to 1965

(Please check appropriate answer and comment when applicable)

(DDS = Discount Department Stores; TDS = Traditional Department Stores)

Ques No.	Competitive Event	Do You Attribute Any Differences Between Charts I-II to This Competitive Event? Yes / No		Do You Attribute Any Differences Between Charts III-IV to this Competitive Event? Yes / No	
1	*Number of DDS:* (underscore appropriate answer)				
a	The number of DDS firms (stayed same, increased, decreased)		Comment:		Comment:
b	The number of DDS units (stayed same, increased, decreased)		Comment:		Comment:
	Please answer following questions yes or no. Yes / No				
2	In changing the *merchandise price-lining* in your classification did DDS				
a	Shift upward entire price-range?		Comment:		Comment:
b	Shift emphasis upward within the range?		Comment:		Comment:
c	Drop some lower prices and add others to top of range?		Comment:		Comment:
3	In changing the *advertising price-lining* in your classification, did DDS				
a	Shift upward entire price-range?		Comment:		Comment:
b	Shift emphasis upward within the range?		Comment:		Comment:

Effect of Competitive Events (Continued)

Ques. No.	Competitive Event	Do You Attribute Any Differences Between Charts I-II to This Competitive Event?			Do You Attribute Any Differences Between Charts III-IV to this Competitive Event?		
		Yes	No	Comment:	Yes	No	Comment:
c	Drop some lower prices and add others to top of range?			Comment: _____			Comment: _____
4	Did DDS change merchandise price-lining in other ways?						
a	Other: _____			Comment: _____			Comment: _____
b	Other: _____			Comment: _____			Comment: _____
5	Did DDS change advertising price-lining in other ways?						
a	Other: _____			Comment: _____			Comment: _____
b	Other: _____			Comment: _____			Comment: _____

IN RESPONSE TO THIS DISCOUNT DEPARTMENT STORE COMPETITION

Ques. No.	Competitive Event	Yes	No	Comment:	Yes	No	Comment:
6	Did you alter your merchandise price-lining?						
a	Did you (underscore where applicable) add or drop any categories of merchandise?			Comment: _____			Comment: _____
b	Did you lengthen or shorten the price-range?			Comment: _____			Comment: _____

Effect of Competitive Events (Continued)

Ques. No.	Competitive Event	Yes	No	Do You Attribute Any Differences Between Charts I-II to This Competitive Event?	Yes	No	Do You Attribute Any Differences Between Charts III-IV to this Competitive Event?
c	Did you shift emphasis from one price-zone to another within the range?			Comment:			Comment:
7	Did you alter your advertising price-lining?						
a	Did you shift emphasis to higher price-zones within the range?			Comment:			Comment:
b	Did you shift emphasis to lower price-zones within the range?			Comment:			Comment:
8	Number of TDS:						
a	The number of TDS firms (stayed same, increased, decreased).			Comment:			Comment:
b	The number of TDS units (stayed same, increased, decreased).			Comment:			Comment:
9	IN RESPONSE TO DISCOUNT DEPARTMENT STORE COMPETITION						
a	Did TDS alter their merchandise price-lining?			Comment:			Comment:
b	Did TDS alter their advertising price-lining?			Comment:			Comment:

203

APPENDIX C

TABLE A-1

Changes in Population in Major Trading Area of Stores Studied as Compared with United States

Trading Area	1950 Index No. 1946=100	1955 Index No. 1946=100	1960 Index No. 1946=100	1965 Index No. 1946=100
Monroeville	107.6	115.2	122.2	127.5
Haverford	117.4	134.7	143.0	153.9
Keelim	107.8	118.9	128.9	137.6
Freeport	106.9	107.3	104.2	107.4
U.S. total: 1946 = 100	107.2	116.9	127.2	137.0
U.S. actual: 1946 = 141,936 (000,000)	152,271	165,931	180,584	194,572

SOURCE: For U.S. total figures, *The Statistical Abstract,* 1966, Bureau of Census, U.S. Dept. of Commerce. For population bases for trading area, *Sales Management Buying Power Guide,* for respective years. Such data will always be found in the year subsequent to the year stated in this chart. Population for 1946 is estimate of population as of 1/1/47, as stated in May, 1947, issue; population for 1950, May, 1951, issue as of 1/1/51; population for 1955, May, 1956, issue as of 1/1/56; population for 1960, May, 1961, as of 1/1/61; population for 1965, June, 1966, as of 12/31/65.

TABLE A-2

Changes in Total Net Effective Buying Income in Trading Areas Studied as Compared with United States

Trading Area	1950 Index No. 1946=100	1955 Index No. 1946=100	1960 Index No. 1946=100	1965 Index No. 1946=100
Monroeville	140.1	185.3	231.1	289.5
Haverford	154.8	213.8	265.8	334.8
Keelim	119.7	160.7	203.2	252.5
Freeport	140.4	154.5	197.7	227.7
U.S. total: 1946 = 100	141.7	188.5	254.1	327.9
U.S. actual: 1946 = $140,968 (000,000)	$199,680	$265,683	$358,122	$462,050

SOURCE: *Sales Management Buying Power Guide* for respective years. See Table A-1. Totals for United States obtained by multiplying Monroeville area percentage of United States for respective years by absolute figure for that area.

The term *Effective Buying Income* is defined by *Sales Management* as "the equivalent of the U.S. Government definition of disposable income available for spending in the various states." (1966 edition, *Buying Power Guide,* p. 224.)

TABLE A-3

Changes in Retail Sales in Major Trading Areas of Stores Studied as Compared with United States

Trading Area	1950 Index No. 1946=100	1955 Index No. 1946=100	1960 Index No. 1946=100	1965 Index No. 1946=100
Monroeville	132.9	170.7	190.2	246.7
Haverford	153.0	211.1	244.4	330.4
Keelim	121.4	155.8	180.0	217.5
Freeport	153.4	168.5	184.6	205.3
U.S. total: 1946 = 100	140.2	179.4	214.3	277.2
U.S. actual: 1946 = 102,488 (000,000)	143,689	183,851	219,529	283,950

SOURCE: For United States totals, *Historical Statistics of the United States*, U.S. Department of Commerce, Series T 23-48. For trading areas studied, *Sales Management Buying Power Guide* for year following specified date. See sources for Table A-1.

TABLE A-4

Changes in General Merchandise Sales in Major Trading Areas of Stores Studied

Trading Area	1950 Index No. 1946=100	1955 Index No. 1946=100	1960 Index No. 1946=100	1965 Index No. 1946=100
Monroeville	94.9	120.4	148.2	217.3
Haverford	119.5	203.8	249.7	429.1
Keelim	128.6	168.3	196.7	309.7
Freeport	95.3	125.8	148.0	188.6
U.S. total: 1946 = 100	113.1	162.5	202.8	299.7
U.S. actual: 1946 = $14,792,350 (000)	$16,729,130	$24,036,102	$30,008,302	$44,336,966

SOURCE: *Sales Management Buying Power Guide* for year following specified date. See sources for Table A-1.

TABLE A-5

Changes in Income Distribution Among Families in Major Trading Areas of Stores Studied Compared with Total United States as Measured by Changes in Percentage of Households by Income Groups

Item	1955	1960	1965
$0,000–$2,499			
Monroeville	100	41.0	61.0
Haverford	100	38.5	49.4
Keelim	100	37.5	60.2
Freeport	100	31.1	76.8
U.S. total*	100	75.8	61.5
	*U.S. total figure is for $0,000–$2,999.		
$2,500–$3,999			
Monroeville	100	66.9	46.1
Haverford	100	66.8	52.4
Keelim	100	77.9	49.7
Freeport	100	51.2	51.2
$4,000–$6,999			
Monroeville	100	107.5	77.6
Haverford	100	114.4	86.3
Keelim	100	101.9	81.5
Freeport	100	123.8	93.1
U.S. total*	100	84.1	70.5
	*U.S. total figure is for $3,000–$6,999.		
$7,000 and over			
Monroeville	100	162.6	211.7
Haverford	100	191.7	249.4
Keelim	100	171.9	222.1
Freeport	100	201.0	252.8
U.S. total	100	179.5	222.5
$10,000 and over			
Monroeville	N.A.	100	168.6
Haverford	N.A.	100	176.8
Keelim	N.A.	100	175.9
Freeport	N.A.	100	144.6
U.S. total	43.4	100	157.2
Median family income	100.0	127.3	148.3
Median family income	$4,420	$5,625	$6,556

SOURCES: Figures for U.S. totals extracted from *Pocket Data Book*, Bureau of Census, U.S. Department of Commerce, December, 1966, p. 191, Table 233. Median income figures from *Statistical Abstract*, 1966, p. 336, Table 472. The figures under column headed "1965" are for 1964. Figures for trading areas studied are from *Sales Management Buying Power Guide* for 1955, 1960, and 1965 (published in editions one year later). Actual percentages of households by income groups were converted to an index of 1955 = 100. This source does not delineate $7,000 and over for 1955 as it does for 1960 and 1965, as seen. In the case of Monroeville the chart indicates that the percentage of households in the $0,000 — $2,499 group in 1960 was 41 percent of the percentage of 1955; that, in 1965 the percentage of households in this income group had risen to 61 percent of the percentage in 1955. The significance is, of course, related to the increased population as shown in Table 1. By the same token, in this case, the percentage of households in the $7,000 and over group in 1960 had risen to 211.7 percent of the percentage with that income in 1955.

Sales Management offers this additional explanation: "Net Cash Incomes of Households: measure of cash income available to households after taxes, . . . it differs from Effective Buying Income in that it excludes all non-cash items such as imputed rentals, imputed value of food and fuel, etc." *Sales Management* has consolidated and refined the Bureau of Census thirteen classes of gross income into five net cash income classes, projected to the year 1965. The percentage figure is cash income only and thus understates real income in farm areas; the percentage is for number of households and not for number of dollars.

The new statistics testify that we are becoming more and more affluent at the high end of the income scale. Nationally, households earning over $10,000 now account for 51.3 percent of total cash income.

Notes

Chapter I

1. Malcolm P. McNair, "Change and Challenge in the Department Store Industry" (Speech delivered at testimonial dinner in his honor, October 5, 1964, New York City).

2. Fabian Linden, ed., *Expenditure Patterns of the American Family* (New York: The National Industrial Conference Board, 1965), p. 7.

3. Robert D. Entenberg, *Effective Retail and Market Distribution* (New York: The World Publishing Company, 1966), pp. 19-23. Based on U.S. Census and Survey of Current Business data, he estimates that in 1965 consumer expenditures were divided as follows: 44.1 percent were allocated to nondurables and 41.7 percent to services. Although he offers no explanation why the total exceeds 100 percent, it can be assumed this is due to aggregation and rounding. He also comments on the trends in these three categories when compared with 1948. Respectively, nondurables represented 55.6 percent; durables, 12.5 percent; and services, 31.9 percent of all consumer spending. For additional interpretation of these trends see Malcolm P. McNair and Eleanor G. May, *The American Department Store, 1920-1960* (Boston: Harvard University Press, 1963), pp. 6-9; also see *The Business of Department Stores,* Technical Paper No. 7 (New York: The National Industrial Conference Board, 1959), pp. 4-7. Corroboration of these estimates and trends can be found in the revenue reports published by states imposing a tax on retail sales.

4. Delbert J. Duncan and Charles F. Phillips, *Retailing Principles and Methods* (7th ed.; Homewood, Illinois: Richard D. Irwin, Inc., 1967), p. 5.

5. *Ibid.*

6. A. Hamilton Chute, *A Selected and Annotated Bibliography of Retailing* (Austin, Texas: Bureau of Business Research, University of Texas, 1964). A more recent publication is *A Bibliography for Students of Retailing* (New

209

York: The Earl B. Puckett Fund for Retail Education, Inc.) A distinguished group of scholars and practitioners prepared both a basic and a comprehensive bibliography.

7. Duncan and Phillips, *op. cit.*; Fred M. Jones, *Retail Management* (Homewood, Illinois: Richard D. Irwin, Inc., 1967); William R. Davidson and Alton F. Doody, *Retailing Management* (New York: Ronald Press, 1966) ; and Entenberg, *op. cit.*

8. Included in this series are articles frequently quoted in the literature, namely, Ross M. Cunningham, "Brand Loyalty–What, Where, How Much?" *Harvard Business Review,* XXXIV, 1 (January-February, 1956); Gerald B. Tillman and Bruce Blomstrom, "Soft Goods Join the Retail Revolution," *Harvard Business Review,* XXXVIII, 5 (September-October, 1960); Malcolm P. McNair and Eleanor G. May, "Pricing for Profit," *Harvard Business Review,* XXXV, 3 (May-June, 1957).

9. For an interesting application of strategy concept to retailing, see Louis P. Bucklin, "Retail Strategy and the Classification of Consumer Goods," *Journal of Marketing,* XXVII, 1 (January, 1963) , 50. He extends Copeland's classification of goods–convenience, shopping, specialty–to stores based upon patronage motives and proposes a strategy based upon market segmentation. Also see David Carson, "Guide for Constructing a Merchandising Policy," *Journal of Retailing,* XXXVII, 4 (Winter, 1961-1962) , 24-31. For another analysis see Barkev Kibarian, "Why Department Stores Can Meet Discount-House Competition," *Journal of Retailing,* XXXVI, 4 (Winter, 1960-1961), 201-204, 224. He urges department stores to alter accounting and pricing concepts and to adopt a contribution-to-profits approach. Strategy may be unsuccessful. See Harry L. Hansen, "Creative Marketing Strategy," *Proceedings, Boston Conference on Distribution, 1959,* Boston, especially pp. 56-57. He urges simplicity in both formulation and communication of marketing objectives.

Typical of the increasing attention to the subject of image by academicians and practitioners are the following: George S. Odiorne, "A Search for Objectives in Business–The Great Image Hunt," *Michigan Business Review,* XVIII, 1 (January, 1966) , 19-25; Richard C. Christian, "Industrial Marketing: How Important Is the Corporate Image?" *Journal of Marketing,* XXIV, 2 (October, 1959) , 79-81. For literature more germane to retailing see Stuart U. Rich and Bernard D. Portis, "The Imageries of Department Stores," *Journal of Marketing,* XXVIII, 2 (April, 1964) , 10-16; Pierre Martineau, "The Personality of the Retail Store," *Harvard Business Review,* XXXVI, 1 (January-February, 1958) ; and George Fisk, "A Conceptual Model for Studying Customer Image," *Journal of Retailing,* XXXVII, 4 (Winter, 1961-62), 1-8.

10. The forces which cause stores to change, which prompt some observers to declare that a revolution is at hand, have occurred before. See Joseph Mayer, *The Revolution in Merchandise* (New York: Greenberg Publishers, 1939) , p. 32. "The Revolution in Merchandise took place as a direct consequence of the fundamental change in consumer psychology which, in turn, was a consequence of the World War which had shaken human society to its very foundations." McNair claims that the root causes of the current " 'retail

revolution' . . . all had their beginnings well before (World War II)." See Malcolm P. McNair, "Significant Trends and Developments in the Postwar Period," in A. B. Smith, ed., *Competitive Distribution in a Free High Level Economy and Its Implications for the University* (Pittsburgh: University of Pittsburgh Press, 1958), p. 5.

11. Bureau of the Budget, *Standard Industrial Classification Manual* (Washington, D.C.: USGPO, 1963), supplement to 1957 edition.

12. Jones, *op. cit.,* pp. 6-7. Also, see William R. Davidson, "The End of the Discount House," *Department Store Economist,* December, 1961, pp. 24-28. Also see Stanley C. Hollander, "The One-Price System–Fact or Fiction," *Journal of Retailing,* Fall, 1955, for explanation of definitions of discounting and examples of discounting prior to 1950. For a more comprehensive economic study of this aspect of retailing see doctoral dissertation by same author entitled "Discount Retailing" (Graduate School of the University of Pennsylvania, 1954).

13. *Discount Merchandiser,* June, 1966, p. 3.

14. *Ibid.,* pp. 30-48.

15. *Study of Organization in Multi-Unit Department and Specialty Stores* (New York: Retail Research Institute, The National Retail Merchants Association, 1961), p. 3.

16. This is one of the most frequently quoted simplifications in retailing. It is found in numerous articles, texts, and trade association reports.

17. Edmund D. McGarry, "The Merchandising Function," in Reavis Cox, Wroe Alderson, and Stanley J. Shapiro, eds., *Marketing Theory* (Homewood, Illinois: Richard D. Irwin, Inc., 1964), pp. 233-36. McGarry adds: "The merchandising function comprises the various activities undertaken to adapt the product to the users' ideas of what is wanted. This function adjusts what is practical to produce to what consumers want. . . . At the retail level it includes the selecting of appropriate assortments of goods for the retailer's particular clientele as well as the location and presentation of these goods in a manner convenient to customers."

18. Duncan and Phillips, *op. cit.,* p. 189.

19. Jones, *op. cit.,* p. 514. Duncan and Phillips, *op. cit.,* 6th ed., 1963, p. 461.

20. Davidson and Doody, *op. cit.,* p. 390.

21. Jones, *op. cit.,* original ed., 1957, p. 385.

22. The American Marketing Association defines advertising as "any paid form of nonpersonal presentation and promotion of ideas, goods, or services by an identified sponsor." Ralph S. Alexander, ed., *A Glossary of Marketing Terms* (Chicago: American Marketing Association, 1960), p. 9.

23. John A. Howard, *Marketing Management* (rev. ed.; Homewood, Illinois: Richard D. Irwin, Inc., 1963), pp. 4-7.

24. See William J. Stanton, *Fundamentals of Marketing* (New York: McGraw-Hill, 1964), p. 300. Stanton summarizes the forces causing change for retailers as (1) the changing consumer markets served by retailers, (2) the retailers' own constant search for more effective and profitable methods, and (3) the manufacturers' realization that they need mass-marketing methods to keep up with mass production of goods. See Duncan and Phillips,

op. cit., p. 8. They attribute these changes to four basic factors: (1) the huge volume of consumers' goods, (2) the rise in population and consumer purchasing power, (3) shifts in consumption patterns, (4) the suburban movement, aided by widespread use of the automobile. See Wroe Alderson, *Dynamic Marketing Behavior* (Homewood, Illinois: Richard D. Irwin, Inc., 1965), pp. 237, 214. He sees the retailer as a marketer subject to changes in his resource market as well as in his customer market. "The retailer must adjust to his environment, few having the power to change it . . . and no matter how impressive innovations may be in such adaptation the retailer's operation continues to be that of moving merchandise which someone else has designed or invented." See Davidson and Doody, *op. cit.,* at pp. 9, 10. They reiterate these themes, adding that "retailing is both a formative influence and an adaptive aspect of our culture. It is adaptive in the sense that retailing firms must be dynamically responsive to the changing wants and circumstances of consumers if such firms are to survive and grow." See Stanley C. Hollander, *Restraints Upon Retail Competition* (East Lansing, Michigan: Bureau of Business and Economic Research, Michigan State University, 1965), p. 85. He has set forth a series of changes in social, political, and economic conditions which act as constraints upon the retailer. For example, he notes that "the customer's set of expectations as to service and quality and assortment is susceptible to change through forces both inside and outside of retailing . . . control exists mainly in the sense that the retailer cannot afford either to lag too far behind or to get too far ahead of the public's expectations concerning merchandise, service, or selling methods."

25. Fabian Lindin, *op. cit.,* p. 8.

26. George Katona, *The Mass Consumption Society* (New York: McGraw-Hill, 1964), p. 9.

27. *Ibid.,* p. 13.

28. Charles J. Collazzo, Jr., "Effects of Income Upon Shopping Attitudes and Frustrations," *Journal of Retailing,* XLII, 1 (Spring, 1966), 2.

29. McNair, "Significant Trends and Developments in the Postwar Period," *op. cit.,* p. 5.

30. See footnote no. 9.

31. Stewart Thompson, *Management Creeds and Philosophies: Top Management Guides in Our Changing Economy* (New York: American Management Association, Research Study No. 32, 1958), p. 7.

32. Wroe Alderson, "An Approach to a Theory of Planning," in William S. Decker, ed., *Emerging Concepts in Marketing* (Chicago: American Marketing Association, 1963), p. 259.

33. Wendell R. Smith, "The Role of Planning in Marketing," *Business Horizons,* II, 3 (Fall, 1959), 55.

34. *Ibid.,* p. 56.

35. Stanley C. Hollander, "Retailing: Cause or Effect," in Decker, *op. cit.,* pp. 228-29.

36. Herbert Landsman as quoted in Philip J. Reilly, *Old Masters of Retailing* (New York: Fairchild Publications, Inc., 1966), p. vii.

37. Wroe Alderson, *Dynamic Marketing Behavior* (Homewood, Illinois: Richard D. Irwin, Inc., 1965), p. 234.

38. *Women's Wear Daily,* June 29, 1965, p. 7.

39. Pierre Martineau, "The Personality of the Retail Store," *Harvard Business Review,* XXXVI, 1 (January-February, 1958), 47.

40. "Study of Organization in Multi-Unit Department and Specialty Stores," *op. cit.,* pp. 7-11. This includes a concise history and development of organization in the department store industry.

41. See J. R. Clagg, Jr., "A Store Image Study Involving Factor Analysis," *University of Houston Business Review,* Spring, 1963, pp. 21-38. See W. Bruce Weale, "Measuring the Customer's Image of a Department Store," *Journal of Retailing,* XXXVII, 2 (Summer, 1961), 47. See also Charles J. Collazzo, Jr., *Consumer Attitudes and Frustrations in Shopping* (New York: Retail Research Institute, National Retail Merchants Association, 1963), pp. 30, 113-14.

42. Alfred H. Daniels, "Fashion Merchandising," *Harvard Business Review,* XXIX, 3 (May, 1951), 51-60. This is regarded as a classic article on fashion by a practitioner.

43. Stuart U. Rich and Bernard Portis, "Clues for Action from Shopper Preferences," *Harvard Business Review,* XLI, 2 (March-April, 1963), 132-49.

44. F. E. Brown and George Fisk, "Department Stores and Discount Stores: Who Dies Next?" *Journal of Marketing,* XLI, 3 (Fall, 1965), 15-27.

45. *Women's Wear Daily,* October 19, 1965, p. 1.

46. Walter Gross, "Strategies Used by Major Department Stores to Compete with Low-Margin Retailers" (Ph.D. dissertation, New York University, 1963). An article based upon this appeared in *Journal of Retailing,* XL, 2 (Summer, 1964), 11-18.

47. *Women's Wear Daily,* December 22, 1965, p. 1.

48. Edward A. Filene, *The Model Stock Plan* (New York: McGraw-Hill, 1930); see especially chap. 12, pp. 164-85.

49. Charles M. Edwards and William H. Howard, *Retail Advertising and Sales Promotion* (rev. ed.; New York: Prentice-Hall, Inc., 1943), pp. 140-43.

50. *Ibid.*

Chapter II

1. Paul Snider, manager of research projects, New York, American Management Association, letter, December 9, 1963.

2. Delbert J. Duncan and Charles F. Phillips, *Retailing Principles and Methods* (7th ed.; Homewood, Illinois: Richard D. Irwin, Inc., 1967), pp. 15-22, cite as major responses by retail institutions to environmental changes: advent and flourishing of the discount house; growth of small, convenience-type stores; increase of department store branches; increase of leased operations; wide-spread "scrambled merchandising." Robert D. Entenberg, "The Changing Competitive Position of Department Stores in the United States," in Stanley C. Hollander, ed., *Explorations in Retailing* (East Lansing, Michigan: Bureau of Business and Economic Research, Michigan State University, 1964), pp. 23-25, analyzes changes in department store merchandising relative to classification and assortment strengths. A more

complete development of this will be found in Entenberg's book by the same name, University of Pittsburgh Press, 1961.

3. Sam Flanel, *Operating Results of Department and Specialty Stores in 1964* (New York: Controllers' Congress, National Retail Merchants Association, 1965).

4. Malcolm P. McNair and Eleanor G. May, *The American Department Store, 1920-1960* (Boston: Harvard University Press, 1963), p. 15.

5. "Neustadt Information Bulletin," New York, 1966, p. 1. As explained later in the text this service is not widely known. There are few references to it in the literature and even among trade associations. Among these few, one is contained in an address by Violet Symons, publicity director, Gimbel's, Pittsburgh, at the Sales Promotion session of the 43rd annual convention of the National Retail Merchants Association in 1954: "The Neustadt studies are our most valuable working tool in our advertising planning. We compare our classification advertising with that of our competitors and with stores in nine other metropolitan areas. It helps us to locate merchandise, timing, and price-lining errors."

6. "Department Store Inventory Price Indexes," Revised Methodology and Historical Series, January, 1941 to January, 1966. Washington, D.C., U.S. Department of Labor, Bureau of Labor Statistics.

7. Based on a review of Neustadt price zones for 77 commodities advertised at retail from 1945-1965. Source: Market Research Department, *The Monroeville Gazette.*

Chapter III

1. *Market Publication,* No. 1, March 8, 1954, p. 36.

2. *Ibid.*

3. Interview with Harold McBride, corporate vice-president for personnel, Staplinger's, April 19, 1966.

4. *Monroeville Gazette,* Staplinger file, 1944. No specific date given.

5. Interview with Harry Parrish, vice-president, general merchandise manager, Staplinger's, May 12, 1966.

6. Interview with Mrs. Harriet Grimes, vice-president, Staplinger's, May 13, 1966.

7. *American Family News,* no date given, extracted from Staplinger file, *Monroeville Gazette.*

8. *Market Publication No. 4,* February 23, 1954, p. 6.

9. *Ibid.*

10. Grimes, *op. cit.*

11. Interview with Ed Strong, vice-president, sales promotion, Staplinger's, April 19, 1966.

12. Parrish, *op. cit.*

13. Interview with Carl Trine, assistant merchandise manager, home furnishings division, Staplinger's, May 13, 1966.

14. "Plaza Type Shopping Centers in Monroeville," Research Division, *Monroeville Gazette.*

15. William R. Davidson, "The End of the Discount House," *Department Store Economist*, December, 1961, pp. 24-28. Also see Stanley C. Hollander, "The One-Price System—Fact or Fiction," *Journal of Retailing*, Fall, 1955, for explanation of definitions of discounting and examples of discounting prior to 1950.

16. *Discounters Digest*, April 26, 1966, p. 1, published by Dun and Bradstreet, New York, claimed 900 stores and $2.9 billions in sales for 1960, and 2,341 stores and $13.3 billions in sales for 1965. In a special report entitled, "Census Report of the Discount Store Market," no date, p. 2, published by *Chain Store Age*, New York, the claim is 1,116 and 2,347 stores, $2.75 billion and $8.75 billion in sales, for 1960 and 1965, respectively.

17. See Davidson, Hollander, *op. cit.*

18. *Market Publication No. 3.* September 27, 1954, p. 37, speech by Henry Coulder. Discounting is viewed as a horrible menace . . . "taking American business back to the Dark Ages of Merchandising."

19. "The Mart—Discount House or Supermarket?" *Market Publication No. 3*, November 1, 1954, p. 56, quoted in Hollander, *op. cit.*, p. 130.

20. *Monroeville Gazette*, May 8, 1946.

21. Strong, *op. cit.*, interview, May 12, 1966.

22. *Market Publication No. 2*, August 3, 1964.

23. McBride, interview, *op. cit.*

24. Austin Worth, "Current Changes in Retailing" (speech before The Retailers of America, Monroeville, 1957).

25. *Market Publication No. 2*, Staplinger file. Publication undated.

26. Trine, *op. cit.*

27. Worth, *op. cit.*

28. *Market Publication No. 2*, April 12, 1949.

29. Parrish, *op. cit.*

30. Trine, *op. cit.*

31. Grimes, *op. cit.*

32. *Market Publications No. 1*, April 26, 1949.

33. *Ibid.*, November 11, 1949.

34. *Market Publication No. 2*, May 3, 1950.

35. *Market Publication No. 1*, April 1, 1952.

36. *Ibid.*

37. Interview with Mrs. Roberta Bollen, merchandise manager, women's sportswear and budget dresses, Staplinger's, May 12, 1966; and Trine, *op. cit.*

38. *Market Publication No. 1*, May 4, 1949.

39. *Ibid.*, February 26, 1952.

40. *Market Publication No. 4*, February 23, 1954.

41. Parrish, *op. cit.*

42. Strong, *op. cit.*, April 19, 1966.

43. Bollen, *op. cit.*

44. Worth, speech delivered at management conference at Monroeville College, as reported in *Market Publication No. 1*, March 10, 1966, p. 10.

45. Worth, reported in *Market Publication No. 1*, June 16, 1966, p. 18.

46. *Monroeville Gazette* files on Staplinger's, 1957.

47. *Market Publication No. 1*, June 23, 1958.

48. Trine, *op. cit.*
49. *Monroeville Gazette,* Staplinger file, 1966. This same kind of statement was reiterated by several interviewees.
50. *Market Publication No. 2,* April 13, 1965.
51. *Ibid.*
52. A. B. Markson, "Staplinger's Opinion on Discounters in Its Midst," *Market Publication No. 1,* September 27, 1961.
53. *Market Publication No. 1,* June 2, 1966.
54. Strong, *op. cit.,* May 12, 1966.
55. *Ibid.*
56. Parrish, *op. cit.*
57. Trine, *op. cit.*
58. *Market Publication No. 6,* August 30, 1965.
59. McBride, *op. cit.*
60. *Market Publication No. 1,* February 25, 1965.
61. *Market Publication No. 7,* June 17, 1965.

Chapter IV

1. *Study of Organization in Multi-Unit Department and Specialty Stores* (New York: Retail Research Institute, The National Retail Merchants Association, 1961), p. 7.
2. Statement by Richard P. Delzer, former president of The Fair, at a meeting of Credit Management Group, Keelim, Northstate, as reported in *Market Publication No. 2,* May 20, 1941.
3. Excerpted from statement by Carl Delzer, "What The Fair Means," 1925, from files of *Keelim News.*
4. *Keelim News,* January 15, 1933.
5. *Keelim News,* December 13, 1938.
6. *Keelim News,* December 18, 1936.
7. Interview, Delbert Richman, divisional merchandise manager, home furnishings, May 3, 1966.
8. Interview, Tom Lee, publicity director, The Fair, May 2, 1966, and May 3, 1966; the Research Division, *The Keelim News.*
9. *Ibid.*
10. Lee, *op. cit.*
11. *Market Publication No. 1,* January 12, 1966, p. 24.
12. *Ibid.*
13. *Market Publication No. 2,* January 26, 1966; also, "The Keelim Market," published by *Keelim News,* 1967, p. 30.
14. *Keelim News,* Federal Trade Commission, and *Market Publication No. 1,* August 28, 1963.
15. Gilbert Moran, personnel director, The Fair, interview, May 2, 1966.
16. Alfred Reden, buyer, linens and domestics, The Fair, interview, May 3, 1966.
17. Mark Sanders, president, The Fair, interview, May 2, and May 4, 1966.
18. Lee, *op. cit.*

19. Reden, *op. cit.*
20. Richman, *op. cit.*
21. Richman, *ibid.,* Jack Gelier, department manager and buyer, dresses, interview, May 3, 1966; and Mrs. Betty Harper, store fashion coordinator, interview, May 3, 1966.
22. Gelier, *op. cit.*
23. *Market Publication No. 4,* November 27, 1955.
24. Richman, *op. cit.*
25. Reden, *op. cit.*
26. Gelier, *op. cit.*
27. Sanders, *op. cit.*
28. Moran, *op. cit.*
29. Richman, *op. cit.*
30. Wenger, *op. cit.*
31. Lee, *op. cit.*
32. Wenger, *op. cit.* The interviewee would not disclose sales figures. But he did provide the gross margin dollars generated from 1961-1965 ($38,000 to $90,000) and the scale of maintained markup percentages (ranging from 37 percent to 42 percent), both rather positive indications that he had increased sales volume and had traded up.
33. A survey shows that in the West Keelim district, the location of this first branch, income distribution compared respectively with Keelim was: under $4,999, 19.2 percent and 28.4 percent; $5,000-$9,999, 46.6 percent and 54.1 percent; and $10,000 and over, 24.2 percent and 17.5 percent. Source: *Keelim News,* "The Keelim Market," *op. cit.,* 1967 (supplement). The reader should note, however, that these data pertain to an area about which a decision was rendered twenty years earlier. Yet so many similar decisions were made that this seemed relevant.
34. *Market Publication No. 2,* March 26, 1958.
35. *Market Publication No. 1,* February 9, 1966, p. 1.
36. *Ibid.,* March 16, 1958.
37. *Ibid.,* March 21, 1960.
38. *Ibid.,* July 7, 1961.
39. Lee, *op. cit.*
40. *Market Publication No. 1,* February 9, 1966, p. 1.
41. See "NRMA'S Standard Classification," New York, The National Retail Merchants Association, 1967, p. 2.
42. Derived from interviews and from various correspondence files at The Fair.
43. Correspondence files, The Fair, *op. cit.*
44. Wenger, *op. cit.*
45. Harold Spieser, accessories merchandiser, the Hanover Department Store, Hanover, Northstate. Spieser was coat buyer at The Fair from 1949-1956.
46. Gelier, *op. cit.*
47. Wenger, *op. cit.*
48. Richman, *op. cit.*
49. *Market Publication No. 1,* August 28, 1963.

50. Sanders, *op. cit.*
51. *Ibid.*
52. *Market Publication No. 5*, April 25, 1966, p. 26.
53. Reden, *op. cit.*
54. *Ibid.*
55. *Market Publication No. 1*, Nov. 16, 1964, p. 11.
56. Harper, *op. cit.*
57. *Ibid.*
58. *Market Publication No. 1*, May 16, 1966, p. 1.
59. Reden, *op. cit.*
60. *Ibid.*
61. Gelier, *op. cit.*

Chapter V

1. Market Publications files of clipping on Mayfield's. Dates on some of these are not legible. This particular reference contained a statement of the founder's principles.

2. Mayfield's has been a leading profit producer since 1950. *Market Publication No. 1*, March 9, 1966.

3. James Reba, buyer, domestics and linens, Mayfield's, interview, April 26, 1966.

4. *Market Publication No. 1*, July 13, 1960.

5. *Market Publication No. 1*, November 10, 1928.

6. *Market Publication No. 1*, November 5, 1928.

7. *Ibid.*

8. *Market Publication No. 4*, August 3, 1929.

9. *Market Publication No. 7*, February 16, 1942.

10. *Market Publication No. 1*, April 8, 1941.

11. The differences in the variables are: population, Newtown commenced a decline in 1955, reaching in 1965 only 93.2 percent of its 1946 base; net effective buying income, 160.3 percent of its 1946 base by 1965, in total retail sales, 169.6 percent of 1946; and in general merchandise sales, 145.3 percent of the 1946 base.

12. Gerald Adams, vice-president, research director, Mayfield's, interview, March 21, 1966, and correspondence, March 22, 1967.

13. "The True Look of the Discount Industry," *The Discount Merchandiser*, New York, June, 1966, pp. 30-48. Most of the data resource for this issue was furnished by the Center for Business and Economic Research, School of Business Administration, University of Massachusetts.

14. "Census Report of the Discount Store Market," *Discount Store News*, published by Lebhar-Friedman, publishers of *Chain Store Age*, New York. Undated, p. 3.

15. Adam Rudderham, chairman of the board, Mayfield's, interview, April 26, 1966.

16. Reba, *op. cit.*

17. While several executives reiterated this theme the exact quote was extracted from interview data with Rudderham.

18. Rudderham, *op. cit.*

19. Miss Sarah Alexander, publicity director, Mayfield's, interviews, March 22, 1966; and, April 26, 1966.

20. Adams, *op. cit.*

21. Lester Roberts, group merchandise manager, Mayfield's, April 26, 1966.

22. Rudderham, *op. cit.*

23. *Ibid.*

24. Reba, *op. cit.*

25. *Market Publication* files, no specific publication or date identified.

26. *Market Publications No. 1,* September 22, 1952.

27. Rudderham, *op. cit.*

28. *Market Publications No. 1,* November 15, 1966, p. 1.

29. Adams, *op. cit.*

30. *Ibid.*

31. *Market Publications No. 1,* March 23, 1965.

32. Miss Treva Ramy, merchandise coordinator, Mayfield's, interview, April 25, 1966.

33. Alexander, *op. cit.*

34. *Market Publications No. 1,* June 11, 1955.

35. *Freeport News,* September 26, 1962.

36. Mayfield executive (unnamed), quoted in *Market Publications No. 1,* October 26, 1953.

37. Ramy, *op. cit.*

38. Alexander, *op. cit.*

39. "Special Message to Executives–The Mayfield Philosophy and Our Place in the Community," by Gerald Adams.

40. *Freeport News,* Mayfield file, undated.

41. *Market Publications No. 7,* December 29, 1952; also *Market Publications No. 1,* August 15, 1952.

42. Adams, *op. cit.*

Chapter VI

1. Interview with George Penney, home furnishings merchandiser, February 2, 1966.

2. U.S. Bureau of Census, U.S. Census of Population for respective years.

3. Interview with Frank Worthing, Western Avenue store merchandiser and manager, January 13, 1966.

4. Interview, Penney, *op. cit.*

5. Interview with Bernard Sperling, general merchandise manager, February 10, 1966.

6. Interviewers would not disclose or provide data indicating exact profit performance. Investigation of Centerstate Corporation Securities Commission files revealed that during each of the last four years the Kane Company added substantially to its retained surplus. Also, I pieced together such data as pay-

roll costs, payroll as a percentage of total cost, and advertising linage, whereby I could reasonably calculate that Kane's profits approximated those of the 16-firm aggregate figure, as shown in Table III-3. In the gross margin calculations shown in Table VI-2, the comparisons are based upon an index of 1946 = 100. In that year Kane's gross margin percentage of sales exceeded the Harvard average by 1.1 percent. Also, the reader must recall that although Kane's never failed to use this measurement as a merchandising yardstick it did, after 1955, emphasize gross margin dollars as well as gross margin percentage as a basis for merchandising decisions.

7. Interview with Sherman Aamondt, general manager, L. H. Kane Company, January 11, 1966.

8. Interview with Lester Henshaw, president, L. H. Kane Company, January 11, 1966.

9. Aamondt, interview, *op. cit.*

10. Henshaw, interview, February 10, 1966.

11. *Enterprise Advertising Agency,* "Ad Clinic Bulletin," undated.

12. Interview with William Westin, sales promotion director, L. H. Kane Company, January 11, 1966.

13. Henshaw, interview, *op. cit.*

14. Sperling, interview, *op. cit.*

15. *Haverford News,* L. H. Kane Company file, spokesman is not identified.

16. *Ibid.*

17. Worthing, *op. cit.*

18. *Ibid.*

19. Sperling, *op. cit.*

20. Westin, *op. cit.*

21. Interview with Mrs. Nancy Brewster, personnel director, L. H. Kane Company, January 13, 1966.

22. *Haverford News,* in order of events cited, February 10, 1960; November 18, 1960; November 3, 1957.

23. Westin, interview, February 10, 1966.

24. Westin, *op. cit.*

Chapter VII

1. Wroe Alderson, *Dynamic Marketing Behavior* (Homewood, Illinois: Richard D. Irwin, Inc., 1965), p. 234.

2. Barkev Kibarian, "Why Department Stores Can Meet Discount-House Competition," *Journal of Retailing,* XXXVI, 4 (Winter, 1960-1961), 201-204, and 224.

3. Robert D. Entenberg, *Effective Retail and Market Distribution* (New York: World Publishing Company, 1966), p. 215.

4. Louis P. Bucklin, "Retail Strategy and the Classification of Consumer Goods," *Journal of Marketing,* XXVII, 1 (January, 1963), 50.

5. Stuart U. Rich and Bernard Portis, "Clues for Action from Shopper Preferences," *Harvard Business Review,* XLI, 2 (March-April, 1963), 132-49.

6. Alderson, *op. cit.,* pp. 237, 214.

7. Walter Gross, "Strategies Used by Major Department Stores to Compete with Low-Margin Retailers" (Ph.D. dissertation, New York University, 1963). An article based upon this appeared in *The Journal of Retailing,* XL, 2 (Summer, 1964), 11-13.

8. *NRMA's* (National Retail Merchants Association) *Standard Classifications* (New York: The National Retail Merchants Association, 1967). In commenting on the work of a special committee which prepared the NRMA report, J. J. Bliss, executive vice-president and treasurer of the NRMA, said: ". . . we now have a means of increasing customer in-stock service; a vehicle for improving volume, turnover, and profit; a merchandising tool that both the smaller and largest retailers can effectively use." P. 2. The committee observed that "at the classification level where dollar and unit controls overlap, information acts as the communications link between the two controls. If unit records are extended by actual price-line data or by estimated average prices, they will sum up to dollars for the class." P. 25. Sam Flanel, general manager, Controllers Congress, NRMA, remarked: "The intensification of retail competition makes it increasingly important that merchants *really* know what is and is not selling *and* whether coordinated sales potential is being realized in the fullest." P. 44.

9. Correspondence with A. B. Parker, president, Parker Brothers, famous department store in Midwestern United States, dated June 20, 1967. ". . . it would be impossible to obtain any sales percentages by merchandise category for 1960, and the other data are so incomplete that I am afraid the information would just be inaccurate."

Also correspondence with M. M. Heyward, associate director, Planning and Research Division, Consolidated Mercantile Company, July 12, 1967. ". . . records of sales by certain merchandise classes, by price-lines, are prepared and exchanged, usually by relatively few of our stores. What is more, the universe of those reporting is anything but constant . . . as to the future, the proliferation of computer usage by retailers is certainly increasing the practicality of collecting, maintaining, and using such records."

Individual executives who had been interviewed during case research also contributed responses to the investigator's inquiry of why the paucity existed. Names used here are fictitious, as are all names of interviewees.

10. *Ibid.*

11. Mrs. Roberta Bollen, merchandise manager, women's sportswear and budget dresses, Staplinger's.

12. *NRMA's Standard Classifications,"* op. cit., pp. 6-7.

13. Interview with Basil E. Adamy, management consultant, Phoenix, Arizona. Mr. Adamy is a member of the NRMA Merchandise Classification Standardization Committee.

Bibliography

Books

Adams, Richard N., and Preiss, Jack J. *Human Organizations Research: Field Relations and Techniques.* Homewood, Illinois: The Dorsey Press, 1960.

Alderson, Wroe. *Dynamic Marketing Behavior.* Homewood, Illinois: Richard D. Irwin, Inc., 1965.

_____. *Marketing Behavior and Executive Action.* Homewood, Illinois: Richard D. Irwin, Inc., 1957.

Arnold, Edward C. *Profitable Newspaper Advertising: Layout, Copy, and Planning for Retailers.* New York: Harper, 1960.

Britt, Stewart H., and Lucas, Darrell B. *Measuring Advertising Effectiveness.* New York: McGraw-Hill, 1963.

Cheskin, Louis. *How to Predict What People Will Buy.* New York: Liveright Publishing Company, 1957.

Chute, A. Hamilton. *A Selected and Annotated Bibliography of Retailing.* Austin, Texas: Bureau of Business Research, University of Texas, 1965.

Collazzo, Charles J., Jr. *Consumer Attitudes and Frustrations in Shopping.* New York: Retail Research Institute, National Retail Merchants Association, 1963.

Collins, Kenneth. *Successful Store Advertising.* New York: Fairchild Publications, 1959.

Dakins, J. Gordon. *The Facts About Branch Stores.* New York: National Retail Merchants Association, 1961.

Dalrymple, Douglas J. *Measuring Merchandising Performance in Department Stores.* New York: Retail Research Institute, National Retail Merchants Association, 1964.

_____. *Merchandising Decision Models for Department Stores.* East Lansing, Michigan: Bureau of Business and Economic Research, Graduate School of Business Administration, Michigan State University, 1966.

Davidson, William R., and Doody, Alton F. *Retailing Management.* New York: Ronald Press, 1966.

Duncan, Delbert J., and Phillips, Charles F. *Retailing Principles and Methods.* Homewood, Illinois: Richard D. Irwin, Inc., 7th ed., 1967, and 6th ed., 1964.

Edwards, Charles M., Jr., and Brown R. A. *Retail Advertising and Sales Promotion.* 3rd ed. Englewood Cliffs, New Jersey: Prentice-Hall, 1959.

_____, and Howard, William H. *Retail Advertising and Sales Promotion.* New York: Prentice-Hall, Inc., 1943.

Entenberg, Robert D. *Effective Retail and Market Distribution.* New York: The World Publishing Company, 1966.

Fairchild's Financial Manual of Retail Stores. New York: Fairchild Publications, Inc., annual publication since 1928.

Fairchild Publications, Inc. *The Retail Revolution.* New York: Fairchild Publications, Inc., 1962.

Feinberg, Samuel. *What Makes Shopping Centers Tick?* New York: Fairchild Publications, Inc., 1960.

Ferry, John William. *A History of the Department Store.* New York: Macmillan, 1960.

Filene, Edward A. *The Model Stock Plan.* New York: McGraw-Hill, 1930.

_____. *Next Steps Forward in Retailing.* New York: Harper, 1937.

Flanel, Sam. *Operating Results of Department and Specialty Stores in 1964.* New York: Controllers' Congress, National Retail Merchants Association, 1965.

Forrest, Dorsey. *Advertising Practices of Ohio Retailers.* Columbus, Ohio: Bureau of Business Research, Ohio State University, 1949 (Research Monograph No. 55).

Gold, Ed. *The Dynamics of Retailing: Major Trends That Shape the Future.* New York: Fairchild Publications, Inc., 1963.

Heidingsfield, Myron S., and Blankenship, Albert B. *Market and Marketing Analysis.* New York: H. Holt, 1947.

Hollander, Stanley C. *Explorations in Retailing.* East Lansing, Michigan: Bureau of Business and Economic Research, Michigan State University, 1964.

_____. *Restraints upon Retail Competition.* East Lansing, Michigan: Bureau of Business and Economic Research, Michigan State University, 1965.

Holdren, Bob R. *The Structure of a Retail Market and the Market Behavior of Retail Units.* Englewood Cliffs, New Jersey: Prentice-Hall, Inc., 1960.

Howard, John A. *Marketing Management.* Rev. ed. Homewood, Illinois: Richard D. Irwin, Inc., 1963.

Hummel, Francis E. *Market and Sales Potentials.* New York: Ronald Press Co., 1961.

Jones, Fred M. *Retail Management.* Homewood, Illinois: Richard D. Irwin, Inc., 1967.

Judelle, Beatrice, and Jarnow, Jeannette A. *Inside the Fashion Business.* New York: John Wiley, 1965.

Kahn, Robert L., and Canvell, Charles F. *The Dynamics of Interviewing.* New York: John Wiley & Sons, Inc., 1958.

Katona, George. *The Mass Consumption Society.* New York: McGraw-Hill Co., 1964.

Linden, Fabian, ed. *Expenditure Patterns of the American Family.* New York: The National Industrial Conference Board, 1965.

Lombard, G. F. F. *Behavior in a Selling Group.* Boston: Graduate School of Business Administration, Harvard University, 1955.

Mahoney, Tom, and Sloane, Leonard. *The Great Merchants.* New York: Harper & Row, 1966.

Mayfield, Frank. *The Department Store Story.* New York: Fairchild Publications, 1949.

Mayer, Joseph. *The Revolution in Merchandise.* New York: Greenberg Publishers, 1939.

McClure, Leslie W., and Fulton, Paul C. *Advertising in the Printed Media.* New York: Macmillan, 1964.

McNair, Malcolm P., and May, Eleanor S. *The American Department Store, 1920-1960.* Boston: Harvard Graduate School of Business Research, 1963 (Bureau of Business Research Bulletin No. 166).

Merton, Robert K., Fiske, Marjorie, and Kendall, Patrick L. *The Focussed Interview.* Glencoe, Illinois: The Free Press, 1956.

Myrdal, Gunner. *Value in Social Theory.* London: Routledge and Keegan Paul, 1958.

NRMA's Standard Classifications. New York: The National Retail Merchants Association, 1967.

Nystrom, Paul Henry. *Economics of Fashion.* New York: Ronald Press, 1929.

_____. *Retail Store Operations.* 4th ed. New York: Ronald Press, 1937.

Ott, Matthew J. "The Allocation of Resources in Departmentized Stores," in *3 Studies in Retail Research.* New York: Retail Research Institute, National Retail Merchants Association, 1965.

Reilly, Philip J. *Old Masters of Retailing.* New York: Fairchild Publications, Inc., 1966.

Retail Research Institute. *Study of Organization in Multi-Unit Department and Specialty Stores.* New York: The National Retail Merchants Association, 1961.

Rich, Stuart A. *Shopping Behavior of Department Store Customers.* Boston: Harvard University School of Business, 1963.

Smith, Guy C., ed. *The Retailer of Today and Tomorrow.* New York: The American Management Association, 1929.

Smith, Samuel Van Dyke. *The Executive Function of Organization Applied to Branch Department Stores.* St. Louis: Graduate School of Business Administration, Washington University, 1961.

Stanton, Edward M. *Branch Stores: Planning, Merchandising, Operating, Promotion.* New York: National Retail Merchants Association, 1955.

Stanton, William J. *Fundamentals of Marketing.* New York: McGraw-Hill, 1964.

Sternlieb, George. *The Future of the Downtown Department Store.* Cambridge, Massachusetts: Joint Center for Urban Studies of the Massachusetts Institute of Technology and Harvard University, 1962.

Thompson, Donald L. *Analysis of Retailing Potential in Metropolitan Areas.* Berkeley, California: Institute of Business and Economic Research, University of California, 1964.

Thompson, Stewart. *Management Creeds and Philosophies: Top Management Guides in Our Changing Economy.* New York: American Management Association, 1958 (Research Study No. 32).

Tucker, W. T. *Social Context of Economic Behavior.* New York: Holt, Rinehart and Winston, 1964.

Van Tassel, Charles E. *An Analysis of Factors Influencing Retail Sales.* East Lansing, Michigan: Bureau of Business and Economic Research, Graduate School of Business Administration, Michigan State University, 1966.

Wingate, John W., and Friedlander, Joseph. *The Management of Retail Buying.* Englewood Cliffs, New Jersey: Prentice-Hall, 1963.

Wolfe, Harry D., Brown, James K. and Thompson, G. Clark. *Measuring Advertising Results.* New York: The National Industrial Conference Board, 1962 (Studies in Business Policy No. 102).

Publications of the Government, Learned Societies, and Other Organizations

Alexander, Ralph S., ed. *A Glossary of Marketing Terms.* Chicago: The American Marketing Association, 1960.

The Buyer's Manual. Rev. ed. Merchandising Division, New York: The National Retail Merchants Association, 1965.

Buying Power Guide. New York: *Sales Management,* 1946, 1951, 1956, 1961, 1966.

Massachusetts School of Business Administration. *Amherst Proceedings, Mass-Merchandising Management.* Amherst, Massachusetts: University of Massachusetts, 1964.

The National Industrial Conference Board. *The Business of Department Stores.* New York: The National Industrial Conference Board, 1959 (Technical Paper No. 7).

The B. Earl Puckett Fund for Retail Education, Inc. *A Bibliography for Students of Retailing.* New York: 1967.

Retailing Publications: 1952-1956. New York: New York University, Research and Publications Division of the School of Retailing, 1957.

Ross, Arthur M. *The Price Statistics of the Bureau of Labor Statistics.* Statement before Subcommittee on Economic Statistics, Joint Economic Committee, Congress of the United States, May 25, 1966.

1,484 Selected Publications for Retailers. New York: New York University, Research and Publications Division of the School of Retailing, 1952.

Bureau of Labor Statistics. Department of Labor. "Department Store Inventory Price Indexes," Revised Methodology and Historical Series, January, 1941-January, 1966.

Van Dness, Michael G. *Shopping Behavior of Customers in Modified and Conventional Layouts of Retail Stores.* Marketing Economics Division, Department of Agriculture. Washington: U.S. Government Printing Office, 1964.

Periodicals

Bayton, James A. "Motivation, Cognition and Learning: Basic Factors in Consumer Behavior," *Journal of Marketing,* XXII (January, 1958), 282-89.

Bliss, James J. "The Shape of Things to Come: Retailing in 1970," *Stores,* January, 1966, pp. 12-15.

Brown, F. E., and Fisk, George. "Department Stores and Discount Stores: Who Dies Next?" *Journal of Retailing,* XLI (Fall, 1965), 15-27.

Blandkertz, D. F. "The Basement Store Customer," *Journal of Marketing,* XV (January, 1951), 336-40.

_____. "Shopping Habits and Income," *Journal of Marketing,* XIV (January, 1950), 572-78.

Bucklin, Louis P. "Retail Strategy and the Classification of Consumer Goods," *Journal of Marketing,* XXVII (January, 1963), 50-55.

_____. "Testing Propensities to Shop," *Journal of Marketing,* XXX (January, 1966), 22-27.

Carson, David. "Guide for Constructing a Merchandising Policy," *Journal of Retailing,* XXXVII (Winter, 1961-1962), 24-31.

Christian, Richard C. "Industrial Marketing: How Important Is the Corporate Image?" *Journal of Marketing,* XXIV (October, 1959), 79-80.

Clegg, J. R., Jr. "A Store Image Study Involving Factor Analysis," *Business Review, University of Houston,* X (Spring, 1963), 21-38.

Cunningham, Ross M. "Brand Loyalty, What, Where, How Much?" *Harvard Business Review,* XXXIV (January-February, 1956), 116-28.

_____. "Customer Loyalty to Store and Brand," *Harvard Business Review,* XXXIX (November-December, 1961), 127-37.

Daniels, Alfred H. "Fashion Merchandising," *Harvard Business Review,* XXIX (May, 1951), 51-60.

Davidson, William R. "The End of the Discount House," *Department Store Economist,* December, 1961, pp. 24-28.

Downs, Anthony. "A Theory of Consumer Efficiency," *Journal of Retailing,* XXXVII (April, 1961), 6-12.

Entenberg, Robert D. "Environmental Change Underlying the 'Retail Revolution'–Implications for the Future," *Pittsburgh Business Review,* XXXIV (February, 1964), 5, 11-12.

Fisk, George. "A Conceptual Model for Studying Customer Image," *Journal of Retailing,* XXXVII (Winter, 1961-1962), 1-8, 54.

Gross, Walter. "Strategies Used by Major Department Stores to Compete with Low-Margin Retailers," *Journal of Retailing,* XL (Summer, 1964), 11-18.

Heidingsfield, Myron S. "Why Do People Shop in Downtown Department Stores?" *Journal of Marketing,* XIII (April, 1949), 510-12.

Hill, Edward W. "Corporate Images Are Not Stereotypes," *Journal of Marketing*, XXVI (January, 1962) , 72-75.
Hollander, Stanley C. "The One-Price System—Fact or Fiction," *Journal of Retailing*, XXXI (Fall, 1955) , 127-44.
Kibarian, Barkev. "Why Department Stores Can Meet Discount-House Competition," *Journal of Retailing*, XXXVI (Winter, 1960-1961) , 201-206.
Martineau, Pierre. "The Personality of the Retail Store," *Harvard Business Review*, XXXVI (January-February, 1958), 47-55.
McNair, Malcolm P., and May, Eleanor G. "Pricing for Profit," *Harvard Business Review*, XXXV (May-June, 1957) , 105-30.
Odiorne, George S. "A Search for Objectives in Business—The Great Image Hunt," *Michigan Business Review*, XVIII (January, 1966) , 19-24.
Purvis, L. E., and Greene, W. F. "A Technique to Measure Purchase Influence," *Journal of Marketing*, XXV (July, 1961) , 38-48.
Rich, Stuart U., and Portis, Bernard D. "The Imageries of Department Stores," *Journal of Marketing*, XXVII (April, 1964) , 10-16.
Schmalz, Carl N. "On Retailers Agenda: Better Downtowns, Sharper Store Images," *Stores*, January, 1966, pp. 17-18.
Smith, Wendell R. "The Role of Planning in Marketing," *Business Horizons*, II (Fall, 1959) , 53-57.
Tillman, Gerald B., and Bruce Blomstron. "Soft Goods Join the Retail Revolution," *Harvard Business Review*, XXXVIII (September-October, 1960) , 133-43.
Weale, W. Bruce. "Measuring the Customer's Image of a Department Store," *Journal of Retailing*, XXXVII (Summer, 1961) , 40-48.
Wittreich, Warren J. "Misunderstanding the Retailer," *Harvard Business Review*, XL (May-June, 1962), 147-59.
Weiss, E. B. "Marketing Through Tomorrow's 100 Top Department Stores," New York: Doyle, Dane Bernback, Inc.

Essays and Articles in Collections

Alderson, Wroe. "An Approach to a Theory of Planning," in William S. Decker, ed. *Emerging Concepts in Marketing*. Chicago: American Marketing Association, 1963.
Christian, Richard C. "Evaluating Industrial Advertising—Realistically and Objectively," *Advertising Research Foundation*. New York: in *Proceedings*, 7th Annual Conference.
Entenberg, Robert D. "The Changing Competitive Position of Department Stores in the United States," in Stanley C. Hollander, ed. *Explorations in Retailing*. East Lansing, Michigan: Bureau of Business and Economic Research, Michigan State University, 1959.
Hansen, Harry L. "Creative Marketing Strategy," *Boston Conference on Distribution, 1959.* 31st Annual, Boston, Massachusetts, 54-57.
Hollander, Stanley C. "Retailing: Cause or Effect," in William S. Decker, ed. *Emerging Concepts in Marketing*. Chicago: American Marketing Association, 1963.
McGarry, Edmund D. "The Merchandising Function," in Cox, Reavis,

Alderson, Wroe, and Shapiro, Stanley J. eds. *Marketing Theory*. Homewood, Illinois: Richard D. Irwin, Inc., 1964.

McNair, Malcolm P. "Significant Trends and Developments in the Postwar Period," in A. B. Smith, ed. *Competitive Distribution in a Free High Level Economy and Its Implications for the University*. Pittsburgh: University of Pittsburgh Press, 1958.

Ott, Matthew J. "The Allocation of Resources in Departmentized Stores," in *3 Studies in Retail Research*. New York: Retail Research Institute, National Retail Merchants Association, 1965.

Wingate, John W. "Contemporary Trends in Retailing," in Delbert J. Duncan, ed. *Conference of Marketing Teachers from Far Western States, Proceedings*. Berkeley, California: University of California, 1958.

Unpublished Materials

Gross, Walter. "Strategies Used by Major Department Stores to Compete with Low-Margin Retailers." Ph.D. dissertation, New York University, 1963.

Hollander, Stanley C. "Discount Retailing." Ph.D. dissertation, University of Pennsylvania, 1954.

Kahn, Henry S. "Comparative Financial Data: Major Department Stores and Other Leading Merchandisers." Chicago: Harris Trust and Savings Bank, 1965.

McNair, Malcolm P. "Change and Challenge in the Department Store Industry." Speech delivered at testimonial dinner in his honor, October 5, 1964, New York City.

Sprague, Richard E. "The Retail Store of 1970." Address to the Store Presidents Conference, The National Retail Merchants Association, 1965.

Symons, Violet. "Successful Sales Planning." Address to the National Retail Dry Goods Association, New York, January, 1954.

Tannenbaum, Louis. "Institutional Advertising Can Build a Better Business for Retailers." Address at National Retail Merchants Association, May 13, 1964.

PUBLICATIONS OF THE DIVISION OF RESEARCH

MSU Business Studies

ELECTRONICS IN BUSINESS
Gardner M. Jones

ELEMENTARY MATHEMATICS OF LINEAR
PROGRAMMING AND GAME THEORY
Edward G. Bennion

EXPLORATIONS IN RETAILING
Stanley C. Hollander

MARGINAL ASPECTS OF MANAGEMENT PRACTICES
Frederic N. Firestone

HISTORY OF PUBLIC ACCOUNTING IN THE UNITED STATES
James Don Edwards

CONTRIBUTIONS OF FOUR ACCOUNTING PIONEERS
James Don Edwards
Roland F. Salmonson

LIFE INSURANCE COMPANIES IN THE CAPITAL MARKET
Andrew F. Brimmer

BUSINESS CONSULTANTS AND CLIENTS
Stanley C. Hollander

THE AUTOMOTIVE CAREER OF RANSOM E. OLDS
Glenn A. Niemeyer

ELECTRONIC COMPUTATION OF HUMAN DIETS
Victor E. Smith

MSU International Business and Economic Studies
MICHIGAN'S COMMERCE AND COMMERCIAL POLICY STUDY
John L. Hazard

INTERNATIONAL DIMENSIONS IN BUSINESS
Recent Readings from BUSINESS TOPICS

MANAGEMENT DEVELOPMENT AND EDUCATION IN THE
SOVIET UNION
Barry M. Richman

THE UNITED STATES OVERSEAS EXECUTIVE:
HIS ORIENTATIONS AND CAREER PATTERNS
Richard F. Gonzalez and Anant R. Negandhi

STEEL AND ECONOMIC DEVELOPMENT: CAPITAL-OUTPUT
RATIOS IN THREE LATIN AMERICAN STEEL PLANTS
David G. Greene

ALTERNATIVE COMMERCIAL POLICIES—THEIR EFFECT
ON THE AMERICAN ECONOMY
Mordechai E. Kreinin

INSTITUTION BUILDING IN BUSINESS ADMINISTRATION—
THE BRAZILIAN EXPERIENCE
Donald A. Taylor

THE OPTIMAL STAGING AND PHASING OF MULTI-PRODUCT CAPACITY
Harold H. Wein and V. P. Sreedharan

EDUCATION FOR BUSINESS IN A DEVELOPING SOCIETY
Amar N. Agarwala

MSU Public Utilities Studies
DEVELOPMENT OF SEPARATIONS PRINCIPLES IN THE
TELEPHONE INDUSTRY
Richard Gabel

PERFORMANCE UNDER REGULATION
Harry M. Trebing, editor

MID-CONTINENT AREA POWER PLANNERS
W. Stewart Nelson

RATE OF RETURN UNDER REGULATION:
NEW DIRECTIONS AND PERSPECTIVES
Harry M. Trebing, and R. Hayden Howard, editors

MSU Public Utilities Papers
SELECTED STRUCTURE AND ALLOCATION
PROBLEMS IN THE REGULATED INDUSTRIES
Manley R. Irwin and Milton Russell

*Set in Linotype Baskerville and Coronet Bold display heads
Printed on Lakewood Natural Offset Antique
Bound in Holliston Mills cloth
Printed by Lithocrafters, Ann Arbor, Michigan*